# "THEY JUST NEED TO GET A JOB"

## 15 MYTHS ON HOMELESSNESS

# MARY BROSNAHAN

BEACON PRESS, BOSTON
MYTHS MADE IN AMERICA

BEACON PRESS
Boston, Massachusetts
www.beacon.org

Beacon Press books
are published under the auspices of
the Unitarian Universalist Association of Congregations.

27  26  25  24      8  7  6  5  4  3  2  1

This book is printed on acid-free paper that meets the uncoated paper ANSI/
NISO specifications for permanence as revised in 1992.

Text design by BookMatters

*Library of Congress Cataloguing-in-Publication Data is available for this title.*
Paperback ISBN: 978-0-8070-0697-9
E-book ISBN: 978-0-8070-0698-6
Audiobook: 978-0-8070-1724-1

*For Quinn*

# CONTENTS

*Preface: The Function of Myth* • vii

*Introduction: Anita* • 1

**CHAPTER 1: A BRIEF HISTORY OF HOMELESSNESS** • 7

MYTH 1: "Homelessness Is Inevitable and Intrinsically Unsolvable" • 7

**CHAPTER 2: THE ROOTS OF AMERICAN HOMELESSNESS** • 30

MYTH 2: "Homelessness in America Is a Relatively New Phenomenon" • 30

MYTH 3: "Helping the 'Worthy' Poor Is the Best Way to End Poverty and Homelessness" • 30

**CHAPTER 3: HOMELESSNESS IN THE TWENTIETH CENTURY** • 64

MYTH 4: "Ronald Reagan Created Modern Homelessness" • 64

MYTH 5: "Most Homeless People Are Mentally Ill and Dangerous" • 74

**CHAPTER 4: OFFERING AID CREATES MORE NEED** • 85

MYTH 6: "If You Build It, They Will Come" • 85

MYTH 7: "There Is No Shortage of Help Available for the Homeless—They Just Need to Access It" • 93

MYTH 8: "Handouts Create Homelessness" • 97

MYTH 9: "Homeless People Just Need to 'Get a Job' to Lift Themselves Out of Homelessness" • 111

MYTH 10: "Homeless People Just Need to Learn to Save" • 114

CHAPTER 5: WHO WE THINK OF WHEN WE THINK OF THE HOMELESS • 117

MYTH 11: "Runaways Really Aren't Homeless" • 117

MYTH 12: "Homeless People Are Single Adults Living on City Streets" • 126

CHAPTER 6: BARRIERS AND SOLUTIONS • 133

MYTH 13: "People Need to Prove That They're Worthy of and Ready for Assistance" • 133

MYTH 14: "Investments in Social Housing Have Proven to Be Failures" • 159

CHAPTER 7: RESISTANCE VS. REVOLUTION • 177

MYTH 15: "There's Really Nothing I Can Do to Make a Meaningful Difference" • 177

*Acknowledgments* • 197
*Notes* • 199

# PREFACE:
# THE FUNCTION OF MYTH

The original purpose of myth was to explain the inexplicable—to offer answers to life's most profound questions, from "How do we come into existence?" to "Why do we die?" They provided powerful narratives around our most evocative feelings, fears, and desires. Their stories transmitted common values and aspirational arcs across generations, through millennia. They endure because they convey fundamental truths about the human condition. They get inside people and compel them to action. Joseph Campbell, beyond his influential writings on the earliest metaphysical and cosmological realms of myth, underscored the modern-day sociological purpose of myth: to pass down ethical codes and shared values that dictate prevailing social structure.[1] In short, myths reveal who gives the orders and why.

While Homer created epics through which he sought to convey truth,* the advent of scientific reasoning four hundred years later rendered the term "myth" as synonym for "fictional tales of superstition or fantasy, symbolic stories…without proof."[2]

This book addresses common myths about homelessness on both levels—cultural narrative and fictional tale. It dismantles the wall of lies and half-truths that has been built up over the past half century—a wall

---

*Writing around the seventh or eighth century BCE, Homer himself understood these two different categories and the intimate connection between them. In perhaps the most famous scene from *The Iliad*, Achilles, enraged by Agamemnon's deceit, cries out to Odysseus, "I hate like the gates of Hades / the man who says one thing and hides another inside him. / So, when I speak, I will say what is on my mind." (*The Iliad*, Book IX)

that has distanced us emotionally from the suffering of our homeless neighbors and has dammed away any promise of investments in lasting solutions.

The first section provides a historical overview of housing instability, starting with the enclosure of the British Commons, through the Industrial Age, and the waves of emigration to what would become the United States. The contours of each of these eras were shaped enormously by English Poor Laws, which were molded by Calvinistic axioms of "worthy" versus "unworthy" paupers. This false dichotomy remains the most destructive yet enduring and influential of narratives.

From there, we examine the history of homelessness in the US, including the foundational myths of our nation, encoded in the creation of our Constitution and the more recent deregulation of our capitalistic system. We also look closely at specific groups of people without homes: homeless youth, our neighbors struggling with severe and persistent mental illness, those living in emergency shelter, and our neighbors living rough on our streets and in other public spaces. We also unpack the policies that function to systematically dehumanize Americans without housing, often with the expressed intent to destroy them by erasure.

Each of these individual myths falls squarely in the modern definition of "myth" as lie or falsehood. But collectively, they also fulfill the ancient purpose of myth—to explain, or in this case, more precisely, justify, the unexplainable. How can we allow hundreds of thousands of Americans to live and die on our streets? These myths, as a whole, serve to shift responsibility away from the systemic causes of homelessness and onto homeless people themselves. When we tell each other these myths, the intended result is to deaden us to our neighbors' plight and obscure the structural violence they endure, perhaps the most grotesque repercussion of unregulated, late-stage global capitalism.

The ultimate goal of leveling these destructive myths is to give us the space that is essential to constructing a truthful counternarrative—one based in facts and that bolsters significant investment in proven, housing-based solutions. Although some of the details herein are centered in New York (owing to my decades of work in New York City and State), this book and its recommendations are national in scope, as meaningful reform is needed urgently at every level of government.

# ANITA

Throughout the mid-1990s, New York mayor Rudy Giuliani unleashed a series of police raids to sweep homeless encampments off the streets. In the wake of one of those blitzes, I spent a freezing February morning driving around the East Bronx with my colleague Michael Polenberg, looking for and speaking with the men who had been rousted and scattered by the New York Police Department. What neighborhoods had they been purged from? Where were they sleeping now? Were they able to find food and places to stay warm? We gave out blankets, coats, woolen socks, and subway tokens. We also gave directions to the Coalition for the Homeless office on Chambers Street, as most of the men had lost essential items in the raids—birth certificates, welfare cards, steel-toed work boots, personal photos, and correspondence—and our Crisis Intervention Team wanted to help in any way possible. Whenever we asked if they had slept recently in NYC's vast emergency shelter system, most said that they'd been robbed, harassed, or physically assaulted there, often by shelter security or staff. And, to a man, everyone seeking shelter had been forced to go to intake at Bellevue Men's Shelter on East 30th Street and wait until after midnight to be transported to Wards Island, a no-man's-land in the East River. Once there, they were given a bed at 2 or 3 a.m., only to be awoken a few hours later at 7 a.m. and told to take a bus and subway "back to intake," to repeat the intentionally cruel process for days, sometimes weeks, on end. Active deterrence was the City's guiding principle: make it as hard as humanly possible to get a stable shelter placement while simultaneously directing frontline police to break up groups of more than three people bedding down together on the streets and other public spaces.

Soon after we returned to Chambers Street that afternoon, Michael poked his head in my office door. "Hey, I don't know how to say this..." as his voice trailed off. "I have a woman in my office and I really don't have any idea what to do..." Michael had worked for years at the Coalition and had seen it all, so I was surprised to see him so rattled.

"I think she might be mentally ill. I can't understand anything she's saying. And she's got a tiny baby with her."

Michael and I walked back to his small cubicle, where he split his time between advocacy and crisis work. There, sitting in a folding chair, hunched over her baby, was a large Black woman, looking listless and exhausted, rocking back and forth. Michael handed me her intake form. Her name was Anita.

"Hi, I'm Mary," I said, extending my hand. She glanced up and slowly lifted up her hand. No grip, but a swell of tears. I sat down next to her so that I could look more closely at the baby. He was tightly swaddled and as perfectly clad as any three-week-old can be. "Anita," I asked, "where are you from?"

She stared back blankly.

"Where did you two sleep last night?"

"Staten Island," Anita answered. That set off a deluge of jagged sobs. Her crying set the baby off too.

I can't remember what I said next, probably the usual reassurance that whatever was going on, we were going to help make it right. We had a modest food pantry along with clothes and diapers on hand. But what I do remember is this: how fucking hot it was in that cubicle.

Our offices were in a crumbling loft building in Lower Manhattan. The windows were single-paned—so thin the wind would blow papers off the windowsill—but the interior cubicles were stifling on even the coldest days as heat poured out unregulated from ancient radiators. The child, swaddled as he was, was sweating. A light green crocheted cap tightly crowned his red face.

"Your baby seems a bit hot," I offered.

"Yes," Anita replied and unwrapped the blanket. Beneath, his clothes were clean and he looked well-fed. But equally important, Anita and I were communicating.

Freed from the blanket, the baby's wail came down a notch from full throttle, but he was still obviously uncomfortable. I instinctively reached over for his cap.

"Maybe let's take this hat off..." As I gently pulled it off, Anita went into near hysterics, and with the hat off, I saw why: the baby's hair was terribly matted, twisted in small clumps around his scalp.

"You see? You see? My baby's hair...it's so tangled....I can't even get a comb to unknot it, it's so matted," she sobbed as she ran her hand over the snarled clusters. Michael had slipped out and gotten a glass of water and I passed it to Anita. I rubbed her back and tried to assure her it was okay. Everything was going to be okay.

Each of us has a breaking point. We really don't know where it is until we reach it. Anita had met hers. Over the next few minutes she explained that she had fled her husband in the Bronx a couple weeks earlier when his fists, usually aimed at her, narrowly missed the infant. She'd spent two days in a chair at the central intake office for homeless families. She and her baby were assigned to a run-down hotel in Staten Island—a world away for the Bronx native—with no heat or hot water, making it impossible to wash the baby's hair. That morning she had run out of the baby wipes she had been using to keep her child and herself clean.

"Look at this....Look at my baby....This will never come undone now....Once it gets like this, you can never undo these mats. You understand?"

We gradually came up with a game plan, from the immediate (using office scissors to snip off the tops of the matted knots) to the necessary (taking her downstairs to Duane Reade to buy baby shampoo and formula, as the stress had made her milk dry up) to the critical (calling the head of family services for New York City's homeless services, demanding that she be moved immediately to a domestic violence shelter in East Harlem). Slowly, a vague sense of hope began to form on her face.

As we stood in the store sorting out the formula situation, Anita suddenly turned and said, "Look at me!" She pulled at the front of her overcoat, held closed by one of those large old-fashioned diaper pins; it was several sizes too big, but the sleeves only reached a few inches past her elbows. "I look like a bag lady. When I left the apartment, I didn't even grab my winter coat. The girl next door at the hotel was so nice, she gave me this."

Anita wasn't "severely mentally ill," as many might initially assume. She was suffering from serious PTSD, pushed to the brink of a nervous breakdown by a cascade of events—including domestic violence and forced relocation to a place with no heat or hot water, inaccessible by subway—all with a newborn, her first, to protect.

Anita's experience—along with those of hundreds, perhaps thousands, of other homeless people I've had the great privilege to meet over many years—has led me to champion personalism as the framework in which to create what Peter Maurin of the Catholic Worker movement envisioned: "a society where it is easier for people to be good."[1] Put simply, personalism is the idea that every person is unique, complex, and valuable—and inherently worthy of a safe, decent place to call home.

The Coalition for the Homeless was founded in 1979 in the wake of its founders bringing the class-action suit *Callahan v. Carey* against the City of New York, establishing what has come to be known as a "right to shelter." The lawsuit's lead plaintiff, Robert Callahan, had been sleeping on the city streets, unable to secure a bed at what was then the only municipal men's shelter on East 3rd Street. One of the Coalition's cofounders, lawyer Bob Hayes, based his legal argument on an obscure clause in the New York State Constitution, which had been added in the aftermath of the Great Depression, which stated that "aid, care and support of the needy are public concerns and shall be provided by the state."[2] The interpretation of the word "shall" loomed large in the court proceedings, and in the end, Mayor Koch's administration settled the lawsuit with a consent decree guaranteeing that men who met the poverty threshold established by the State of New York, or were homeless due to "physical, mental or social dysfunction," must be provided a shelter bed. The founding culture of the Coalition was one of social justice, not charity; the mission was to put ourselves out of business by ending, not just ameliorating, homelessness. But as Dorothy Day, cofounder of the Catholic Worker movement, put it decades earlier, "Once you start talking about a problem, people show up, looking for help."

I joined the Coalition for the Homeless in New York City in February 1989 and became its leader nine months later. Over the next thirty years I worked alongside and got to know countless thousands of homeless New Yorkers. Their courage and tenacity propelled the work of everyone at CFH, which runs a wide array of services, from a mobile feeding program to a summer sleepaway camp for homeless kids, from job training for homeless moms to affordable housing for families and single adults. But the central work that animated the Coalition for the Homeless was groundbreaking advocacy. Our guiding mission was singular and radical: not to simply provide services but to put ourselves out of business by solving the problem, permanently.

Modern mass homelessness exploded across the US more than forty years ago. The ranks of homeless Americans have recently surged to an all-time high, while additional untold millions hover near the complete destitution that eviction brings. And yet, as Anita and myriad others remind us, we know what works. Six years after Anita first visited the Coalition's office, she returned. After staying in a domestic violence shelter, Anita and her child were eventually placed in a NYCHA (public housing) apartment in Manhattan's Chelsea neighborhood, and she had found a part-time job at a nearby bodega. The son I had remembered was actually a girl—the spitting image of her mother. Anita showed up one afternoon with Brianna, proudly wearing her first school uniform, in tow. I was then heavily pregnant with my own son, not yet fully realizing what a sacrifice it was for them to make the three-hour round-trip trek from Brianna's charter school in Queens to downtown Manhattan. Anita didn't want anything from me other than to show off her daughter and say, "Can you believe it?" as much to herself as to me.

Yes, I can. I've seen, firsthand, the unparalleled difference that decent permanent housing makes in the lives of our neighbors in distress.

Why is housing so important? What makes having a home so vital to our ability to thrive? Why is its absence so catastrophic? Home is the place we leave each morning and return to at the end of each day. It's the space where we rest and make ourselves whole in order to face the world. Our homes are the staging grounds for our most profound and intimate experiences. Home is where we celebrate our triumphs and grieve our most painful losses. The sanctuary of home gives us not only respite, but perspective: imagine delighting in the peace and beauty of a long night's snowfall without a place to call home. Take away home and you lose something much more than the physical structure. For author Pierce Brown, home is "where you find light when all grows dark."[3] It's been said that the first prayer uttered by humans was for shelter.

This book traces the arc of homelessness in America since our country's inception, showing that our failed response to the current crisis is undeniably rooted in the punitive, Victorian-era assumption that there are two distinct classes of poor people: the deserving (a relative few) and the undeserving (the vast majority). This is just one of the many destructive myths surrounding homelessness.

The need to rebuke these myths has never been more urgent. They are pervasive, woven into the fabric of our nation's founding documents, masquerading as values, amplified time and again by elected leaders, sowing fear and hatred against our homeless and indigent neighbors. Debunking these myths, as we will do in the pages that follow, is paramount to leveraging the popular mandate needed to fund the affordable, housing-based solutions that will finally bring our unhoused neighbors home, for good.

# CHAPTER I

# A BRIEF HISTORY OF HOMELESSNESS

**MYTH 1** **"HOMELESSNESS IS INEVITABLE AND INTRINSICALLY UNSOLVABLE"**

When I began working at the Coalition for the Homeless in 1989, I saw a lot that stunned me, in good ways and bad. The bad, I'd expected when I signed up: the physical collapse of an elderly woman who had avoided shelters at all costs, trying for months to subsist in a shuttered subway entrance; the meltdown of a man who'd had all his belongings—birth certificate, dry clothes, and the last photo of his dead sister and grandmother—destroyed in an NYPD raid; the toddler whose untreated chronic sinus infections had left her partially deaf. The good were unexpected moments of grace: The seven-year-old boy who, after I handed him a few sheets of paper and an eight-pack of crayons while his mom and I worked on getting their food stamps reinstated, looked at me and grinned: "How did you know?" "Know what?" "That I'm the best drawer in my class." Or the man who delivered a pilfered interoffice envelope to the security desk, labeled "For Mary (NOT the tall one)!" Inside was a pristine, poster-sized subway map from the 1970s that he had repainted in wild, beautiful colors. Everything flowed into one stop, Grand Central, which was marked with concentric hearts.

But one thing I hadn't seen coming happened several months after I started, in the form of a group of high schoolers interested in volunteering with our mobile feeding program. Once I had finished explaining the genesis of the program (a woman, dubbed Mamma Doe, found dead of malnutrition in Midtown) and basic logistics (one team covered uptown Manhattan, the other Chinatown and parts south), the Q&A session turned quickly, with brazen teen candor:

"Well…what's it really like? Scary or sad?"

"If I sign up and can't deal, who's there to take over then?"

And, cutting to the chase: "This guy on my block—he's been there forever. Like I never *not* see this guy Frank any day we go his way."

I initially thought the student, José, was asking if there was anything more the Coalition could do for Frank. But as the questions continued to come at me, I realized that it hadn't even occurred to José that we might be able to get Frank off the streets. Neither José nor any of his classmates were old enough to remember a time before homelessness seemed inevitable and unsolvable.

Before. Less than two decades before, homelessness in New York was almost entirely confined to a few blocks on the Bowery. Before countless adults were "living rough" in every neighborhood, in every season. Before families with young children were being quartered at decrepit welfare hotels. Lou Reed had a number-one hit that same year, "Dirty Blvd.," describing the squalor: "This room cost $2,000.… Somewhere a landlord's laughing till he wets his pants."* I'm not exactly sure why these teens stunned me so. I had moved to New York after college, in 1984, a few years after modern mass homelessness had emerged, but it wasn't until I left for several months to work on the 1988 presidential campaign and returned home that the full impact of the crisis hit me. Before that, I had been more like those kids: usually limiting my concerns to immediate personal safety, avoiding direct interaction with homeless folks, and minimizing eye contact to proactively short my emotional circuit. Troubling in a different way were the

---

* When a *Rolling Stone* reporter compared Reed's savage take to that of Spanish poet Federico Garcia-Lorca, Reed shot back: "Lorca, of course, was writing during the first year of the Depression, and I think that today we're heading toward another one. I also feel that the people who run things have knowledgeably and intentionally fucked the people who can't possibly defend themselves—the aged, the poor, the young, the old, women. Lorca was livid about the situation, and so am I." Jonathan Cott, "Lou Reed: A New York State of Mind," *Rolling Stone*, October 27, 2014.

older, longtime New Yorkers beginning to develop a collective battle fatigue. A friend who was finishing his fellowship at Bellevue's psychiatric unit likened this mounting burnout to the well-documented emotional numbing experienced by nurses working in burn units: a similar repeated exposure to intense misery. To say that homeless people were everywhere was no exaggeration: An estimated 36,000 homeless adults were bedded down in nearly every doorway across dozens of blocks on upper Madison Avenue.[1] The inner walls of Penn Station's vast corridors were lined with people—hundreds—"sleeping rough" each night. In parks, subway stations, trains, and nearly every other type of public space, it was more common than not to encounter neighbors without a home.

The creeping normalization of modern mass homelessness began to morph very publicly into—and, I would say, significantly fanned the embers of—what the press described as a "backlash" against homeless people. Business leaders like Mort Zuckerman pulled no punches in their assessment of our unhoused neighbors (he even went so far as to mock them in a cameo appearance as a surly homeless man in Irwin Winkler's 1999 film *At First Sight*).[2] Proposed solutions for the crisis included shipping homeless people to an island in the middle of the East River for "re-education" (this from the legendary journalist and erstwhile liberal Pete Hamill in 1993).[3] This pattern was replicated across the country. The Department of Justice's June Kress analyzed the crisis in "Homeless Fatigue Syndrome: The Backlash Against the Crime of Homelessness in the 1990s."[4] And in the aftermath of a vote by the DC Council to weaken the right to access emergency shelter, Mitch Snyder—a personal hero to me and many others and "the nation's best-known advocate for the homeless," according to the *New York Times*—died by suicide.[5]

That high schoolers' Q&A introduced me to an entire generation who knew nothing other than visible, abject poverty at every turn. In the three decades since, the government's failure to invest in cost-effective, housing-based solutions has fueled this fatalism mightily. But homelessness is neither inevitable nor unsolvable. The greatest obstacle to ending modern mass homelessness is the dust of cynicism that has settled on it.

To understand this cynicism, it's helpful to unravel the two major strands that directly contributed to it: the wholesale destruction of truly affordable housing throughout the '70s and '80s—over a quarter million units in New York City alone—and the intentional nature of the crisis. Americans have become unhoused in increasing numbers "by design."

## STOKING THE FLAMES: THE ADVENT OF MODERN HOMELESSNESS, 1975–1990

Single room occupancy (SRO) housing was first developed in cities across the US as early as the 1880s. The small, furnished rooms with shared bathroom and kitchen facilities for decades provided low-cost housing, mostly to single men. In New York, they were usually located within tenement and larger buildings. As Malcolm Gladwell put it, "SROs sprang up early in the century in New York and other major American cities as short-term housing for the working poor. But they soon acquired an unsavory reputation."[6] There was an almost immediate, hard-line call to rein in this housing of last resort. In 1889, Thomas Byrnes, chief inspector of the nascent NYPD, penned an essay, "Nurseries of Crime," opining that such housing was "largely frequented by thieves and other criminals of the lowest class, who lodge in these resorts regularly and here consort together and lay their plans for crimes of one sort or another."[7] As for any new arrival in town who might stay in such accommodations, "In nine cases out of ten—I am quite confident that this proportion is not too large—he turns out a thief or a burglar, if, indeed, he does not sooner or later become a murderer." Byrnes's solution was as caustic as his assessment: "This is not a case for a palliative; as Emerson would say, it is a 'case for a gun'—for the knife, the blister, the amputating instruments." His cure was an attempted unabashed bureaucratic overreach: "In my judgment, based on many years' experience, the lodging-house business should be under the immediate supervision of the police, since they are the officials who practically enforce the laws, and because they have better opportunities than any others for ascertaining the character of persons and places."

In 1890, a year after Byrnes's essay appeared, journalist Jacob Riis published his landmark work of photojournalism, *How the Other Half Lives*, which exposed squalid living conditions, resulting disease, and early deaths in New York City tenement buildings.[8] Riis had honed his journalist craft as a crime reporter and, not surprisingly, was a vocal critic of Byrnes, who had garnered "a reputation as a champion of the rich and powerful."[9] By documenting "the filth, disease, exploitation, and overcrowding that characterized the experience of more than one million immigrants," Riis pushed "tenement reform to the front of New York's political agenda."[10] His efforts spurred the first major building codes in 1901 and even prompted a new friend, Theodore Roosevelt, Byrnes's successor at the helm of the NYPD, "to close down the police-run poor houses" in 1896. However, *How the Other Half Lives* also heralded a new brand of "muckraking journalism" that sensationalized the slums under the guise of enlightening the middle and upper classes to the destitution there. Architectural historian Paul Groth traces the evolution of Riis-era reformers—"self-appointed" wealthy businessmen or their wives, "who volunteered their time…for the public good," and who, because of their class origins, "attacked the problems of SRO living as moral and cultural failures."[11]

Groth emphasizes the darker side of these urban reformers, writing that their calls to reform housing codes through the 1940s "were informed by class biases, social prejudices, and varying degrees of xenophobia and racism." Their agenda became increasingly anti-SRO, and they were ultimately instrumental in eradicating this critical reserve of low-end housing. Their well-intentioned disdain for the decrepit living conditions of the poor often masked a growing unease with indigent people themselves.

New York City continued to grow by leaps and bounds, its population more than doubling in a half century—from 3.4 million (in 1900) to 7.9 million (in 1950)—and housing expanded accordingly. In the mid-1940s, as more than 7.6 million US servicemembers returned home from World War II, housing occupancy rates reached new all-time highs across the nation. This postwar housing shortage made most municipalities turn a blind eye to marginal housing conditions. SROs were ascendent in major urban housing markets, including New York. By the mid-twentieth century, there were upward of 200,000 SRO units in the city. However, the mid-1950s saw New York's housing policy turn uniformly against SROs. Brian Sullivan and Jonathan Burke observed in the *City University of New York Law Review*: "Beginning around 1955, and continuing for nearly three decades thereafter, the City attempted to eliminate SRO housing."[12]

The arrival of families—as opposed to the traditional single male tenant—in SROs was a turning point. Malcolm Gladwell notes that when "poor families—particularly, and not inconsequentially, immigrant families—began moving into the new SROs in large numbers," public resentment of this housing type reached its peak. "Landlords began chopping up one- and two-bedroom apartments to make SROs, alarming city officials," writes Gladwell. "In a few celebrated cases, chaotic conditions resulted when owners on the Upper West Side of Manhattan rented SROs to families with children, largely Latino immigrants."[13]

### GOVERNMENT-ENGINEERED HOMELESSNESS

In 1954, New York City passed Local Law 24, which banned any new construction of SROs and prohibited carving up large apartments for conversion into single-room units. The City of New York established the J-51 tax abatement program the following year, which gave tax incentives to building owners if they proactively converted their existing SRO units into commercial hotels, offices, or market-rate apartments.

The results were predictable. Thousands of single-occupancy units were quickly converted into larger apartments, which—because J-51 specifically allowed the new units to be untethered from any type of rent stabilization or regulation—commanded far more expensive rents. Many of these conversions happened in marginal neighborhoods, particularly Manhattan's then economically diverse Upper West Side, and pushed longtime residents out of previously affordable communities. Displacement as precursor to gentrification is not unique, but the scale at which luxury housing flourished during this period was. This surge in upscale housing, birthed from a diminution of affordable units, significantly increased the rent burden for lower- and working-class households.

Many assume these shifts were the yield of pure market forces, but in fact, exponential housing insecurity was engineered by government. Sullivan and Burke offer the critical summary: "The interplay between market forces and government policy was dynamic: landlords, responding to market and government signals, quickly emptied and converted the most desirable buildings."[14] Whatever remaining SRO buildings were occupied by tenants with rent-regulated leases, yielding far less income and thus viewed by owners as a poor investment. Those buildings were not maintained, and Sullivan and Burke conclude, "As the condition of these SROs deteriorated, tenants who could afford to leave moved out."[15] Eventually, the only tenants left were extremely low-income individuals. The result was an overwhelming concentration of people least able to compete in the housing market: minimum-wage workers, the unemployed, those on welfare, and patients discharged from State psychiatric hospitals that were being massively downsized around this time.[16] "The City's tax policies," explain Sullivan and Burke, "gave owners an extra push to remove these tenants and convert the remaining buildings, effectively putting SROs out of business."[17]

In sum, New York effectively banned new SRO construction by altering building codes, provided tax incentives for owners to convert SROs to unregulated apartments, and prohibited SRO leases for families. The fallout from these policies reached its apex in the late 1970s, "which were particularly disastrous for SROs."[18]

The downward spiral of deteriorating conditions, spurred by tax policy and new zoning restrictions was succinctly summarized by Anthony Blackburn in an interview with the *New York Times*: "There were terribly deteriorated buildings…which could be incredibly valuable if they were rented to young professionals." Blackburn also noted that throughout the '70s and '80s, landlords forced SRO tenants out "by creating unimaginably dreadful conditions in the building. They turned the heat off, they let units to prostitutes [and] drug dealers. Some hired thugs to simply throw tenants out."[19] By the City's own admission, the J-51 program encouraged a large number of landlords to burn down their own properties as a last resort to remove tenants.[20]

## DISPOSSESSION BY FIRE

Another equally pivotal cascade of events sparked New York's modern homeless crisis: the unprecedented widescale destruction of multifamily complexes of affordable housing, particularly in the Bronx. Between 1970 and 1980, "seven different census tracts in the Bronx lost more than 97 percent of their buildings to fire and abandonment and 44 tracts... lost more than 50 percent."[21] As with the SRO debacle, neglect and intentional governmental engineering were precursors to the destruction of tens of thousands of affordable homes in the Bronx.

In the years after World War II, Robert Moses—New York's famed urban planner from the 1920s through the 1960s—spearheaded slum-clearing efforts throughout Manhattan, the Bronx, and Brooklyn, demolishing low-income neighborhoods and replacing most with massive high-rise public housing projects. This resulted in the displacement of hundreds of thousands of people, overwhelmingly poor people and people of color.[22] Many of these families migrated to outer-borough neighborhoods, traditionally populated for generations by low-income Jewish, Irish, and Italian communities. The population of the Bronx swelled by over 100,000 in the 1960s alone. The borough's housing stock largely consisted of prewar buildings and was carved up to accommodate the influx of mostly Black and Puerto Rican New Yorkers.[23] Landlords typically made little effort to maintain—let alone upgrade—the physical structures, electrical wiring, or plumbing necessary to ensure the basic safety of the expanding tenant base. In the 1960s, in response to the increased fire hazard conditions specific to these packed, decaying neighborhoods, additional firehouses were opened in close proximity.[24]

## "LADIES AND GENTLEMEN, THE BRONX IS BURNING"

During Game 2 of the 1977 World Series, in what many consider a defining moment in American history, ABC Sports helicopters hovering

above Yankee Stadium in the Bronx panned over to the horizon, cap-
turing a spectacular building fire against the clear October night sky.
Although broadcaster Howard Cosell never actually said the infamous
words, "Ladies and gentlemen, the Bronx is burning," he and his cohosts
did return repeatedly to, and provide commentary on, live shots of the
raging fire throughout the game.[25] In deconstructing Kurt Vonnegut's
repetitive use of the phrase "So it goes" in *Slaughterhouse-Five*, Salman
Rushdie gleaned that "sometimes a phrase…can catch the imagina-
tion so powerfully—even when misquoted—that it lifts off from the
page and acquires an independent life of its own. 'Come up and see
me sometime' and 'Play it again, Sam' are misquotations of this type."[26]
Likewise, in the days and weeks that followed, news outlets around the
world ran a cribbed version of the faux quote, spawning the headline
"The Bronx Is Burning!"

The narrative given by these news stories was bleak: low-income
Bronx residents were so alienated and dysfunctional they were setting buildings on fire for entertainment, for thrills, or as some form of
protest. Though their explanation was false, it's little wonder why journalists readily adopted it. New York City administrators had a covert
agenda of "planned shrinkage," a disinvestment strategy that intentionally withdraws essential services from the poorest neighborhoods, particularly those with the least political power. This strategy, first seeded
in Robert Moses's mammoth housing projects, was successfully amplified in 1970 by Daniel Patrick Moynihan, then senior advisor to President Richard Nixon, in his infamous "benign neglect" memo to the
commander in chief.[27] Moynihan argued that the government should
withhold key resources from low-income, predominantly Black areas
such as the Bronx. The biggest takeaway from his document: "*Fires are
in fact a leading indicator of social pathology for a neighborhood. They
come first. Crime, and the rest, follows.*" (Emphasis his.)

Moynihan offered no evidence whatsoever to back his racist analysis. (The section of his memo titled "Social Alienation" literally begins:
"With no real evidence," and continues: "I would nonetheless sug-
gest that a great deal of the crime, the fire setting, the rampant school

violence, and other such phenomenon in the black community have become quasi-politicized. Hatred—revenge—against whites is now an acceptable excuse for doing what might have been done anyway.") Nonetheless, his theories were adopted wholeheartedly as fact when the *New York Times* decided to print the memo, in its entirety, on its front page on May 1, 1970.[28] Moynihan's memo concludes with the singularly disturbing policy prescription: "The time may have come when the issue of race could benefit from a period of 'benign neglect.'"

In the context of the early 1970s, "benign neglect" was barely veiled code for shrinking urban populations by cutting or eliminating infrastructure funds for everyday services such as water, sewage, and transportation, as well as reducing Medicaid and Social Security Disability Insurance (SSDI) benefits and housing funded by Housing and Urban Development (HUD). The Republican Nixon administration adopted this tactic with the aim of weakening urban Democratic strongholds. They also revised formulas for federal block grants, redirecting overall funding from Democratic cities to Southern states—increasing funding to solidifying the emerging Republican voting bedrock.

Urban epidemiologists Deborah Wallace and Rodrick Wallace, sifting through documents obtained via 1973 Freedom of Information Act (FOIA) requests, observed: "Since, to Moynihan, pathologies express themselves as malicious false alarms or arson, 'benign neglect,' when applied to fire service, meant not answering alarms in poor minority neighborhoods." In New York City specifically, "benign neglect" would soon, as the Wallaces wrote, take the form of withdrawing "essential services from sick neighborhoods which were seen as unable to survive or undeserving of survival.... Of course, the neighborhoods diagnosed as 'sick' were all poor and nonwhite."[29]

Documents from the Wallaces' FOIA requests also revealed extensive correspondence between Moynihan and the RAND Corporation (which Moynihan used to prop up his flawed logic). RAND, best known then for falsifying body counts and generating specious mathematical models to prolong the Vietnam War (exposed by Daniel Ellsberg via the

Pentagon Papers in 1971) would soon pivot to play a role in obliterating huge swaths of the Bronx.[30]

When New York City began to recognize the very real possibility of impending bankruptcy in 1971, Mayor John Lindsay engaged the RAND Corporation to study ways to cut unneeded or redundant expenditures. Joe Flood's authoritative and riveting book, *The Fires: How a Computer Formula, Big Ideas, and the Best of Intentions Burned Down New York City—and Determined the Future of Cities*, notes that the following year, "RAND recommended closing 13 [fire] companies, oddly including some of the busiest in the fire-prone South Bronx, and opening seven new ones, including units in suburban neighborhoods of Staten Island and the North Bronx." In perhaps the most misguided and shortsighted analysis ever, RAND "created computer models that used *response times* as the most important variable in their equations, and suggested that areas with already low response times could afford to have firehouses closed."[31] (Emphasis mine.)

Firehouses had been added to densely packed Bronx neighborhoods throughout the 1960s to forestall fire tragedies in the borough's deteriorating buildings. But beginning in 1972—at a time when fire fatalities were already at an all-time high—using the flawed logic and computer models generated by RAND, the City closed thirty-five fire companies in high fire-incidence neighborhoods, which Flood notes "inherently increased response times and endangered residents."[32]

With the firehouses closed, in 1974 alone over four thousand suspicious fires were recorded in New York City.[33] Perhaps Cosell's apocryphal tagline was embraced so thoroughly because it provided a perfect shorthand to convey government abnegation on the grandest scale and its staggering results: the Bronx hemorrhaged 97 percent of its buildings to fire in the 1970s. This catastrophe was not limited to the Bronx. As Dartmouth University's Bench Ansfield notes, in "predominantly Latinx sections of [Manhattan's] Lower East Side, 57 percent of residents were displaced by fire, eviction, and landlord abandonment between 1970 and 1980." Because the fires were mostly set at night, "many parents [instructed] their children to wear shoes to bed, while suitcases filled with essential possessions sat expectantly by the front door."[34]

All this unfurled in near parallel with the City's J-51 program, which Sullivan and Burke estimate eliminated nearly two-thirds of its remaining SRO units, amplifying "market forces [already] pushing landlords away from SRO housing.... By the 1980s, the consequences of the anti-SRO crusade were painfully evident: harassment, homelessness, and misery."[35] By the City of New York's own admission, the J-51 program encouraged a large number of landlords to burn down their own properties, as a last resort, to remove tenants.[36] In total, by 1980, over 80 percent of housing stock in the Bronx had been torched, and an estimated 250,000 people displaced as a result.[37] The era of seemingly intractable homelessness had arrived.

## CASE STUDY: JAY AND STUART PODOLSKY

Amidst this mosh pit of thuggery and arson, one example that stands out is Jay and Stuart Podolsky, brothers whose criminal enterprises to capitalize on the city's most marginal residential real estate were so brazen that in the 1980s they garnered the moniker "Terror Lords" from the *New York Post*. Throughout their childhood, their father, Zenek Podolsky, had spent his workdays cutting meat, his evenings at the local Democratic clubhouse, and his weekends acquiring Coney Island rooming houses. Between 1970 and 1978, according to a document filed by District Attorney Robert Morgenthau in an unrelated case years later, "almost all were burned down in over 125 suspicious fires." The elder Podolsky was never charged with a related crime, and he profited when the government condemned the properties for urban renewal. Podolsky used the condemnation windfalls to expand. Every Friday, he and his seven children talked real estate over Sabbath dinner. The family philosophy was summed up by the Ayn Rand–inspired name of the company he used to acquire one Brooklyn building: Fountainhead Associates.[38]

My personal introduction to the Podolskys came in the aftermath of a criminal case brought against them. In 1983, the Podolsky brothers purchased three brownstone buildings on Manhattan's West 77th Street occupied by mostly senior citizen tenants. They promptly brought in a gang of "professional vacators" to terrorize the residents into leaving so that they could convert the buildings into luxury condos. The thugs were paid a $600 bonus for each apartment emptied, including one in which a longtime tenant, an elderly woman, died from pneumonia after they illegally cut off her heat. The brothers were indicted for these crimes and in 1987 pled guilty to a total of thirty-seven felonies. In order to avoid serious prison sentences, they agreed to give the three buildings to the Coalition for the Homeless to repair—and ensure they would be permanently affordable housing.[39] One of my first major projects at the Coalition was to help guide extensive renovations in those nearly gutted buildings, returning them to their former glory. But as we'll see in later chapters, the Podolskys regrouped following their plea deals and to this day continue to reap a massive fortune providing dangerously substandard shelter for homeless New Yorkers.

It is impossible to overstate the staggering impact of the City of New York's misguided SRO policy. The demise of New York's SROs is not a tale of private market real estate trends run amok. It was "not the inevitable result of impersonal or unalterable market forces. City policy, acting dynamically with market forces, is responsible for [creating the resulting] crisis."[40] New York City's SRO count dropped from 200,000 in the 1950s to just 46,744 by 1993 and roughly 35,000 by 2002.[41] (Nonprofit groups grew that number to an estimated 40,000 by 2020; most of the post-1983 units have been modified into what's known as "supportive housing," with on-site mental health and other support services.)

There is an uncontested relationship between this wholesale destruction of New York's most affordable housing and the sudden, dramatic appearance of homeless single adults on the streets and other public spaces in the late 1970s and early '80s. A 1980 study of homeless men living in public shelters confirmed that fully 50 percent of them had resided in SROs immediately before seeking shelter.[42] Certainly, other factors are relevant: stagnant wages, increasing poverty and unemployment, and—as we'll discuss in detail in chapter 3—the discharge of more than 125,000 indigent psychiatric patients from State hospitals between 1955 and 1980. But the unprecedented, policy-engineered destruction of low-cost housing obliterated the final bulwark that had kept our most vulnerable neighbors from literal homelessness. New York's story of dwindling SROs and torched inner-city neighborhoods had parallels across the nation: similar stark diminutions of affordable housing and increased homelessness have been documented across urban and rural America over the past four decades.

But there is a second perhaps equally important thread that is essential to understanding the entrenchment of modern, mass homelessness: the othering of the visibly poor. This may present as a psychological phenomenon, but its roots are economic, and they run deep. The remainder of this chapter looks at the seeds of this othering in the US's founding principles and documents, how it has been fully realized in our financial system, and how increasing income inequality drives interclass alienation. (In chapter 2, we'll take a deeper dive into the religious and ethical mythology imported from abroad that continues to blunt our ability to advance proven solutions to homelessness and enduring poverty.)

## THE FINANCIALIZATION OF THE AMERICAN ECONOMY

The year of my eye-opening meeting with the high schoolers, 1990 was a capstone for three full decades of tectonic shifts in the US economy. Once largely manufacturing driven, the economy became dominated by financialization, in the wake of unprecedented rollbacks in financial regulation. The unparalleled economic growth in post-WWII America had been fueled by our robust manufacturing sector, which in 1950 accounted for nearly a third of gross domestic product (GDP). The financial sector that same year totaled just 12 percent. Financial institutions were a (far more regulated and) relatively small sector of the economy and their task was to distribute unused assets. But by 1990, manufacturing had shrunk to 19 percent and finance had begun its steady ascent, growing to 16 percent.

This sea change began in the 1970s. As Noam Chomsky elegantly puts it, there was at that time "a concerted effort on the part of 'the masters of mankind,' 'the owners of the society,' ... to increase the role of financial institutions—banks, investment firms, and so on." This decade ushered in the lifting of Depression-era regulations specifically enacted to prevent the catastrophic economic downturns seen in the boom/bust cycles of the 1800s, as well as that which spawned the Great Depression. This deregulation was tremendously destabilizing—sparking "huge increases in flow of speculative capital ... because of enormous changes in the financial sector from traditional banks to risky investments, complex financial instruments, money manipulation, and so on," according to Chomsky.[43]

Chomsky drills down on the implications of this deregulation and financialization, using General Electric as an example: once synonymous with light bulbs and computers, "by the 1970s General Electric could make more profit playing games with money than they could by producing [goods] in the United States. You have to remember that General Electric is substantially a financial institution today. It makes half its profits just by moving money around in complicated ways." Perhaps most disturbing, Chomsky adds, "It's very unclear that [GE is] doing anything that's of value to the economy."[44]

An integral piece of financialization is the offshoring of production. This is all overtly intentional. In the aftermath of huge societal upheavals in the 1960s, Chomsky notes, "The trade system was reconstructed with the very explicit design of putting working people in competition with one another all over the world. What it's led to is a reduction in the share of income on the part of working people." American workers were thrust into competing with already exploited workers in developing countries. Of course, highly paid workers in the legal and financial sectors managed to escape this fate because they're not "placed in direct competition with the rest of the world. Far from it ... Capital is free to move, but the workers aren't."[45]

Intrinsic and essential to this newly engineered economy is an approach that increases worker insecurity. In 1999, then Federal Reserve chair Alan Greenspan in his *Monetary Policy Report to the Congress Pursuant to the Full Employment and Balanced Growth Act of 1978* explicitly stated that, to the power establishment, a successful economy was one based on "the consequence of *greater worker insecurity*."[46] (Emphasis mine.) By keeping workers increasingly insecure, they're less likely to unionize and push for a living wage and better conditions. The seeds of alienation throughout most of society are thus intentionally sown. That undercurrent of seismic economic shifts underlay the first wave of public anti-homeless sentiment in 1990.

Before the 1970s, when the majority of US employment was generated by manufacturing sectors, the financial well-being of those companies was predicated on their workers being able to afford the goods they produced. To debunk another myth: Henry Ford didn't really say that he paid his workers five dollars a day so they could afford the cars they were building—rather, as reported in the *Saturday Evening Post*, he arrived at that number during a series of meetings with his managers.[47] In 1914, Ford was paying workers $2.34 for a nine-hour shift when he told his deputies, "Figure out how much more we can give our men." The managers timidly added increments of twenty-five cents an hour, with Ford dismissing their figures again and again as "Not enough." After many a back-and-forth, he urged the group to double the rate at which they'd started, for a total of $4.80 per day.

"Why don't you make it five dollars an hour and bust the company," griped one of the managers.

Ford replied, "Fine! We'll do that!"

According to the *Post*, when Detroit's other manufacturers heard the news of Ford's five-dollar day, they were "panicking and predicting various disasters," believing they would be forced to relocate because matching the wage would bankrupt them. They even posited that Ford's own workers would be "demoralized by this sudden affluence." Let that sink in and marinate.

Ford explained that his rationale for the dramatic wage hikes was employee retention and consistency of workmanship. In the *Post*'s analysis, "Ford believed he was buying a higher quality of work from all his employees." It would also bolster his ability "to retain workers who could handle the pressure and the monotony of his assembly line." Ford himself wrote in his book *Today and Tomorrow* (1926): "The owner, the employees, and the buying public are all one and the same, and unless an industry can so manage itself as to keep wages high and prices low it destroys itself, for otherwise it limits the number of its customers."[48]

Harley Shaiken, a labor economist at the University of California, Berkeley, underscores that while Ford's primary motivation wasn't to pay his employees enough to buy a car, the $5-dollar day was nonetheless "a game changer," because what it "gave us was an industrial middle class and an economy driven by consumer demand." Ford's experiment in higher wages increased productivity, and that's also a win for business: "That positive feedback loop gave rise to a broad, prosperous middle class."

Shaiken notes that, in contrast, "*today, overwhelmingly employers view the lowest wage as the most competitive wage.*" (Emphasis mine.) "There are very real economic pressures out there that push down on wages," he says. "So it's not a simple story, but that doesn't mean that there isn't a core truth into what Ford found."

In Chomsky's analysis, the enormous shifts wrought by financialization began in the 1970s but really took off in the 1980s. Importantly, he flags the practical and moral underpinnings of these changes: "Keep in mind, there are two entirely different sets of rules for any dire consequences for the wealthy versus the working-class or poor Americans."[49]

This became abundantly clear when in 1984 President Reagan gave a then unprecedented bailout to banks like Continental Illinois. Rather than let the bank fail as a result of its own ineptitude and gross speculative practices, Reagan handed them $7.5 billion—then, the biggest US government bailout. His successor, fellow Republican George H. W. Bush, went on to sign off on a staggering $126 billion bailout for the savings and loan industry in 1989. In fact, the federal government's own postmortem pinned the cause of what became known as "the S&L debacle" on the fact that "most political, legislative, and regulatory decisions in the early 1980s were imbued with a spirit of deregulation."[50] And the blame is not limited to Republicans alone: from the mid-1970s onward, the top leaders of the financial sector seeded cabinet-level appointments in each administration, Republican and Democrat alike.

Interviewed in 2019, Chomsky remarked, "The American Dream, like many ideals was partly symbolic, but partly real." The financialization of the economy significantly shifted capitalism's intrinsic risks and burdens to the working class. The 1950s and '60s, widely considered to be a golden age of economic expansion in the US, saw, according to Chomsky, "pretty egalitarian growth, wherein the lowest fifth of the population was improving about as much as the upper fifth." That is in sharp contrast with the current state of the global economy. Now "we're well on our way into an international plutonomy," says Chomsky, where a small number of people are amassing tremendous wealth. For the few that control increasingly vast wealth, the fate of the working-class consumer matters far less than it did in Ford's day, "because most of them are not going to be consuming your product anyway, or at least not on a major basis. High salaries and high bonuses are doled out to the wealthy—here and abroad. What about the rest? There's a term coming into use for them, too—they're called the 'precariat' "—a portmanteau of "precarious" and "proletariat" that expresses the increased economic instability of working people around the world.[51]

### "THE OPPOSITE OF LOVE IS NOT HATE, BUT SEPARATION."*

These changes have powerfully undermined our innate sense of connectedness, compassion, solidarity. Chomsky raises the alarm about this new economic order as a direct threat to our democracy: "Solidarity is quite dangerous from the point of view of the masters: You're only supposed to care about yourself, not other people. This is quite different from the people they claim to be their heroes, like Adam Smith, who based his whole approach to the economy on the principle of sympathy." Sympathy is a hardwired human trait, according to Chomsky, "but today it has to be driven out of people's heads. Unlike Smith, at all costs

*John Berger, *And Our Faces, My Heart, Brief as Photos* (New York: Vintage, 1992).

you've got to be for yourself and follow the vile maxim, 'don't care about others.'" This increased atomization reinforces the continual othering of the visibly poor.

"It's taken a lot of effort to try to drive these basic human emotions out of people's heads," Chomsky summarizes. "And we see it today in policy formation," including recent Republican attacks on Social Security from the floor of Congress and on the presidential campaign trail. "Social Security is based on the principle of solidarity—caring for others. I pay payroll taxes so the widow across town can get something to live on," he says. (We'll revisit this example in the next chapter, but notice how even Chomsky chooses the example of widows, who, like orphans, are universally deemed among the "worthiest" of the poor.) As it relates to homelessness and skyrocketing housing insecurity, "for the poor, [the attitude is] let market principles prevail. Don't expect any help from the government."

This is the bedrock of neoliberalism, and its roots are deeply entrenched. "It has the dual character which goes all the way back in our economic history," Chomsky says. "There are one set of rules for the rich—and the opposite set of rules for the poor." One important difference today, however, is the lack of class awareness among the middle and lower classes: "[During the nineteenth-century Industrial Revolution,] in the US, people were very conscious of class, and overwhelmingly regarded wage labor as not very different from slavery—different only in that it was temporary." "[Nowadays,] in the interest of power and privilege, it's good to drive those ideas out of people's heads," observes Chomsky. "You don't want them to know they are an oppressed class."

This cultural shift was orchestrated by business leaders and coincided with massive deregulation financialization, all with a single goal: to strip away the guardrails of the social safety net adopted in the wake of the catastrophic Great Depression. The most significant of these, the Glass-Steagall Act of 1933, had separated commercial and investment banks and created the Federal Deposit Insurance Corporation, or FDIC. That act, along with other legislation of the period, had helped successfully stabilize the US economy through its mid-century golden age. All were predicated on the ideal of solidarity: together, we are stronger. The separation of investment and commercial banks curbed the ability of the wealthy to gamble freely with the money of the poor, prioritizing a base level of common welfare. This ideal transcended political parties. In 1934, President Franklin D. Roosevelt, in one of his radio addresses, "On Moving Forward to Greater Freedom and Greater Security," quoted a conservative Republican senator from New York, Elihu Root: "The relations between the employer and the employed, between the owners of aggregated capital and the units of organized labor, between the small producer, the small trader, the consumer, and the great transporting and manufacturing and distributing agencies, all present new questions for the solution of which the old reliance upon the free action of individual wills appear quite inadequate."[52]

At the conclusion of this stirring address, FDR quoted another Republican, Abraham Lincoln: "The legitimate object of government is to do for a community of people whatever they need to have done but cannot do at all or cannot do so well for themselves in their separate and individual capacities."

## MODERN PROGRESSIVES IGNORE HOUSING

Missing from Chomsky's, and indeed from virtually all progressive economic analyses of the financialization of our economy, is how that financialization was led by and fueled the commodification of housing—the unprecedented shift away from housing for the sake of shelter and into a vehicle for investment and wealth creation. The advent of home-as-investment-vehicle was a direct by-product of economic financialization. As more complicated financial instruments grew, the finance sector revenues generated were increasingly invested in real estate, which drove housing prices up. For the average homeowner (who actually managed to accrue equity in their home), this bullish real estate surge meant their home became their main vehicle to amass wealth. This led some middle-class American homeowners to roll over whatever equity they had accumulated into more expensive homes—or even purchase second or third homes, believing the housing market would continue to expand indefinitely. Banks, now freed of pre-1970s regulations, were all too happy to extend mortgages to folks who really couldn't afford to maintain the upgraded (or speculative) homes should the market contract. Deregulation was essential in allowing banks and investment groups bundled these "subprime" mortgages into larger securities that gained a veneer of respectability from the more stable assets included. The rating agencies moved in lockstep, giving high bond ratings to these toxic stews of mostly housing investments, precipitating the 2008 collapse of the US housing bubble and the Great Recession, which brought the global economy to near collapse.

The decades-long march to financialize the housing market stripped housing of its essential—I would argue sacred—role to provide shelter. Leilani Farha, former United Nations Special Rapporteur on the Right to Adequate Housing, put it best: "I believe there's a huge difference between housing as a commodity and gold as a commodity. Gold is not a human right, housing is."[53]

## FAILURE FUELS FATALISM

It turned out that those high schoolers in 1990 had a lot more resting on their shoulders than I'd initially grasped. In their short lifetimes, the only New York City they'd ever known was one that had destroyed over 250,000 units of its most affordable housing via policies that magnified destructive market forces. As a result, an estimated 36,000 destitute adults were made homeless and living rough on city streets by the 1980s.[54] The established, ongoing financialization of the US economy made it far less likely that these teens would find decent, living-wage jobs with benefits to help carry them through adulthood. And the financialization of housing was just beginning to do similarly spectacular damage to their odds of securing a decent home for themselves and their children. The popular press narrative was that New York, like many other parts of the country, had bottomed out economically in the 1970s and a new, hopeful tide would lift everyone to new levels of prosperity. But the turbocharged '80s laid its own stealth framework for the greatest wealth polarization ever seen, amassing enormous amounts of capital into the hands of a relative few, and spading economic insecurity for working-class and poor Americans. Class consciousness was actively suppressed, with the notable exception of our most visibly poor neighbors. Like the existential point of no return that climate scientists warn we are approaching, a similarly bleak point economically is rapidly approaching. There are no more citizens, only consumers. And homeless people are a glaring, unavoidable reminder of the basic human decency sacrificed in the era of neoliberalism—or, as it's increasingly (more accurately) called, "late-stage capitalism."

At every level of government—federal, state, and local—the sharp surge in homelessness between 1975 and 1990 birthed numerous much-hyped homeless commissions, task forces, blueprints, and "robust/enhanced/targeted" housing policies. But because these were knowingly designed and underfunded to "manage" (not solve) a full-blown humanitarian crisis, they yielded mostly stopgap Band-Aids.

It wasn't entirely surprising, then, that a small but vocal minority began to blame the problem on homeless victims themselves. Failure fuels fatalism. It's far easier to move away from compassion and solidarity when the steady drumbeat of news declares, in essence, that nothing works. Accepting that narrative gives us a convenient off-ramp from having to care and is oddly self-soothing. Normalcy of a sort sets in. It is too hard, we tell ourselves, to acknowledge the humanity of people struggling literally to live another day. How much easier simply to surrender hope and replace it with a cleaner-cut explanation that "those people" we once saw as neighbors might really just be responsible for their own fucked-up situation. It's *their* "bad choices," not larger economic forces, and certainly not the most obvious explanation: as untold thousands of cheap homes were destroyed in record time, those least able to compete were left without any place to turn.

When people first appeared on the streets carrying everything they owned, it was startling. Now, when you step out of your door, you expect someone to appear, needing something. Asking for your leftover sandwich or a subway swipe or some water, just three more dollars so he can crash at a Bowery flophouse, anything you can spare to replace the shoes stolen last night from under his pillow at a shelter with a thousand other homeless men (this last plea made as the gentleman walked barefoot from subway car to subway car). Now, no one bothers to look up. The sheer scale and depth of suffering were seemingly everywhere, escalating.

Poet, artist, and author John Berger challenged us to realize that how we look at anything is a choice. How are we choosing to look at our homelessness neighbors? Do we even see them? What those teens were grappling with was an unprecedented shift in enduring, visible poverty. As Berger explained in 1991: "The poverty of our century is unlike that of any other. It is not, as poverty was before, the result of natural scarcity, but of a set of priorities imposed upon the rest of the world by the rich. Consequently, the modern poor are not pitied... but written off as trash. The twentieth-century consumer economy has produced the first culture for which a beggar is a reminder of nothing."[55]

The good news is that if we've engineered a system that traps ever greater numbers of our neighbors in homelessness, we can very well reverse-engineer our way out. This book is an attempt at cataloging not only myths surrounding homelessness, but what bolstered their construction. We'll see that the current wave of mass homelessness is different—but neither inevitable, nor unsolvable. It hinges on hope.

*Hope is not a form of guarantee; it's a form of energy,*
*and very frequently that energy is strongest*
*in circumstances that are very dark.*

—JOHN BERGER[56]

# CHAPTER 2

# THE ROOTS OF AMERICAN HOMELESSNESS

**MYTH 2** "HOMELESSNESS IN AMERICA IS A RELATIVELY NEW PHENOMENON"

**MYTH 3** "HELPING THE 'WORTHY' POOR IS THE BEST WAY TO END POVERTY AND HOMELESSNESS"

Examining the past contextualizes our present harsh realities, but more importantly, it provides a road map of where things went astray. This excavation has never been more urgent, given the unsympathetic attitudes so many hold against our homeless neighbors and the ruthless policies now unfolding across the nation attempting to criminalize their very existence. "Cruelty is the point!" (the rallying cry that activists have taken up to condemn such policies) aptly and tragically describes much of America's homeless strategy since our nation's inception.

In this chapter, we will trace the historic arc of homelessness in the US—including fluctuations tied to the ebb and flow of wartime economies—and debunk misconceptions that it is a purely modern problem. Homelessness has waxed and waned throughout US history, but unlike homelessness of the modern era (the late 1970s to the present), previous surges in homelessness were directly tied to postwar conditions or economic depressions.

We will also look at the historical roots of the modern-day impulse to judge destitute people for their circumstances and force them to "prove" that they deserve aid. This mindset can be traced back to the colonial-era Calvinist myth of the "worthy" versus "unworthy" poor, which itself informed seventeenth-century English Poor Laws. In all historic periods—Elizabethan, colonial, modern—this punitive approach has failed to solve the problem of poverty or its most visible manifestation: homelessness. Yet it continues to animate current debate, with an emphasis on moving our most marginalized neighbors out of sight rather than up, out of destitution.

The most destructive aspects of the Calvinist belief system have endured and serve most importantly to emotionally distance the domiciled from the visibly impoverished—preventing us from fully investing in humane solutions proven to work.

These two myths must be considered in tandem, as they are a double helix, entwined deep within our nation's DNA.

## MODERN-DAY ALMONERS

Just how ingrained is the misguided belief that there are "worthy" versus "unworthy" poor? When I joined the Coalition in the late 1980s, my wonderful predecessor, Jayne Davis, explained that because she was leaving to get married and move to South Carolina, I was to take over her role as an "almoner."

"I'm sorry....almoner?" I asked, as Jayne handed me an envelope from something called the Havens Relief Fund Society. Inside was a letter addressed to me, confirming that the fund had accepted Jayne's recommendation to induct me into their secret society of "almoners." The letter was short, referring mostly to the enclosed report form, which I was to file when I distributed grants to recipients, and the initial check for $10,000. A pamphlet, mimeographed on light blue paper, summarized the history of the society's founder, Charles Gerard Havens. In 1871, Havens had set aside money to help people who, with one-time assistance, could avoid or escape destitution.

Because I was inducted into the society at a time before New York City had established funds specifically for one-time assistance with rental arrears, I and many other almoners, scattered throughout other nonprofit agencies and religious groups across the city, gladly used Havens funds to help working individuals or families on the brink of catastrophe. We used the funds to cover everything from brokers' fees and first month's rents, to course costs for securing a commercial vehicle license, to steel-toed work boots required for union jobs in plumbing or construction. The society's most important point was that these funds be used *only* for one-time assistance and *only* to ensure that the recipient would be stably employed and/or economically independent from that point on.

"Beware of chronic pauperism," the pamphlet trumpeted. "Never reveal the source of this funding, lest grantees become dependent on additional help."

As we'll see later as we trace the chronology of American homelessness, the timing of Mr. Havens's initial investment coincided with a particularly acute increase in housing insecurity. The limits Havens placed on the type of help the fund could provide, as well as the term "almoner" itself (giver of "alms," or charitable aid to the needy), thread together many of our culture's durable, false assumptions that many, if not most, poor people will game any reasonable assistance system and that we must be assiduous in ferreting out these maligners.

## PROTECTING "THE MINORITY OF THE OPULENT"

Michael Klarman, in his masterful 2016 analysis, *The Framers' Coup*, details the successful thwarting of American democracy by its own framers.[1] Fearing legitimate democracy, they colluded to effectively prevent it. During the Constitution Convention of 1787, the main framer of our Constitution, James Madison, set young America on a trajectory of enduring inequality when he declared, "The major concern of the society has to be to protect the minority of the opulent against the majority."

As stunning as that pronouncement is, the larger context of Madison's remarks reveals his specific, troubled reasoning: "The landed interest, at present, is prevalent; but in process of time, when we approximate to the states and kingdoms of Europe—when the number of landholders shall be comparatively small, through the various means of trade and manufactures, will not the landed interest be overbalanced in future elections, and unless wisely provided against, what will become of your government?"

Doubling down on this imagined existential threat to his landowning ruling class, Madison argued, "In England, at this day, if elections were open to all classes of people, the property of landed proprietors would be insecure. An agrarian law would soon take place." He concluded, "Our government ought to secure the permanent interests of the country against innovation. Landholders ought to have a share in the government, to support these invaluable interests, and to balance and check the other."

Cribbing a page from Aristotle, who had long ago already grappled with the logical inference that the far larger number of poor people in a society would inevitably rise up and take from the wealthy, Madison put forth his remedy: "The senate, therefore, ought to be this body; and to answer these purposes, they ought to have permanency and stability." And so, our Constitution originally mandated that US senators be selected by state legislatures, not by the public. Direct voting for senate seats wouldn't be codified until 1913, with the Seventeenth Amendment to the Constitution. Thus, the very scaffolding of US government was predicated on a conviction that stability is guaranteed, first and foremost, by ensuring the interests of elite landowners.

This underscores just how strongly our framers believed that one's personal economic success (and accrued resources) was evidence of one's superior abilities. Put succinctly by Chomsky, the framers believed that "power should be in the hands of the wealthy, because the wealthy are the more responsible set of men."

To fully appreciate this founding precept and its entanglement with custom, religion, and industry—as well as the unwavering throughline it has made in our monetary, social, and welfare policy—we need to first step back and examine an intentionally overlooked piece of the bedrock of our modern judicial system: the second charter of the Magna Carta.

## THE POOR MAN'S MAGNA CARTA

What is popularly referred to as the Magna Carta is essentially a thirteenth-century political settlement between the British monarchy and its wealthy barons. It codified the principle that the law, not the king, is sovereign. It delineated the rights of citizens to due process; a speedy trial; the writ of habeas corpus; protection against loss of life, liberty, or property; protections from unlawful search and seizure; and the presumption of innocence, all of which later became the basis for the US Bill of Rights.

But the original Magna Carta consisted of two charters. The famous first charter described above, the Charter of Liberties, is only half the story. Long forgotten, but achingly pertinent today, is the second charter, the Charter of the Forest. "Forest" here refers not to heavily wooded lands but rather to Britain's vast tracts of meadows, fields, farmlands, streams, and moors, even to entire villages and shanties constructed to shelter livestock. Signed two years after 1215's Charter of Liberties, the Charter of the Forest originated in a time when most of the land in England, known as "the commons," was held under the auspices of the king. The Charter of the Forest sought to end what were widely viewed as unfair, capricious, and erratic settlements of disputes between the Crown's overseers and the residents living off the land.

The term "commoner" originated in this era, referring to the vast majority of people who, in this pre-capitalist time, did not own land themselves but were understood to have permission to use the land on which generations of their families had lived for activities of basic survival. While the Charter of Liberties established individual rights of elite barons, the Charter of the Forest codified the rights of poor people to lawfully use common land to sustain themselves: to collect firewood, fish, bring their livestock to graze, and cut turf for fuel. It concerned "meat and drink, house and health and simple warmth."[2] Any fences or other enclosures on the commons were almost never boundaries of ownership, but rather small partitions to keep livestock from wandering too far afield.[3] Chomsky highlights the invaluable evolution of the commons across the centuries: "The Forest was no primitive wilderness. It was carefully developed over generations, maintained in common, its riches available to all, and preserved for future generations."[4]

Residents of the commons were not striving to become landowners. They were craftspeople, farmers, reapers, or gleaners. Historian Peter Linebaugh has written extensively about the commons, noting how great works of literature have referenced its importance again and again throughout history. This passage from Edgell Rickword's 1939 *Handbook of Freedom: A Record of English Democracy Through Twelve Centuries* (included in the duffels of British soldiers heading off to World War II) accents this truth poignantly: "It will be noticed how the word 'common' and its derivatives...appear and re-appear like a theme throughout the centuries. It was for the once vast common lands that the peasants took up arms; it was as the 'true commons' that they spoke of themselves when they assembled, and it was the aspiration of men not corrupted by petty proprietorship 'that all things should be common.'"[5] Percy Bysshe Shelley in 1812, just back from Ireland, wrote "the rights of man are liberty and an equal participation of the commonage of nature."[6] In 1903, William Morris concluded a Fabian tract by saying, "The rights of nature therefore and the wealth used for the production of further wealth, the plant and stock in short, should be communized."[7]

Throughout the centuries when the forest was protected as a common good, the economic status of women was relatively elevated. Canadian historian Jeanette M. Neeson has documented the myriad ways in which women of the commons contributed economically and artistically by making baskets, hats, food, and medicines, all from plants, seeds, and berries gathered nearby.[8] Ferns were collected to make soap. Karl Marx noted the harsh effect the eventual enclosure of common land had on women in particular: "Criminaliz[ing] taking wood from forests where gathering of fallen wood was once a customary right. In Germany, as in England, this was a right exercised by women, particularly widows."[9] Neeson concludes that once the commons were eradicated, women were left even more dependent on men's wages.

The eighteenth and nineteenth centuries saw the dramatic expansion of private ownership rights. Land that had been perpetually available for common use was given over to aristocrats and subsequently fenced off. This trend, which became known as the Enclosure Movement, was codified in 1801 when the British Parliament passed the General Enclosure Act. The justification underpinning this seismic shift was that the land could be more efficiently farmed under private ownership. Under this arrangement, former commoners became farming laborers. Relatively few people were needed to plant, harvest, and process crops, which did indeed maximize the profits—profits that went not to the laborers but to the new owners of these legally confiscated lands. These conditions led to the Agricultural Revolution. Those unable to secure farming jobs subsequently migrated, in huge numbers, to more urban areas, marking the shift from an agrarian economy to a wage-making (capitalistic) economy that gave rise to the Industrial Revolution.

The implications of this economic transformation are manifold. Whereas before enclosure, workers had engaged in varied labors in order to derive communal self-sufficiency directly from the fruits of the forest, the motto of the new industrial world seemed to be, as workers at the time put it, "The New Spirit of the Age, Gain Wealth, Forgetting All but Self!" Chomsky, like other critics across time and the political spectrum—from Marx in the mid-1800s[10] to the 2009 winner of the Nobel Prize in Economics, Elinor Olstrom—stress that "women were among those most active and vocal in condemning the destruction of the rights and dignity of free people by the capitalistic industrial system."[11] The aristocracy cast the enclosure of the commons as a step forward for the landless—a new life of increased independence. However, as essayist Eula Biss puts it succinctly in the New Yorker, the "commoners lost, in the bargain...Dispossessed of land, they were now bound to wages."[12]

Modern attitudes toward and treatment of poor and homeless people can be traced back to this great British land grab (the precursor to the subsequent North American land grab from Native tribes). The contempt that led the ruling class and lawmakers to mischaracterize the poor is astounding. Biss writes that commoners were seen as rough, savage, and lazy. Sharing land was viewed as "barbarous" and "[economically] primitive. They had an inexplicable preference for using their free time for sport, rather than for paid labor."[13] Historian Jeanette Neeson, throughout her expansive work, has shown that commoners were in fact industrious. Sadly, Neeson reflects, "What defenders saw as hard work and thrift, critics saw as squalor and desperation."[14]

These specific insults are identical to those lobbed at the Irish by British colonialists in the eighteenth century, forming the rationale to forcibly subjugate their entire realm. By the mid-1700s, Irish Catholics held title to a mere 7 percent of their own country. A century later, from 1845 to 1849, this attitude and accompanying aristocratic farming scheme culminated in the Great Famine, which killed a million Irish people. Over a million more fled to other countries. Many Irish emigrants at sea crossed paths with British vessels overstuffed with grain grown on their motherland's soil, headed to England for export—more than enough to feed those in dire need. Because, Biss poignantly underscores, "*that* grain was grown for profit."[15] (Emphasis mine.)

As in England, the theft of common land and the subsequent savage scramble for survival did not pass without bloodshed. When the potato blight that had caused the Great Famine reemerged in 1879, the Irish Land League, a collective of rural farmers, joined with the Tenant Right League to launch the largest agrarian movements of the nineteenth century: the Irish Land War. The leagues organized successful boycotts of absentee British landlords and physically blocked the evictions of farmers. Blocking evictions reduced widespread homelessness, which helped avert the scale of mass death that had previously reduced the Irish population to a staggering one-third of the pre-famine era.[16]

## PROTESTANT WORK ETHIC'S INFLUENCE ON POOR RELIEF

While researching the Calvinistic branch of Protestant theology for this book, I couldn't help be reminded of the old dating adage "Every relationship is an overreaction to the previous relationship." While it initially rang hollow to me personally the first time I heard it, I did eventually come around to find some truth in it. In the context of historical religious battles, I began to wonder if this axiom could also extend to one's relationship with God—particularly for the consequential change (some might say, overcorrection) in course by Calvinists in the wake of Martin Luther's revolution.

The Reformation sparked by Martin Luther in 1517 made manifest the justified, righteous anger against long-festering corruptions in the omnipotent Catholic Church—chief among which was the sale by the hierarchy of "indulgences," or forgiveness of sins, to wealthy parishioners. Whereas Catholic doctrine required the Church to intercede with God on behalf of believers, Luther's revelation was that people could have a direct relationship with God, read the Bible for themselves (translated from Latin into their own native languages), and cut out much of the middlemen, or more exactly, spiritual overlords, represented by the bloated religious hierarchy of the Church. With a bold theological stroke that would become the foundation of Protestant Christianity, Luther asserted that a person's soul was essentially "saved" when they accepted Jesus Christ as their God. Good deeds or payments to clerics were not what punched your ticket to heaven. Faith in Jesus as Lord and Savior was all that was required.[17]

In 1541, a French Protestant named John Calvin doubled down on Luther's fundamental teachings with a talk in Geneva presenting his own brand of reform. In Calvin's version, God's absolute power extended to a predestination: God, Calvin asserted, in His infinite wisdom has already predetermined who will be saved, and no action that a person takes can alter this. In a perversely circular form of logic, Calvin claimed that committing to his own brand of Protestantism (Calvinism) was proof that you were among those God had predestined to join Him in heaven. Of the biblical pillars of Christianity—faith, hope, love, and charity—Calvinism not only decidedly demoted charity, as had been championed by the Catholics for centuries, it actively frowned upon it.[18] If you happen to do a good deed or two, it was because God inspired you to do so, not because you had made your own choice to follow His teachings. Calvin's doctrines spread quickly through France, Scotland, and the Low Countries (Luxembourg, Belgium, and the Netherlands), all of which became hotbeds of growth for Dutch Calvinism.

A major tenet of Calvinism compelled believers to choose a secular vocation and commit to executing it with as much zeal as possible—another stark contrast to centuries of Catholic aspirations, in which the highest "calling" would be to join the Church as a priest or nun. Max Weber's highly regarded 1904 work, *The Protestant Ethic and the Spirit of Capitalism*, posits that there's a strong (not universal, but extremely strong) agreement among experts that Calvinists were more likely to be professionally successful and accumulate money.[19] Calvinism is on the more austere end of the Protestant spectrum, and in addition to zealous work habits it specifically forbids wasting money, especially on luxuries. Moreover, Weber specifically underscores that "donation of money to the poor or to charity was generally frowned on as it seen as furthering beggary. This social condition was perceived as laziness, burdening their fellow man, and an affront to God; by not working, one failed to glorify God." Weber theorized that modern capitalism had grown "out of the religious pursuit of wealth."

Because Protestantism lacked the Church's relative deep bench of clergy to assure believers that they were in possession of heavenly approval, Weber argues that Calvinists looked for "other signs" that they were saved. Believing you were saved, and having tremendous self-confidence in that belief, "took the place of priestly assurance" of God's grace. "Worldly success became a significant measure of that (essential) self-confidence." At the conclusion of his analysis, Weber crystalizes the trajectory of Calvinism's theology in the concept of "rationalization:" the critical insight that, at some point, "the Calvinist rationale informing the 'spirit' of capitalism become unreliant on the underlying religious movement...leaving only rational capitalism."[20]

As I mentioned, Weber's analysis is not without its detractors, chief amongst whom is economist Henryk Grossman.[21] Grossman's critique, written after Weber's death in 1920, specifically references Marx's work, which "showed that the stringent legal measures taken against poverty and vagabondage was a reaction to massive population shifts caused by factors such as the enclosure of the commons." Grossman's own body of work railed against the "bloody legislation" that had put commoners off their land across Europe. Significantly for homeless relief and the shape it has taken in the US, Grossman specifically correlates enclosure with "the outlawing of idleness and creation of poorhouses they instituted physically [which] forced people from serfdom into wage-labor." Although Grossman's overarching analysis concludes that capitalism "came largely by force and not by any vocational (zeal) regarding an inner-worldly Protestantism," he does entertain the possibility that the Protestant work ethic is used to justify, reinforce, and legitimize the unfair and destructive consequences of rent-seeking economics.

Whether you fully embrace Weber's causal connection between Protestant beliefs and the expansion of capitalism, or whether you favor Grossman's more leftist reading that Calvin's theology provided cultural cover for anti-poor attitudes and policies, there is little denying the impact these beliefs had in the creation of Elizabethan Poor Laws and their direct offspring: poor relief in the US.

## THE RISE AND FALL AND RISE OF HOMELESSNESS IN AMERICA

In March 1990, the US Department of Housing and Urban Development (HUD) announced it would begin conducting a yearly national census of homeless people—a single-point-in-time numeration of Americans who were visibly homeless. The following morning, homeless activist Mitch Snyder—leader of Washington DC's largest shelter, the Community for Creative Non-Violence (CCNV)—responded by dumping a massive load of sand on a bridge, preventing many Virginia commuters from entering DC. Once the two-ton dump trunk had emptied its load, Snyder conveyed this simple but enduring explanation: "It is easier to count grains of sand than homeless people in America."[22] Snyder anticipated accurately, as did many homeless people and those working with them across the nation, that such a census would yield a massive undercount in homeless Americans.

While data is scant on the numbers of homeless people in early America, we can get a sense by looking at the scale of destitution among new arrivals to the colonies. Many of them were shipped over from Britain, guilty of the crime of being poor.

Vagrancy was first outlawed in Great Britain in 1349, in an attempt to increase the labor pool in the wake of the Black Death. Persons deemed able to work but refusing to do so were imprisoned and whipped. In the sixteenth century, Henry VIII upped the punitive ante with his Vagabonds Act of 1530: first-time offenders were whipped until "blood streams from their body," second offenses were met with a whipping and half an ear sliced off, and a third offense led to outright execution (a staggering 72,000 "vagrants" are estimated to have been executed during his reign). Not to be outdone, Edward VI's Vagabonds Act of 1547 declared: "If the slave [apprentice or indentured servant] is absent for a fortnight, he is condemned to slavery for life ... branded on forehead or back with the letter S.... If it happens that a vagabond has been idling about for three days, he is to be taken to his birthplace, branded with a red hot iron with the letter V on his breast, and set to work, in chains, on the roads or at some other labor.... Every master may put an iron ring round the neck, arms or legs of his slave, by which to know him more easily."[23] Of course, Henry VIII's "three-strikes-you're-executed" clause remained in force.

Henry VIII's legacy on the treatment of the poor extended well beyond physical punishment. In the wake of the king's split from the Church, England's Catholic monasteries, previously the main source of relief for the poor, were closed. Prior to the Reformation, the Church had undertaken the seven "corporal works of mercy," dictated in Matthew 25:35: to feed the hungry, give drink to the thirsty, welcome the stranger, clothe the naked, visit the sick, visit the prisoner, and bury the dead.[24] (In more recent Catholic versions, "welcome the stranger" has been replaced with "shelter homeless people.")[25]

The government of Henry's daughter Elizabeth enacted the Act for the Relief of the Poor in 1601, known colloquially as the Elizabethan Poor Law, to take the place of the corporal works of mercy. It formalized the authority of various parishes to levy taxes to provide aid, including food and lodging, for the poor. Significantly, it also separated the needy into three categories: the "impotent poor" (those who could not work—the elderly, infirm, and blind), to be sheltered in almshouses; the "idle poor" (those who were able but refused to work), to be sent to jail or workhouses to do forced manual labor; and the "able-bodied poor" (those who were capable and willing to work), to be given materials to make sellable goods. It also delineated two types of relief to take the place of corporal works of mercy:

- Outdoor relief—people were given aid (such as food and clothing) in their own homes
- Indoor relief—people were relegated to institutions: hospitals, almshouses (shelters without mandated labor), workhouses (shelters with forced labor), or orphanages[26]

The parallels between these British groupings and relief schemes and those in America are detailed later in this chapter.

The cleaving of the "worthy" from "unworthy" of the poor by monarchs reverberates beyond historic relic: in May 2023, when Prince Charles was coronated as king of the United Kingdom, he was presented with the Jewelled Sword and pledged, in part, to "help and defend widows and orphans,* restore the things that are gone to decay, maintain the things that are restored, punish and reform what is amiss, and confirm what is in good order."[27]

### "NEW WORLD" HOMELESSNESS

The escalating harshness of the British criminal system eventually formed a direct pathway to early homelessness in North America. The Vagabonds Act of 1597 introduced penal transportation as an alternative to execution. Convicts could "choose" to be shipped across the Atlantic and enter into "bond service" (indentured servitude). England's catastrophic crop failure in 1597, coupled with the hardships brought by the enclosure acts, had left countless thousands homeless and destitute, triggering a massive increase in the "vagabond" population and

---

* Widows and orphans were consistently deemed worthy of relief throughout the evolution of Poor Law history.

setting the stage for waves of forced, indentured migration to the "New World."

Historian Anthony Vaver estimates nearly three-quarters of those arriving between the first British settlers in the early 1600s and the American Revolution of 1776 were "slaves, convicts or indentured servants." During the eighteenth century, a quarter of British immigrants were convicts, "most of them ending up in the labor-hungry colonies of Maryland and Virginia."[28] Between 1718 and 1775 alone, British colonialists bundled more than 16,000 Irish criminals and vagabonds together for shipment to the New World, along with an estimated 34,000 native Englishmen sentenced to transport and forced servitude.

Vaver notes, "Most of the people who ended up being transported to America for their crimes were petty criminals who mainly came out of the ranks of the destitute poor. The economic situation in England generally offered those who could not find work two choices: They could either sell themselves into indentured servitude in America or risk continued stealing and be forcibly shipped to America anyway."[29]

The best source of data for homelessness in early America therefore derives not only from surviving records of forced migration and indentured servitude but also from subsequent vagrancy convictions on American soil. Although there is likely a correlation between total number of homeless and such convictions, the latter were hugely influenced by the size and sophistication of any given locality's law enforcement. Before the mid-nineteenth century, most policing was local and based on "the informal constable-watch system." By 1850, many cities sheltered homeless men overnight in police stations or precinct units and also kept running counts of nightly censuses of these "tramp rooms." In his definitive overview, *Down and Out, on the Road,* historian Kenneth Kusmer estimates that "between the mid-19th and mid-20th century, a substantial portion of the American public joined the ranks of the 'down and out' at some point in their lives. Although we'll never know exactly how many homeless people existed [over this span], their numbers must surely number in the millions."[30]

As grim as that sounds, we do know that the colonial-era proportion of homeless people to domiciled people was far smaller than in subsequent eras.[31] The eventual geographic spread and overall growth of homelessness in early America was not uniform: the ranks of the homeless in Northern urban areas increased much more quickly than in rural areas and the antebellum South. Pre-Revolution skirmishes with Native Americans often forced rural settlers into Boston. Similar conflicts with other tribes and the French rendered frontier families homeless and sent them packing back east toward New York and New England. According to Kusmer, the ranks of homeless swelled significantly "in the decades immediately before and after the American Revolution...the effects of warfare were probably the most important cause of homelessness."[32]

## EARLY AMERICAN RELIEF PROGRAMS

Early relief for indigent Americans closely followed the outlines created by the Elizabethan Poor Laws (1601) and Britain's Law of Settlement and Removal (1662), the latter of which predicated eligibility for any assistance on proof of established residency, a requirement that most US states have maintained to this day. If one met the threshold for residency, one was then placed into one of three categories:

- vagrant, also known as "sturdy beggar"
- involuntarily unemployed
- helpless (disabled, elderly, widowed, or orphaned, also known as "impotent poor")

These three categories condense into the two essential groups that animate nearly all debate surrounding today's American relief programs: *worthy* (those able and willing to work, along with those unable to work due to physical limitations) and *unworthy* (those with substance use issues and those able but unwilling to work—the lazy, willful). Historian John Hansan notes that at first "colonial legislatures, then State governments adopted legislation patterned after English Laws," thus sketching out our American tradition of public responsibility: "The most popular means for caring for the poor in early America... included: the contract system, auction of the poor, the poorhouse and relief in the home, or 'outdoor relief.'"[33]

In the contract system, the government paid a lump sum to a farm or landowner to care for a poor person. "The process of 'auctioning the destitute resulted in an individual or family being placed with (whomever bid) the lowest amount of public funding needed to care for them," explains Hansan. Both the contract and auction systems mostly flourished in rural areas, Hansan concludes, because "evidence that the practice of entrusting the care of the poor to the lowest bidder essentially legalized abusive behavior and near starvation existence."[34]

Since the contract and auctioning schemes were nearly entirely rural, the vast majority of relief afforded to indigent folks in early America was either via institutions, including the poorhouse ("indoor relief"), or payments made directly to individuals and families, which they would use for subsistence in private housing ("outdoor relief"). Poorhouses, an umbrella term that included almshouses and workhouses, epitomized the essential Calvinistic teaching that idleness was antithetical to what pleased God. As Hansan explains, in poorhouses, "the necessity of working every day would be a deterrent for able-bodied persons who were simply lazy or shiftless; and the regimen of daily life in a congregate setting would instill habits of economical and virtuous living." In short, the poorhouse was predicated on the bogus belief that people were indigent "because of moral weakness or self-indulgence."[35]

But things got complicated in the colder months for the many localities operating poorhouses. Far less work was available in the winter, swelling the ranks of the poor greatly. Even more problematic, folks who (under the Elizabethan prescript) fell firmly in the "worthy" category of poor—homeless children, widows caring for children, frail elders, people with disabilities—were thrown in with the "unworthy," cheek by jowl. In other words, as the scale of need grew, the system of using poorhouses to separate the long-term destitute from those temporarily destabilized broke down, necessitating the mixing of the "worthy" and the "unworthy" poor. Eventually, even more funds were needed to separate the two categories of desperately poor Americans.

In the mid-nineteenth century, the filth and utter deprivation within poorhouses became widely publicized, leading to calls for reform. Hansan underscores the growing evidence of unseemly death rates, "disease, illicit births, lack of discipline, graft and mismanagement," and posits that the tipping point came when it became clear the "costs of maintaining poorhouses increased [far] beyond... promises of public officials."

The administration of outdoor relief—both on what conditions and the actual amount tendered—varied widely from locality to locality, state to state. Significantly, Hansan notes that this newer form of public assistance "conflicted greatly with Calvinist values," and also tread too close for comfort to the work of private charities, many of which were pet projects used (perversely) to advance the social standings of elite matriarchs in the years approaching the Gilded Age and beyond.[36]

New York State led the way toward abolishing poorhouses. A report from the New York State Senate in 1857 stated unequivocally that the "most efficient and economical" way to support poor New Yorkers and "prevent absolute pauperism" was "the proper and systematic distribution of 'out door' relief." The report specifically parses out "worthy indigent people" as those deserving "to be kept from total degradation" by giving them "provisions, bedding and other absolute necessities at their own homes." The economic argument won the day more than any other, as the report concluded that "half the sum requisite for their maintenance in the poor house would often save them from destitution," and moreover, allow them to work from home (typically doing piecework, laundry, or sewing). This option was laid out in stark contrast to forcing them "into the common receptacles of pauperism, whence it rarely emerges without a loss of self-respect and sense of degradation."

Yet such debates on the relative merits of punitive versus respectful relief programs continue a century and a half later. These same arguments became particularly prominent during Clinton-era welfare reform, and their contours can be seen in current disputes around the funding and siting of temporary congregate shelter and even afford-able permanent housing. Historian Kusmer writes extensively about the timelessness of this debate and the historic underlying misrepresenta-tion of homeless people as "lazy and irresponsible—a deviant group, perhaps incorrigible…outside the mainstream of society." Without question, Kusmer explains, "these views are fundamentally biased… [and] have often functioned to justify persistent class or racial inequi-ties in American society."[37]

In fact, according to Kusmer, our unhoused neighbors have "much in common with other Americans, especially the working class. The fundamental difference that has set them apart from the mainstream is their extreme poverty or vulnerability to economic change."[38] *New York Times* writer Paul Vitello's obituary of the great social scientist and researcher Michael Katz zeroed in on Katz's analysis of the ten-sions between the micro and macro views of poverty: "In the micro view, individuals were the authors of their lives and impoverishment proof of their moral failings. In the macro analysis large historical forces and economic trends—war and peace, the shifting interest of capital—favored some people and disadvantaged others."[39] It's a perfect summation of the grasping selfishness of the American Dream narra-tive. Indeed, the axes upon which homelessness has waxed and waned throughout our nation's history until the mid-1970s are economic re-cession and wartime-related fluctuations in the labor pool, as much as housing supply.

The budding colonial economy's links with the world market cre-ated a template for homelessness to faithfully shadow downturns in in-ternational business cycles. In 1700, New York City had scant evidence of significant poverty, but between 1720 and 1730, Kusmer notes that "New York began for the first time to experience the negative effects of [national and international] economic downturns." Newspaper ac-counts from 1734, he writes, indicate that "many beggarly people wan-der about [New York City] streets" and articles urged the use of public funds to build institutions to incarcerate them. These "wandering poor" were by then a significant presence in all Northern cities, and when wealth inequality skyrocketed in the latter half of the eighteenth century, the number of visibly destitute grew as well. Capitalism's boom/bust cycles increase what sociologist Peter Rossi referred to as the "awareness of the porous line between the down-and-out and the working poor profoundly influencing their understanding of [the] emergent industrial order and their precarious place in it."[40]

Researcher Billy Smith amplifies this essential insight in The "Lower Sort": Philadelphia's Laboring People, 1750–1800: "Laboring people often lived a hand-to-mouth existence, struggling to maximize their family and cut the cost of basic necessities. Those unable to make ends meet are likely to find themselves sleeping in back alleyways and begging on the streets."[41] By nature and physical proximity, laborers' sympathies and actions aligned in natural solidarity with the poorest of their neighbors. When the British fled New York in 1783 after their defeat in the American Revolution, the resulting economic instability was reflected in a huge surge in people sleeping rough. Then mayor James Duane attempted to wield "the Discipline of the Bridewell or House of Employment" in order to "correct and shame" the destitute out of existence, or at least out of sight. But attempts by New York City mayors to outlaw impoverished people out of existence have always failed—from Duane and his successor, Richard Varick, through Rudy Giuliani and Eric Adams. Threats from any mayor made little, if any, dent in the growing problem.

During times of extreme economic calamity—for instance, the depressions of the 1850s—the Calvinistic certainty that one's accrued wealth reflected God's grace was increasingly questioned in popular culture. Writers like Charles Dickens, as well as widely read newspapers, all urged generosity of heart toward the downcast. Kusmer notes, "Impoverished children elicited a particularly sympathetic response." Homeless children of this era were romanticized as "street urchins" throughout art and fiction, "undermining the sharp divisions between the worthy and unworthy poor that organized (religion) and charity tried to establish."[42]

Somewhat surprisingly, up until 1870, women constituted a significant portion of the urban homeless population. Their gradual diminution was not owing to some gender-related immunity to employment shortages and housing scarcity that created more homelessness amongst men. Rather, sociologist Theda Skocpol argues effectively that the Victorian-era redefinition of male and female normatives created an enduring ideology that women were the "weaker sex" and therefore less capable of caring for themselves. This, according to Skocpol, "led to the establishment of numerous institutions to assist women and children" and, ultimately, to the child labor laws and widows' pensions in the twentieth century.[43]

## POST-CIVIL WAR THROUGH THE GREAT DEPRESSION

We've already tracked the surges in homelessness following the American Revolution. The period just before the Civil War saw another marked increase in homelessness. The 1807–08 embargo and the economic downturns of 1817–1823 and 1837–1843 had left vast numbers of "the laboring poor destitute," increasing "the number of homeless persons significantly," notes Kusmer. Antebellum poverty was greatly concentrated in urban areas, prodding many to strike out west to seek work.

Homelessness rose even more sharply after the Civil War—what Kusmer terms "the massive vagrancy problem of the 1870s." Sociologist Nels Anderson, in his seminal 1923 work *On Hobos and Homelessness*, describes his own family's journey to acquire workable farmland during this period: gaining a toehold on the American economic ladder spurred many agricultural workers to aspire to farm ownership.[44] Although this pathway to financial independence would ultimately vanish (as Anderson's father learns firsthand) in the late 1800s, once farmable land became saturated with homesteaders. While midsized towns and cities still had relatively few people sleeping rough, in stark contrast, in large cities, Kusmer notes, "the social and economic foundation... in which the work ethic and mobility through land ownership...were already being undermined."

Not unlike Americans in the Roaring Twenties or New Yorkers in the 1970s, in the mid-1800s the nation was largely ignorant of impending widescale homelessness. Kusmer poignantly reflects the mindset of the time, in which people were certain that "the future would be very much like the present: a predominantly agricultural, locally controlled society with small-scale industry"—a place "where diligent workers could [continue to] obtain economic independence, either as farmers or small capitalists.... The emergence of the tramp in the 1870s was one of the first indications that they were mistaken."[45]

After the Civil War swept thousands of homeless men into the service, many assumed the regimented army life would instill more order on enlisted men—or at least the docility required for factory employment, once veterans came back from the war. But the antithesis emerged. Kusmer credits this to a number of factors. Existing farms and factories were unable to absorb the returning ranks of veterans. Equally significant, destitute veterans turned to brute survival tactics they had acquired during the war. On their tours of duty, soldiers were forced to loot enemy stores and scavenge factories, even private homes, as their companies advanced, just to secure basic provisions. As veterans, they used those same skills to survive joblessness and hunger. Moreover, American society—barely equipped to adequately tend to the physically wounded—had virtually no awareness of the toll of PTSD returning soldiers carried. Two financial panics (that of 1873 and of 1893) bookended a period known as the Long Depression.

These were also the first vets to have traveled great distances on the nation's new railroads. Kusmer observes that "particularly in the north, the movement of troops by rail was a significant part of the war effort... Soldiers traveled in boxcars or cattle cars, herded together much like the animals for whom the conveyances had been designed."[46] Before the immense expansion of the railways from the 1830s to the 1850s, people rarely traveled more than a few miles from home in their entire lives.

The growing ease with which post–Civil War men traveled via the rails, unemployed and unattached, combined with the hand-to-mouth survival skills developed during the worst of combat—all factors combined to create the first massive wave of roaming homeless men in the US. The words "tramp" and "bum" were coined during this time, the former derived from the phrase "on the tramp," the latter a shortening of "bummer," which during the war was a crude slag to scavenging soldiers. Vagrancy was illegal in many states, until the US Supreme Court declared the practice unconstitutional in 1972, and Kusmer notes that immediately after the Civil War, two-thirds of Massachusetts, Pennsylvania, and Illinois prison inmates were veterans. F. B. Sanborn, head of the Massachusetts State Charities Board, noted in 1870: "Vagrancy—which was checked by the war, now seems to be largely on the increase."[47]

Two important takeaways from the Sanborn quote: First, the expansive wartime economy had offered gainful employment and housing to hundreds of thousands of Americans. Second, in the years before and after the war, jail and prison populations swelled across the nation. Michael Katz teases out the important change in the handling of criminals from the colonial era, compared to the mid-1800s: "Criminals (in colonial America) were not punished by long periods of incarceration. Rather, they were held in jail only until trial; if found guilty, they were punished by fines, whipping or execution. . . . By 1850 all of this had changed." Alongside "specialized institutions to care for the mentally-ill, to rehabilitate juvenile delinquents, to educate the blind, deaf and dumb . . . new penitentiaries had been constructed on novel principles," as well as "hundreds of almshouses."[48]

Police stations soon began using their overnight common space to quarter homeless men, becoming some of the first public homeless shelters in the country. In Boston alone, from 1872 to 1874, "lodgers" at these precinct locations swelled by 63 percent to over 57,000. Setting aside those bedding down in their police stations, the ranks of homeless in Boston (including people dossing in private charitable almshouses) was estimated at 98,263—up 300 percent from just two years before. By 1878, yearly usage of these types of emergency shelter had surged to over 200,000 people across Massachusetts. The pattern was replicated in other major cities, including New York City, where arrests for vagrancy doubled over the same period.

It was exactly around this time that Charles Havens set up his fund, enshrining the emphatic rejection of aid to the chronically homeless, the "vagrants" and the "wandering poor" who comprised the vast majority of Americans in most dire need.

Many signal trends emerged during the homeless surges in the antebellum and post–Civil War periods:

- Because of the Victorian ideals noted earlier, rates of homelessness among females did not keep pace with men. In the 1870s, men were routinely sent to police station houses to shelter in the evenings. Stays at other emergency shelters (e.g., "Wayfarers' Lodges") were limited in number and length of stays, and required men to work in exchange for shelter.
- Homeless people during this period were mostly white. Even when the Great Migration began as Black Southerners headed north to find jobs and escape rampant discrimination, unemployment among Blacks was actually lower than that of whites until World War I.
- There was a gradual, as Kusmer puts it, "Americanization of homelessness." In the 1860s, immigrants constituted roughly two-thirds of homeless men quartered at police stations along the East Coast. Not surprisingly, given the unprecedented wave of Irish fleeing famine, Irish men accounted for over half of this group. But by 1900, 70 percent of men seeking emergency shelter in cities along the Eastern Seaboard were native born.
- Single men outnumbered married men by a large margin among the homeless in eastern America throughout this period.[49]

## EAST VS. WEST

Over the thirty-year arc following the Civil War, the US grew into an economic powerhouse, but stark divides emerged in opportunity and resulting wealth. While America was now a nation knit together by railroads, it was still a country of distinct regions. Virtually all the data on American homelessness until the Civil War is amassed through records from municipal lodging houses, poorhouses, and jails in the East. The West was far less densely populated, with agriculture and mining generating most employment. Families continued to migrate westward throughout this period, fueled by several Homestead Acts that gave parcels of land, stolen from Indigenous people, almost exclusively to white families.

Anderson, in *On Hobos and Homeless*, writes that his own family's nomadic experience was, in many ways, "quite prevalent before 1900." Anderson's father was a Swedish immigrant who had spent his first few adult years traveling widely across the US, going wherever he could find work as a bricklayer or as a "mixer of mortar, which most bricklayers were not.... He was a hobo." Anderson underscores that the search for work, more than anything, was the motivating factor in the lives of the hobos and homeless families common throughout the West: "Above all, the hobo was a worker, one who moved from one kind of work to another when and as needed and who went his way when not needed."[50]

After Anderson's parents married, the couple had twelve children and moved (via horse-drawn covered wagon) ten times. "We were a hobo family always in poverty or near it, but only once did poverty get us down," Anderson writes. "We didn't know that word, although we did use the word 'paupers,' in referring to other families." Like countless thousands of other Americans, Anderson's father's dream was "to accumulate the means to set himself up as a farmer." He met a man outside of Spokane, Washington, who offered him equity in some land claimed during the Donation Land Claim Act of 1850. Anderson's father felt that he could farm it "once the tall timber had been cleared away." But "slowly, Father came to the conclusion that one man's lifetime would not be enough to convert the timber claim to a viable farm."

And so, after several months of hard work, they moved on: "What seemed strange, if not impossible two years earlier, they now accepted as the proper thing to do. They had learned how families moved about in the West." What they were learning, "first in the flats by Spokane and then on the timber claim, was the fluidity of life." Most striking is the ubiquity of nomadic families during this era throughout the American

West. Anderson details that, as his family moved from place to place, "One rarely met an adult who was born there. Few of the children… were born there." There were single men amongst these families "batching it." Anderson succinctly puts it, "Hobos all, moving about was a way of life."

The Andersons were among "the land hunters," as his father recalled—those on the move in search of "better land or more land." Mixed among these land hunters were migrant workers harvesting wheat, or picking fruit, or working on "construction projects or in the lumber woods, making the rounds with the seasons." His father was an "alien…not yet a citizen. That sense of being an outsider never left him." That "awareness of being an outsider" made him instinctively sympathetic to the Native Americans they met along the way. He went into partnership with one named Joe Bronjo, one of the oldest surviving tribal leaders. The reservation was where young Nel's "first memories began," and where he "changed from child to boy."

## FROM THE GILDED AGE TO THE PROGRESSIVE ERA

Anderson's account is made gripping by both the details of the survival skills cultivated by every family member (each was expected to contribute his or her own hard labor, regardless of age) and the larger political landscape against which his family endured. During the Panic of 1893, also known as the Cleveland Panic, Anderson paints a vivid image of his father returning from a trip to town with devastating news of the price drops for the crops, pigs, and chickens that he and Joe Bronjo had raised. Anderson writes, "When the panic started, thousands of hobos from all parts of the nation [marched] to Washington to demand the government start a national road building program. But they were not called hobos by many then, rather, many papers…used the term 'industrials.'"[51]

The Cleveland Panic is an important inflection point because it's at the center of the temporal Venn diagram of the Gilded Age (roughly 1870–1900) and the Progressive Era (1890–1920). It is the capstone of many market panics that came in fast succession after the Civil War, including the Panic of 1873, in part sparked when a major bank, Jay Cooke & Co., which was backing railroad bonds, suspended withdrawals. This triggered an unprecedented run on that bank (and, almost instantaneously, many others). The underlying grift of this panic was that the railroad company had used a shell company to inflate costs charged to the federal government, which was underwriting a large part of the capital needed to construct the rails from Minnesota to Seattle.

The Panic of 1873 was also the first international monetary crisis sparked by plummeting silver prices. At the time, thousands and thousands of Americans were flocking to mine silver in western states, only to discover their yields were relatively worthless. The resulting deflation destabilized banks worldwide, following a bubble of then record investments in silver futures. What started as a regional run on banks in Vienna spread to the surrounding cities and countries, amplified in New York after Cooke & Co. and other major US banks began refusing withdrawals.

The federal government responded by adopting a pure gold standard, taking money out of circulation to adhere to it. This greatly constricted the economy and intensified the depth of the worldwide depression.

The US economy was wildly unstable throughout the Long Depression (1873–1896), and measures to tighten the currency drove wages down dramatically. Moreover, thousands of businesses failed, with losses amounting to over $1 billion. The ranks of the unemployed skyrocketed—in New York, fully one-quarter of workers were without jobs. Throughout the 1880s, there were glimmers of hope, but they were crushed when manufacturing and other major sectors collapsed and more New York banks disintegrated.

The Progressive Era and its reforms emerged in response to the excesses of the Gilded Age. Six depressions in the 1800s and Americans began to question if structural inequity was causing destitution, not personal moral shortcomings. They clung tight to the notion of equality as a central tenet of democracy and were increasingly outraged by the massive and increasing divide between the haves and the have-nots.

Night scene from the East Side: Tenement dwellers sleeping on roofs and windowsills, New York City. *Frank Leslie's Illustrated Newspaper*, August 12, 1882.

In 1890, while the average wages for working-class and poor Americans stalled or plummeted, the top 1 percent in the US possessed over a quarter of the wealth. Labor conditions in factories, farms, and western mines were harsh, and those not literally homeless often lived in appalling, overcrowded conditions. Anderson, as he grew older, became aware of tensions between "the settled people" and the single men who lived in the "flats area" (the roughest neighborhoods) of various towns. Once, when his father was giving a mixed report on the quality of local workers of this type, his mother chided him to remember, "Everyone in Lewiston came here in a covered wagon."[52]

This domestic quarrel also played out nationally, as now familiar lines of rhetoric were drawn when labor unions became potent forces in advancing the concerns of working people. A *New York Times* editorial in 1886 detailed a vile proposal by the Westchester County (north of New York City) supervisors for the "cure of tramps."[53] Anyone accused of vagrancy would be soaked in a tank of cold water, the level of which would be held just under the man's head, so long as he makes "vigorous exertions in the way of pumping or bailing. As soon as he remits his exertions he will drown." While the *Times* rejected the plan overall, it gave far more space to condemning the Central Labor Union for vocally decrying the plan as "inhumane and barbarous." Why? Because "this labor union 'recognizes' the tramp as the 'victim of our present economical [sic] system,' instead of recognizing in him, as other people do, the victim of a violent dislike to labor and a violent thirst for rum." The *Times* was more threatened by union solidarity with the unemployed—organized labor's "theory that the tramp is merely a workingman who has been crushed by the capitalist"—than the Westchester proposal, which "carried to its logical conclusion would make vagrancy a capital offense, punishable with death by drowning."

Katz eloquently summarizes the arc of camaraderie between working-class and impoverished Americans, from the early- to mid-1800s and beyond: "Poverty was not unusual among the American working class in the early nineteenth century. In fact, working-class people often were poor at some point in their lives. Thus, no clear line demarcated ordinary working people from those in need of relief."[54] Periodic poverty "was a structural consequence of the great transformation of American life after about the "mid-eighteenth century.... With luck, some people pulled themselves out. They got well or found work. Others were not so fortunate."

Katz concludes that, because people understood that growing economic instability, not individual or moral failing, fueled the eventual crises nearly all families faced, "periods of dependency were normal. Working-class experience was a continuum; no clear line separated respectable poor from paupers."[55]

Decent, affordable housing was a primary goal advanced during the emerging Progressive Era. The fuel for change was the growing collective realization that, as historian Nell Irvin Painter put it, "Gilded is not golden. Gilded has the sense of a patina covering something else. It's the shiny exterior and the rot underneath."[56] For the poor and working class, that rot of inequality struck at the heart of the American promise.

The manifesto for the Progressive Era's widespread political mobilization came from an unlikely source. In 1879, the struggling political economist Henry George, having faced the near-starvation of himself and family, published one of the most influential books ever: *Progress and Poverty*.[57] Second in sales at the time only to the Bible, George's book laid bare the forces that allowed poverty to persist and even increase, despite advances in manufacturing, technology, and transportation. The boom/bust cycles were destroying the economic fabric of the country, enriching the "top 1 percent" (he coined this phrase) at the expense of hardworking, everyday citizens. George brilliantly detailed patterns of maturation in cities. His key insight was that ever-increasing value generated by laborers, using capital (raw materials, tools, machines), was absorbed into the price of urban land. The value of urban land soared, destabilizing regional economies. Wealth accumulated to the landholders, leaving the workers and unemployed poor at greater risk for homelessness, as they could not afford to rent, let alone buy, urban land.

Henry George's theories have gained relevancy in recent years as economists, including Nobel laureate Joseph Stiglitz, have emphasized the central role that urban land value plays in wealth inequality. In his seminal paper "Inequality and Economic Growth," Stiglitz underscored: "Much of the increase in wealth has little to do with savings in the usual sense. Rather it is the result of capital gains—especially the increased value of land—and an increase in the capitalized value of other rents. It is a mistake to confuse capital with wealth."[58] Urban land increasingly absorbs wealth generated by labor and capital, artificially inflating its value and making it prohibitively expensive for laborers.

Adam Smith got it right in 1776 when it came to land, differentiating it starkly from other "commodities," like iron or salmon. From chapter VI in Smith's The Wealth of Nations: "As soon as the land of any country has all become private property, the landlords, like all other men, love to reap where they never sowed and demand a rent even for its natural produce." Smith categorized land as one of three "factors of production," alongside capital (such as a simple horse-drawn tractor or large factory) and labor (from a wage-earning farmhand or factory worker). He asserted that while land is essential to production, it makes no direct contribution. Landowner and landlords derive value from capital and labor without contributing any work. They are essentially parasitic.[59]

Forty years later, in 1817, David Ricardo's "Law of Rent" theory dictated that the value of the soil goes not to the laborer, but to the landlord.[60] Soil, in modern-day terms, is land—and the most valuable soil (or land) renders the biggest profit. Urban land is by far today's most "valuable soil," particularly land in major coastal cities, and as we'll see in chapter 6, that's what explains the relatively high levels of homelessness in places like San Francisco, Los Angeles, and New York City. Smith's three factors of production, bundled with Ricardo's Law of Rent, are the core doctrine of classical economics.

Urban planner and scholar Patrick Condon is masterful at connecting the larger economic theories to the very current distortions they exert on urban housing development. Because wealth is so greatly concentrated, it must be invested, and "urban land has been a very safe bet.

Before rezoning
Land price $1,000,000
Per sq. ft. interior price $1,000

After rezoning
Land price $4,000,000
Per sq. ft. interior price $1,000

**Effect of rezoning on FAR (floor area ration) and land price.** Patrick M. Condon, professor, University of British Columbia.

This form of global, highly speculative 'asset inflation' eventually bids up the price of urban land way beyond its utility for housing or industry, exerting an ever more crushing burden on both entrepreneurs and wage earners." This is the fallout as we continue to move from a "wage-based" to an "asset-based" economy. Condon, based in British Columbia, has written extensively on Vancouver's housing market. We'll revisit other parts of his work in the final chapter, "Resistance vs. Revolution," but it's important to note here this essential finding: Building more units without significant paths for nonmarket developments (either public housing rentals or limited equity cooperatives, which strictly limit speculation) will only exacerbate the escalating trend of inflating prices for urban land. Because housing prices are valued in units—reflecting the interior square footage, when a relatively small building is rezoned, even if the price per interior unit remains equal—the new zoning will allow far greater interior square footage. As a result, the "asking value of the new density allowance is captured by the land owner."[61]

Condon summarizes: "Unfortunately, in all the cases that I've examined throughout North America, what happens when you do a rezoning [with no legitimate path for nonmarket developers] is you let the hungry dogs of land price speculation and inflation loose across the landscape, which undercuts the intention of enhancing affordability." Contrary to the deregulation agenda of real estate–funded YIMBY (Yes in My Back Yard) groups, Condon's research proves that "many [developers] make most of their money by being land owners during the rezoning process."

## WORLD WAR I'S BONUS ARMY AND THE GREAT DEPRESSION

As we've seen in this chapter, mass homelessness is not just a recent phenomenon in our country. But unlike the current forty-plus-years era of modern homelessness, the timing and scale of previous displacements of Americans to the streets hewed closely to shifting economic tides. In the wake of six depressions during the nineteenth century, a Progressive movement was galvanized from a growing understanding and acceptance that structural forces played a far greater role in extreme poverty than mere personal failings. The shift from what might be called "hobos to heroes" was in full ascent during a critical, dramatic post–World War I showdown known as the Bonus War.

When the economy was flush in 1924, a Democratic Congress voted, overriding a veto by President Calvin Coolidge, to allocate bonus pay to veterans who had served in Europe during World War I. Although these bonuses weren't initially intended to be redeemable until 1945, the willingness of veterans to wait evaporated when the implosion of the stock market in 1929 and ensuing Great Depression left thousands of them unemployed and on the brink of complete destitution. In the summer of 1932, more than twenty thousand (some estimates top forty thousand) vets and family members from every corner of the mainland converged on Washington, DC, demanding that Congress amend the legislation to pay them their bonuses immediately.[62] They erected tents, lean-tos, and shacks, and dug in for several weeks in the nation's largest and most racially integrated "Hooverville," homeless encampments across the country named to protest President Herbert Hoover's austerity programs amidst soaring poverty. The nation was overwhelmingly sympathetic to the vets' plight, and on July 19, retired major general Smedley Butler, a two-time Medal of Honor recipient, addressed the vast crowd: "You have just as much right to have a lobby here as any steel corporation.* Makes me so damn mad when people speak of you as tramps. By God, they didn't speak of you as tramps in 1917 and '18!"[63] Newsreel footage and press accounts of Butler's fiery speech flooded the nation. He closed his remarks with: "Take it from me, this is the greatest demonstration of Americanism we have ever had. Pure Americanism. Don't make any mistake about it: You've got the sympathy of the American people."[64]

But just over a week later, on July 28, Hoover unleashed the US military to torch and raze the encampment; the violent footage and press accounts shocked the nation. The *New York Times* reported that only thirty minutes' warning was given to the homeless families before their campgrounds were smashed by tanks and baton- and gun-wielding soldiers on horseback and then quickly set ablaze. A four-column front page *Times* headline "Troops Drive Veterans from Capital" led the paper's account of the destruction: "Amidst scenes reminiscent of the mopping up of a town in the World War, Federal troops drove the army of bonus marchers from the shanty town near Pennsylvania Avenue in which the veterans had been entrenched for months. Ordered to the scene by President Hoover detachments of infantry, cavalry, machine gun and tank crews laid down an effective tear-gas barrage which disorganized the bonus-seekers, and then set fire to the shacks and tents left behind."[65]

In James Clarke's recent analysis of General Butler and the savage rending of the Bonus Army camp, "The news that police and the US military had used force against a gathering of largely peaceful demonstrators who had just won the country's most recent war...was, to put

---

* Butler is taking a well-deserved shot at U.S. Steel, the first American company to reach (in 1929) a $1-billion market cap yet which cut 75 percent of its workforce to part-time hours.

it bluntly, a disaster for the Hoover administration."[66] *Politico*'s Gordon Sander captures the stunning repercussions of "the Bonus March fiasco," as many historians considered it "the death knell for Hoover's reelection campaign": "The sight and sound of his and his top general's troops tear-gassing the pitiful remaining tenants of Bonus City and their weeping families, as shown in biograph theaters around the country, certainly didn't endear him to voters. In November, Hoover lost by a landslide to Franklin D. Roosevelt."[67]

The fate of perhaps the most consequential presidential election in the twentieth century was materially swayed by the gross mistreatment of homeless families by an entrenched (many believed callous) incumbent. Why? Because the Bonus Army demonstrators were avatars for millions of underdogs struggling to survive, former servicemen who peacefully but stubbornly demanded from the government the help they righteously felt was owed them.

Personal and class allegiance—the ability to accept both the humanity and commonality we share with our unhoused neighbors—is what tips the scales in favor of accepting that structural forces, without a doubt, animate the catastrophe of homelessness. As Coalition cofounder Kim Hopper remarked at the critical inflection moment, back in 1990: "Rather than asking what it is about 'them' that makes them homeless, one [should] inquire what it is about 'us' that has enabled homelessness to assume the...unprecedented proportions it has today?"[68]

# CHAPTER 3

# HOMELESSNESS
# IN THE TWENTIETH CENTURY

## MYTH 4 "RONALD REAGAN CREATED MODERN HOMELESSNESS"

As we saw in chapter 2, mass homelessness is not unique to our era, but its roots differ significantly from earlier crises. The misconception that Ronald Reagan single-handedly created our present-day disaster is the most contemporary homeless origin myth. As we'll see below, while Reagan's savage cuts to the federal Housing and Urban Development (HUD) budget accelerated rates of homelessness across the US, a major cause of the dramatic rise in homelessness that occurred during his tenure preceded his administration. Although it's a less tidy narrative, understanding this more complicated timeline is key to bolstering investments in evidence-based, tax-saving solutions.

### DEINSTITUTIONALIZATION AND ITS AFTERMATH

In 1963, John F. Kennedy signed what would be his final bill as president: the Mental Retardation and Community Mental Health Centers Construction Act. It was meant to effect a sea change away from the large state-run psychiatric hospitals (notorious for decrepit conditions, abuse, and neglect) in which mentally ill Americans had long been warehoused and toward humane, effective care within patients' own communities. To that end, the bill laid the groundwork for a vastly improved community-based system of mental healthcare delivery, one with a "wholly new emphasis and approach for care" for Americans with mental illness.

The massive state hospitals targeted for dismantling had actually been created in the wake of a reform movement more than a century earlier, when mental health advocate Dorothea Dix toured the "institutional explosion"[1] of jails, poorhouses, and small hospitals across several states, appalled by the utter squalor in which the most vulnerable were forced to live. Dix successfully advocated for the creation of asylums, or state hospitals, initially small facilities that functioned as short-term treatment sites, offering legitimate care over brute incarceration. The first was established in Massachusetts in 1840. More were then created across New Jersey, Illinois, and up and down the East Coast. The arc of Dix's remarkable advocacy culminated in 1854, when her hard-won state-level reforms were proposed at the federal level with the Land-Grant Bill for Indigent Insane Persons, which would have given ten million acres of federal lands to individual states upon which to build asylums.[2] It was passed by both chambers of Congress, but President Franklin Pierce, a staunch states' rights advocate, vetoed the popular legislation, insisting, according to historian Graham Warder, it "represented an unwarranted expansion of federal authority into areas more properly the responsibility of the states, local government, or private charity."[3]

The historical context to this stunning rebuke is significant. The veto came on the heels of extraordinary federal land grants that had been handed to private railroad companies, allowing them to expand their profit-making enterprises.[4] There was also a succession of soon-to-be codified homesteading acts, which would give white Americans hundreds of thousands of acres of federal land upon which to farm, mine, build housing, and establish businesses.[5]

In the absence of federal support to provide long-term stability of the "indigent insane" (those without resources and whose families were too poor to provide for their basic needs), ever more patients were ejected from the hodgepodge of local care and remanded to the State. In the 1870s, State hospitals briefly took a step toward decency and adequate care. But by the 1960s, the New York Times notes "most of them held upwards of 3,000 people [and had] morphed into human warehouses."[6]

As we saw in the previous chapter, because the government refused to provide basic sustenance for destitute people lacking the skills, employment, or kinship network necessary to survive, they were shunted into almshouses, jails (for violators of vagrancy laws), reform "schools" (for unaccompanied minors), municipal lodging houses (essentially local police stations, repurposed overnight into congregate shelters), private charitable enterprises (almost always for single women or mothers with children), orphanages, and a relative handful of beds in hospitals. This abiding three-card monte shuffling of vulnerable people between institutions and localities, along with Pierce's veto, converged—I would argue by design—to exacerbate the ghastly conditions in groaning state sanitariums.

The Kennedy-era reforms sought to undo the consolidation of misery in state facilities by redesigning the mental health system to align with the core values of community-based treatment. With the advent of new psychotropic medications (the first of which, Thorazine, an antipsychotic, was approved by the FDA in 1954), mental health advocates argued for local, evidence-based treatment, which would be more humane and restore health and dignity to our neighbors living with severe, chronic mental health issues. Kennedy's plan included building 1,500 mental health centers nationwide to provide a spectrum of services, from emergency response teams and inpatient facilities, including hospitalization capacity, to ongoing outpatient treatment. The centers were envisioned as "as single point of contact for patients in a given catchment area who needed not just access to psychiatric care but also help navigating the outside world."[7]

Essential to any potential success of this grand gambit was an intrinsic expectation that states would take the massive savings realized in shuttering psych hospitals and use those funds for both these centers and housing for those on disability. Because of this assumption, the Kennedy bill did not include any long-term funding, only grants for upfront costs related to site acquisition, planning, construction, and initial staffing. A humanitarian time bomb was set ticking when states instead diverted the funding toward tax cuts, pensions, and other more politically popular priorities.

President Jimmy Carter doubled the federal investment in Kennedy's scheme in 1980, but in a particularly cruel echo of history, Ronald Reagan subsequently repealed the funds, repackaging them into block grants over which states had wide discretion.[8] As they did nearly a century before, states' rights once again trumped ensuring basic human decency. But the floodgates of deinstitutionalized patients had opened long before Reagan's tenure and continued shedding people in need of long-term support; when Reagan took office, the population at state psychiatric hospitals had already plummeted by 80 percent since the advent of psychotropic medication.[9] But from the 1950s through the mid-1970s, a cushion of inexpensive housing provided a retaining wall between deinstitutionalized patients and the streets. Frontline service providers of the era commented that patients were routinely discharged with their meager belongings and a single refill for medication. When they ran out of medication, began to decompensate, and subsequently were evicted for nonpayment of rent, the relatively high vacancy rates in the cheapest housing meant that many would literally walk around the corner and find another room to rent, using disability or public assistance benefits. When the pool of affordable SROs and apartments began to recede in the 1970s—either through conversion or outright destruction—thousands of visibly poor people were forced to bed down in streets, parks, and other public spaces. They seemed to appear out of nowhere, but the seeds of their utter destitution had been planted almost two decades earlier.

## THE CASE OF BILLIE BOGGS (JOYCE BROWN)

My arrival at the Coalition coincided with the public unraveling of a mentally ill homeless woman in New York named Joyce Brown, known as Billie Boggs in court proceedings.[10] She became infamous as her story was amplified by the national press. The battle waged in the late 1980s pitted New York City's mayor, who attempted to launch a new city-run program under which Brown became the first forcibly hospitalized and medicated homeless person, against civil liberty lawyers who fought furiously to have her "freed."

Joyce Brown's story echoed that of countless people I met over the years at the Coalition. She had grown up in the suburbs outside of Newark, with no symptoms of psychological distress until her twenties. Her three sisters had taken turns caring for her throughout the early part of the 1980s, trying to keep her housed, fed, and stable between their homes in Elizabeth, New Jersey. But Brown's deteriorating mental health and increasingly irrational verbal tirades made it impossible for her to hold steady work. Her illness continued to escalate, and she began using heroin and cocaine to self-medicate. In December 1984, she was hospitalized for three weeks in New Jersey, then released with a prescription for 350 milligrams of Thorazine to be taken three times each day. With the help of county social workers, she qualified for Social Security disability benefits.

By spring 1986, Brown's sisters were worn out by her unpredictable behavior and implored her to see a psychiatrist for ongoing help. The final day with her sisters ended bitterly, with Brown angrily lashing out at them, "I'm not insane. I'm intelligent." After packing a small bag, she left for New York City. Like so many families of people with severe and persistent mental illness (SPMI), the sisters made multiple efforts to track Brown down, combing police precincts, shelters, and even the medical examiner's office, all to no avail.[11]

Brown soon became well-known on Manhattan's tony Upper East Side, living for months on end on a heating grate in front of the Beekman movie theater. She frequently lashed out at people verbally, and sometimes physically. She particularly targeted Black men who worked in the area, believing they were trying to pay her for sex. She panhandled, demanding quarters. If people tried to give her dollar bills, she angrily tore them up, burning them, or urinating on them.

At the time, then mayor Ed Koch was touring the city with a team from a City-run homeless outreach program, Project HELP (Homeless Emergency Liaison Project), which provided clothing, food, psychiatric and medical services, and transportation to emergency rooms and intake shelters. When he asked about the proportion of people hospitalized, he was told roughly 60 percent. Koch found that estimate incredible, given that he saw dozens of the same people each time he went out. When the workers explained that hospitals were not able to keep patients if they weren't deemed dangerous, Koch soon began pushing his law department to reexamine these limits and research ways to extend the City's ability to forcibly hospitalize homeless people with mental illness.

The standard against which they were pushing had been established in 1975, when the US Supreme Court issued a landmark ruling, *O'Connor v. Donaldson*, involving Ken Donaldson, who had been involuntarily committed by his parents for nearly fifteen years.[12] The court ruled that a person could not be held against their will if they posed no threat of danger to themselves or others—a threshold that has held for nearly five decades.

In 1983, the New York State Legislature had attempted and failed to expand the threshold of people considered actively homicidal or suicidal. Undeterred, the Koch administration's top lawyer presented the mayor with an argument based on case law that might allow them to shift this standard temporally—from present to future tense. They would begin forcibly hospitalizing people who, rather than being an imminent threat to themselves or others, were deemed a *potential* threat "in the reasonably foreseeable future." This approach had shades of the Philip K. Dick novella *The Minority Report*, a cautionary tale that reflects the slippery moral and philosophical slope of predictive detention. Unlike in Dick's fiction, Koch's attempt to shift the legal standard from current to presumed threat was playing out not in some distant dystopian future but in the present day.

In September 1987, Koch announced that he had cordoned off an entire wing of Bellevue Hospital; 18 West was a new ward for mentally ill New Yorkers who were to be targeted for forced treatment under this much broader standard of forced detention.[13] At several press availabilities, when asked about the new program, Koch specifically mentioned "the woman in front of the Beekman theater."[14] He had met Brown on one of his tours with the outreach team and had been informed that she'd been taken to Metropolitan Hospital five times, but on each occasion, the attending psychiatrist had not believed she was dangerous. In promulgating new City regulations, Koch's commissioner urged clinicians to remember that "the law recognizes a concept of 'serious harm' that is significantly broader than actively suicidal conduct. *Significant, passive self-neglect meets the 'serious harm' standard as well.*"[15] (Emphasis mine.)

Joyce Brown was picked up on October 28, 1987. She was the first person to be forcibly hospitalized under the new program, transported to the new Bellevue ward, and given, without option, a tranquilizer (Ativan) and an antipsychotic (Haldol). The following morning, she called a number on a flyer from the New York Civil Liberties Union and soon met its executive director, Norm Siegel, and a staff attorney, Robert Levy.

The shitstorm that ensued captivated New York and eventually the entire nation. The facts and history are straightforward: Brown's lawyers prevailed at the trial court level, but that ruling was then overturned by the appellate court. As the case dragged on, Brown was detained at Bellevue for months, refusing medication and showering only four times. The Koch administration returned to New York's state supreme court (the trial level), seeking to force Brown to take medication. A different judge assigned to the case appointed a new psychiatrist to evaluate Brown. Dr. Francine Cournos from Columbia University told the court Brown "suffered from mental illness...either paranoid schizophrenia or mania" and that medication would have "a good chance of improving [Brown's] hostility and irritability." But she also counseled that reconnecting Brown with her "network of people" she had developed over the past months would help her mental health improve. The judge agreed and told the administration it could not force medication on the patient.[16] In the face of this, the City released Brown from the Bellevue psych ward.

Brown was an instant celebrity when she walked out of Bellevue in mid-January 1988.[17] She appeared on several local television outlets that day and on *60 Minutes* and *The Phil Donahue Show* in the follow-ing weeks. A month later, she gave a talk at Harvard Law School. She was photographed answering phones at the NYCLU's front desk and declared, "I was incarcerated against my will...a political prisoner. The only thing wrong with me was that I was homeless, not insane."[18]

And yet, a few months later Brown was still living on and off at the Traveler's Hotel near Times Square, in a room rented for her by her lawyers. She was also frequently seen sleeping on the streets near Port Authority, panhandling, and assaulting passers-by. A year later, she had returned to her old location in front of the Beekman Theatre.

For most people, understandably, their attention to Brown's plight faded with the TV lights. But after subsequently cycling in and out of jail and hospitals (for physical ailments), in 1991, Joyce Brown finally found peace and stability in an apartment with on-site social services, an arrangement known as "supportive housing." Joan Olson, the pro-gram director, described Brown as "frail" when press made inquiries and shielded her from the constant scrutiny that dogged her for years.[19]

Brown's story—often distilled into a battle between "individual rights" and the public's "quality of life"—was so stark, so pitched, it siphoned public attention and the political will to fund supportive housing models at a scale approaching the obvious, and rapidly grow-ing, need. Although Brown's New York story is discussed in the past tense, these same battle lines are lately redrawn in several states with different legal underpinnings—on a collision course in federal court. California governor Gavin Newsom's recent directive to render any person unable to care for themselves under state conservatorship is a frighteningly similar attempted end run around this exact legal and policy paradigm.

The simple but profound takeaway from Brown's story is that a permanent home is the foundation for any person's stability, especially for people with severe mental illness who often have co-occurring sub-stance use disorders. Recovery from either condition rarely follows a straightforward trajectory, which is why case management support is essential. Long-term success is predicated on the certainty that, should symptoms relapse and require short-term hospitalization, a resident's home will still be there for them.

This practical middle road was—and continues to be—drowned out in the din of simplistic dueling narratives of civil liberties versus law and order.

Policy correctives must also be informed by the invaluable lived experience of the families of people struggling with SPMI. Their yearslong heroic efforts to support their loved ones lend a more nuanced, informed take, which aligns with what Brown's sisters reiterated again and again: "The person you think you're seeing is not what you think." It isn't the sanitized, standard advocacy message you expect from activists, but it doesn't make it any less valuable or relevant.

I've seen the situation that Brown's sisters described countless times in the Coalition's Crisis Intervention Program. Any frontline clinician dedicated to daily work with unhoused people will tell you that calling 911 and asking the police-led emergency services workers to forcibly take someone to the hospital is truly the last recourse: it's unpredictable and ugly, and most important, likely to destroy invaluable, hard-won trust built up over days, weeks, even years. But it *is* sometimes necessary. There is a role for hospitalization, both in the short term for stabilization and longer term for severe cases. At the Crisis Intervention Program, staff rarely pulled that trigger—perhaps every two months or more, and only when, despite our best efforts, not calling would create an even more dire situation.

The other reason calling 911 is often a losing move is that, however agitated, threatening, or delusional a person is, when the police show up, the person will almost certainly be able to pull themselves together for several minutes and present as lucid, either on-site or once they've been transported to the hospital. And that means they won't wind up being hospitalized or often even transported. They end up not getting the help they genuinely needed, and in the aftermath, you're dealing with a huge, often irreparable hole shot through the relationship.

Oddly, one of Koch's VPs at Health and Hospitals Corporation, Dr. Luis Marcos, explained this conundrum succinctly during Joyce Brown's trial. I didn't often agree with Marcos, but I did with his response to the NYCLU lawyers, who pointed out how cogent Brown had been on the witness stand: "People who don't know about mental illness very often think a mentally ill person has to sound confused. She is mentally ill, not mentally retarded. Mental illness does not affect intellect. As soon as her attention is focused, with her lawyers, on the witness stand, on television, she sounds fine. When she isn't [focused], she goes into her inner world and her more bizarre behavior comes out."[20]

## THE WAY FORWARD

The path out of this decades-long nightmare is the full funding of the community-based model outlined in the Kennedy plan. We also desperately need to reverse the closure of inpatient psychiatric beds. In New York State alone, the number of certified inpatient psychiatric beds dropped 12 percent between 2000 and 2018, with New York City bearing 72 percent of that decline. This is happening while both population and resulting need has increased. Without enough long-term beds, patients increasingly wind up in the carceral system. States including New York need to reverse the trend in decertification of inpatient hospital beds. Future bed closures must be tied to corresponding increases in housing and quality services, including comprehensive hospital discharge planning, all of which are now woefully inadequate. As examined in detail below, a driving force in these devastating bed closures is economic pressures related to the relative pittance of reimbursement that hospitals receive for providing long-term psychiatric care—an intentional feature, not a bug, of our nation's Medicaid system.

People used to largely assume that folks living rough on the streets refused to enter emergency shelter because they are "too crazy" to realize they need help. But in shelters, mentally ill people are considered easy prey; they're sized up the minute they come through intake. As one homeless friend confided in me, "I may be crazy, but I'm not stupid. I've went in the shelters three times and got the hell beaten out of me and robbed every time. Those guys see me come in—and they're on me day and night." And in New York, the intake portion of the shelter system is intentionally composed of larger and more remote congregate facilities. When you place 1,200 men on Wards Island in the middle of the East River, you can be sure it will be impossible to provide adequate security, let alone meaningful casework or access to public transportation for work or healthcare.

In short, the inability of outreach workers to convince a homeless street dweller to come into a massive, chaotic shelter system is rarely a communication problem. When outreach workers offer the standard van ride to an intake shelter, people make what they see as a rational choice—taking their chances on the streets over risking the dangers and indignity of congregate shelter. Want a different outcome? Start offering a different option: A private room with a door that locks. Privacy. Security. Dignity.

### MYTH 5 "MOST HOMELESS PEOPLE ARE MENTALLY ILL AND DANGEROUS"

It's increasingly rare that homelessness makes the news without being tethered to crime or "quality of life" issues. Politicians across the spectrum increasingly (and seamlessly) conflate homelessness and crime, amplifying the myth that homeless people are uniformly deranged and dangerous. In fact, mentally ill people comprise a minority of the homeless population: studies dating back to 1980 have consistently shown an estimated one-quarter to one-third of homeless single adults suffer from SPMI, including schizophrenia, schizoaffective disorder, bipolar disorder, and major depression/anxiety disorders.[21] Those rates are higher for homeless women, for those who are chronically homeless, and for our neighbors sleeping rough.

There is a complex, two-way relationship between homelessness and mental illness, as Peter Tarr explains: "An individual's mental illness may lead to cognitive and behavioral problems that make it difficult to earn a stable income or to carry out daily activities [needed to sustain stable housing. However,] individuals with mental illnesses often find themselves homeless primarily as the result of poverty and a lack of low-income housing." What's more, homelessness can have lasting traumatic effects on people already struggling with existing mental illness.

Homelessness itself and the amount of time "spent homeless can lead to higher levels of psychiatric distress, higher levels of alcohol use and lower levels of perceived recovery."[22]

Press coverage of homelessness reaches its inevitable, frenzied apex whenever a homeless person is accused of a violent crime, leaving the public with an unerring image of public menace. Civil rights attorney Scott Hechinger and others have written extensively about sensationalized journalism, which distorts crime trends in order to boost circulation and ratings.[23] The homeless man as proxy for danger is ubiquitous in daily media coverage of crime. Yet, homelessness has been shown to be associated with a *reduced* risk of felony arrest and an increased risk of arrest for misdemeanor arrests (typically petty theft, trespassing, and other crimes related to survival). The dearth of community-based psychiatric services and supportive housing, combined with inadequate discharge planning, contribute directly to higher rates of rearrest among homeless men. Researchers at the University of South Florida found that "being male, being homeless, having an involuntary psychiatric evaluation, and not having outpatient mental health treatment in the previous quarter independently increased the odds of... misdemeanor arrests." Meanwhile, "being Black, being in a younger age group, having a nonpsychotic diagnosis, and having a co-occurring substance use disorder diagnosis were all independently associated with felony arrests."[24]

The data shows that homeless people are far more likely to be the *victim* of crime than their domiciled counterparts. A meta-analysis by Professor Laurence Roy and her team at McGill University points to six studies showing homeless people with severe mental illness were far more likely to be preyed upon at staggering levels, with "the prevalence of victimization [lifetime rates] ranging between 73.7 percent and 87.0 percent...Significant correlates of victimization included female gender, history of child abuse, and depression."[25]

Central to (but rarely discussed openly) the crisis of mental illness among homeless Americans is the tremendous racial disparity in the rates of diagnosis for psychotic disorders—schizophrenia, in particular.

A 2014 literature review spanning twenty-four years of research on psychiatric diagnoses and race by Robert Schwartz and David Blankenship documents "a pervasive pattern wherein African American/Black consumers" are diagnosed with psychotic disorders at "a rate of on average three to four [times] higher than Euro-American/White consumers." In state hospitals, the disparity is even greater, with Black patients nearly five times more likely to be diagnosed with schizophrenia than their white counterparts. This, "despite the absence of genetic evidence indicating a true increase in prevalence in this population."[26]

That last fact is so obvious yet profound, that it's crucial to pause a moment and let it sink in. I recall in the months before joining the Coalition being thunderstruck by the implications that the vast majority of seriously mentally ill people I saw in the subway system or sleeping in public spaces were Black men. I thought, *Unless you believe there is an epidemic of schizophrenia in the Black community, this is insane.* Although seldom scrutinized in the detail it deserves, the ramifications of racial disparity in diagnosis and corollary lack of early/appropriate treatment are truly catastrophic.

Correct diagnosis is critical to care, as Schwartz and Blankenship note, as it's "considered to be the springboard of triage and treatment decisions." The researchers highlight cultural biases that often lead to misdiagnosis, either over-diagnosis (assigning a disorder when none is present) or misidentification (assigning a diagnosis for a different condition), which can cause tremendous harm to the patient. In particular, there is widespread distortion of "deviant behaviors... behaviors which a clinician deems unusual or out of the norm either statistically or from their own perspective, [which] do not constitute mental disorders. Moreover, a culturally expectable or acceptable pattern of cognitions, psychological or emotional states, or behaviors does not warrant a mental disorder diagnosis." Misdiagnosis often results "when culturally normative behavior is mistaken for psychopathology."[27]

Beyond correcting assessment instruments and retraining clinicians, a multitude of other factors, far more unwieldy, play into the misdiagnosis paradigm. Within the carceral system, among forensic psychiatric consumers, "Euro-Americans were 78 percent less likely to be diagnosed with a psychotic disorder than African Americans. High levels of education were associated with decreased odds of being diagnosed with psychotic disorder while length of stay in the forensic psychiatric facility increased those odds."[28] Perhaps most significant, Black Americans account for more than half of all behavioral hospitalizations; whites accounted for just 23 percent. When discharged, Black patients were twice as likely to have been given a primary psychotic diagnosis than white patients.[29] The relative economic insecurity of Black households and their resulting lack of capacity to accommodate a family member struggling with mental health issues relegates a larger portion of Black Americans to rely on state or municipal hospitals, where they are far more likely to be misdiagnosed, mis-medicated, and discharged to the streets.

Just as many wrongly assumed that diversifying the ranks of police would significantly curb brutality directed at Black citizens, diagnosis distortion by Black clinicians mirror those of their white colleagues.[30]

The ramifications of this misdiagnosis trend are far-reaching and tragic. Psychiatrist Jonathan Metzl's 2011 authoritative appraisal of the bias and its toll, *The Protest Psychosis: How Schizophrenia Became a Black Disease*, painstakingly details the many factors contributing to misdiagnosis and the disastrous outcomes—mis-prescribed psychotropic medication, alienation from appropriate mental healthcare, increased familial estrangement and homelessness, and potential death (from homeless-related exposure or illness to stigma-induced suicide).[31] Beyond clinicians mistaking culturally normative behavior for psychopathology, underdiagnosis of both mood disorders—particularly bipolar and major depressive disorders—contribute to the overdiagnosis of schizophrenia among Black Americans. Stigma associated with mental illness symptoms, combined with the lack of access to basic healthcare effectively block early intervention, as well as appropriate diagnosis and vital treatment for countless thousands of our Black neighbors, many of whom become homeless.

## KENDRA WEBDALE AND THE ADVENT OF OBSERVED OUTPATIENT THERAPY

In January 1999, a twenty-nine-year-old homeless man named Andrew Goldstein pushed a thirty-two-year-old aspiring journalist named Kendra Webdale in front of an oncoming Manhattan subway train, killing her instantly. It's hard to overstate the impact of this grisly crime on the public psyche, both in New York and nationally. Officials' attempts to prevent similar acts set in motion a trajectory of legal maneuvers that continue to unfold over twenty years later. The primary solution, flawed in both its conception and implementation, has done little to ensure either personal safety or public order.

The immediate remedy offered up, in August 1999, was New York State's Kendra's Law, which mandated assisted outpatient therapy (AOT) for patients discharged from state psychiatric facilities who (a) are perceived as noncompliant in taking prescribed psychotropic medication and (b) have a history of violence. The "assisted" part of AOT means the patient must be observed actually taking their medication. Studies of compliance with AOT in the years since enactment show its efficacy is largely dependent on stable housing or stable mental health shelters in which daily dosing of mandated medication can be reliably observed. Yet the State offered no additional funds for supportive housing.

The law passed despite Michael Winerip's masterful investigation for the *New York Times Magazine* in May 1999, detailing a jarring series of facts: Andrew Goldstein had made myriad attempts to secure psychiatric treatment for himself in the years, months, and even days leading up to the murder. Winerip put it simply: "He wanted help. When a mental patient kills, there is often an outcry for tougher commitment laws, but this was not the problem in Goldstein's case. He signed himself in voluntarily for all 13 of his hospitalizations [from 1997 to 1999 alone]. His problem was what happened after discharge."[32]

In just one example of the scope of bureaucratic ineptitude, Goldstein had made his way to Creedmoor State Hospital in 1997, asking for long-term hospitalization. But census reductions from State budget cuts resulted in him being referred instead to an ER, from which he was released the next day. Over the next two years, every time Goldstein was discharged from short- and long-term psychiatric hospitalizations, well-meaning staff searched for an appropriate placement in a supportive facility, as both they and he knew he shouldn't be alone. "But everywhere they looked they were turned down," Winerip wrote. "They found waiting lists [at] state hospitals, waiting lists for [state-funded] group homes, waiting lists for a state-financed intensive-case manager" (someone to visit him daily to make sure he was taking his medication and getting by).[33]

Hospital staff could find no openings for supportive housing, because as noted by Winerip, "openings are rare since Governor Pataki financed no new [residences] in his first four-year term." As is still so often the case today, the last time Goldstein was hospitalized—just a few weeks before killing Webdale—his discharge had been initiated after three weeks because of financial pressure by Pataki's mental health administrators to free up the bed. Like so many before and after him, Goldstein left the hospital with a week's worth of medication and written instructions to find a new counseling center. He never made it there.

Winerip's summary bears repeating in full: "There is a long list of institutions and individuals who should be held accountable for what happened to Goldstein and Webdale, but at the top of that list belong Governor Pataki and the State of New York, for it is the states that, for the last 150 years, have had primary responsibility for citizens who are seriously mentally ill, and it is the states, beginning with deinstitutionalization in the 1950s, that have persistently shirked that responsibility."[34]

This cycle of abuse by neglect continues to this day. A personal example from late 2021: After getting my first Covid vaccine at Harlem Hospital, I ducked into a tiny private restroom on the second floor. As I washed my hands, I noticed a small stack of papers on the ledge above the sink. They were discharge papers, an hour old, left behind by a psychiatric patient. Stapled to the bottom was one pink piece of paper with basic subway and bus instructions (in English and Spanish, blurry from generations of mimeographing the original) to Bellevue Men's Shelter on Manhattan's East Side.

A little over a month later, in January 2022, Michelle Go, a forty-year-old advertising executive on her way to work, was shoved to her death at the Times Square subway station. Her assailant, like Goldstein, had a long history of homelessness and mental illness. *New York Times* reporters noted that Martial Simon had spent years on an "endless circuit of hospitals and jails, outpatient psychiatric programs and the streets."[35] A few months after the murder, he was deemed unfit to stand trial and was remanded to a nearby New York State forensic psychiatric unit, where he remains.[36]

And it's not just a New York problem. Every state has significantly defunded mental healthcare since the 1950s. Dorothea Dix, the renowned nineteenth-century advocate, shamed several states into recognizing the "insane persons confined... in cages, closets, cellars, stalls, pens! Chained, naked, beaten with rods, and lashed into obedience."[37] Michael Winerip put it perfectly: "Though a moralist, Dix understood that it was all about money."[38]

The sad irony, of course, is that the law named after Kendra Webdale likely would not have even applied to her assailant, Goldstein. The most significant, enduring lesson is that it wasn't a lack of legal authority to compel his or others' compliance with forced treatment, it's the lack of capacity in hospitals and in supportive housing across the nation that allows this disgrace to persist and grow.

The prime sponsor of Kendra's Law, Governor George Pataki, put in play a dynamic that continues the divisive arguments over the forced hospitalization of Joyce Brown in 1987. California governor Gavin Newsom in 2022 pushed through a bill with a similar aim: to lower the threshold for state mandated treatment, taking it from the US Supreme Court's established "threat to oneself or others" to anyone with severe psychiatric disability unable to "care for themselves."[39] Anyone deemed noncompliant will be forcibly hospitalized.

Newsom's plan—aside from egregious civil liberty and moral concerns—is a financial house of cards. There are not nearly enough facilities in which to house those he wants to force into treatment. Billions of dollars of investment would be needed to reopen shuttered inpatient psychiatric beds and build supportive housing units for patients upon discharge. A therapist I know who had worked ten years ago in a Northern California clubhouse-type program, providing mental health services via a drop-in setting, recently told me that the program had been mandated by State officials to keep detailed notes on what was commonly referred to as the "100K Club"—clients who had cost the State $100,000 or more in outreach/hospital/jail costs over the previous two years. The therapist, one of the most even-keeled, unflappable people I know, had this to say about Newsom's plan: "That's . . . that's just laughable. They don't even have the capacity to begin to hospitalize that number of people—and if they did, it would bankrupt the state."

In February 2022, New York State adopted frighteningly similar language to Newsom's plan as it renewed and expanded Kendra's Law. New York governor Kathy Hochul, spurred by Mayor Eric Adams's nearly daily press conferences held in subways or subway entrances, allowed her mental health commissioner (a holdover from Andrew Cuomo's administration) to release a letter to localities, directing police and front-line staff to take into custody "persons who appear to be mentally ill and who display an inability to meet basic living needs, even when there is no recent dangerous act." Note the parallels to California's inclusion of "self-neglect."

Eric Adams's chief police/public safety advisor is Bill Bratton, former police commissioner under mayors Rudy Giuliani and Bill DeBlasio. A top goal of his has long been "disappearing" homeless people. AOT is just another tool to that end. Since Kendra's Law was modified in 2022 to envelop vastly more mentally ill homeless New Yorkers, the number of AOT orders has surged. Manhattan saw the largest year-to-year increase among the boroughs, at a whopping 25 percent. Not surprising, since it aligns "with Adams and Hochul's focus on targeting police and 'outreach' services to the epicenter of transit hubs," and closest proximity with media outlets.[40] Making homeless people disappear from Manhattan by pushing them into the less visible outer boroughs is a page from the original Giuliani/Bratton handbook. The practical problem is that it makes it far more difficult to deliver lifesaving services, including food, warm clothing, and healthcare.

Predictably, Black people are impacted disproportionally: of the roughly 3,500 people statewide who currently have an AOT order, 38 percent are Black (Black people comprise only 17 percent of the state population). Of AOT enrollees, 70 percent are diagnosed with schizophrenia and 15 percent with bipolar disorder, and roughly half have "co-existing alcohol or substance use disorder."[41]

## FOUR DECADES OF GASLIGHTING

Back-to-back investigative deep dives by Amy Julia Harris and Jan Ransom of the *New York Times* in November and December 2023 detailed the massive failures in the mental healthcare system. Their first exposé was the result of examination of hundreds of recent case files across public (New York City and State) and private systems. It shows how, again and again, the major arteries of our mental healthcare system—the shelter system, psychiatric hospitals, and outreach teams—fail to meet the most obvious needs of our neighbors with profound mental illness.[42]

The *Times* documented case after case in which unhoused people with severe mental illness sought, even begged for treatment, only to be turned away or sent to the street or to general population shelters, where they subsequently committed violent assaults. It was a bracing indictment of the disarray within the mental health and homeless systems, and each of these recent cases echoes the pattern of neglect and outright expulsion documented by Michael Winerip over twenty years earlier when Andrew Goldstein murdered Kendra Webdale. And again in 2022, when Martial Simon killed Michelle Go in a similar subway shoving.

Winerip's sage insight that reformer Dorothea Dix "understood that it was all about money" is etched in each of the ten cases detailed in the November exposé. The greatest driver of massive gaps in our mental healthcare system is money. Psychiatric hospital beds have been cut, and those closures "have been spurred by federal policies [that] discourage keeping people for long-term mental health care by reducing reimbursement rates from Medicaid and other insurers. Hospitals earned just $88,000 in net patient revenue per psychiatric bed in 2018 compared with $1.6 million per bed for all types of care."[43] Hospitals "have repeatedly erred while being overwhelmed by over 50,000 psychiatric patients per year. At least some of the discharges documented by the *Times* appear to violate federal law requiring hospitals to stabilize patients before releasing them." Patients in severe distress, pleading for long-term help, were often dumped on to the streets. Those sent to the shelter system were not even flagged with psychiatric histories, as low-paid intake workers were not given access to the specialized database with relevant information. Finally, a network of outreach teams often could not provide meaningful services in the midst of "staggering caseloads. Some teams spent just 15 minutes per visit with patients—the minimum amount of time required to bill Medicaid for services."

The erosion of funding following deinstitutionalization is astonishing. In 1963, before deinstitutionalization, New York State "spent about $400 million a year on its psychiatric institutions—the equivalent of about $4 billion today." By contrast, the outreach team approach, heralded in the 1990s as a replacement for state hospitals, has "received, on average, about $120 million a year in state and federal funding in recent years." When contacted by the *Times*, I commented: "The public has been gaslit for nearly four decades. We keep being told something is done, but nothing has changed. There is constant finger-pointing at every level of government and dropping the ball with the hopes that it won't result in another Michelle Go."

Harris and Ransom's December 2023 follow-up—which focused on Kendra's Law, the "gold standard program" that "has been held up as a national model" for assuring that "treatment-resistant" outpatients adhered to medication compliance—was equally detailed and every bit as disturbing. Its headline neatly summarizes the grotesque ineffectiveness of AOT: "Kendra's Law Was Meant to Prevent Violence. It Failed Hundreds of Times."[44] After reviewing tens of thousands of pages of records and interviewing hundreds of people, the *Times* reporters uncovered hundreds of incidents in which Kendra's Law, named to honor the legacy of subway shoving victim Kendra Webdale over twenty years ago, failed to ensure adequate psychiatric care. In addition to crimes committed against strangers, "more than 90 people have killed themselves while subject to Kendra's Law orders in the past decade." Both the November and December 2023 analyses showed the consequences of a woefully underfunded mental healthcare system: "New York State spends about $29 million a year to run Kendra's Law for some 3,800 people—less than one percent of what the state spends to operate the prison system."

CHAPTER 4

# OFFERING AID CREATES MORE NEED

**MYTH 6** "IF YOU BUILD IT, THEY WILL COME"*

As we've seen, the delayed effect of deinstitutionalization on homelessness shows that, while homelessness exploded under Reagan, many seeds of the crisis had already been sown. Most deinstitutionalization had occurred by the mid-1970s, half a decade before Reagan became president. Until the late 1970s, slim cushions of cheap housing throughout the nation kept mass homelessness at bay, or geographically corralled in discrete neighborhoods, the Bowery in New York City, the Tenderloin in San Francisco, and Skid Row in Los Angeles, where residents were typically white, alcoholic men.

But Reagan's role in the unprecedented escalation of homelessness—and its widespread persistence to this day—is nonetheless significant. As we've seen in previous chapters, homelessness has waxed and waned throughout US history, largely following the national, sometimes international, fiscal tides. As HUD researcher Walter Leginski notes, "While there have been temporary lulls, from colonial times forward there has been no period of American history free of homelessness." However, modern mass homelessness is unique in that "the contemporary wave of homelessness has not subsided during good economic times."[1]

*This familiar phrase is from the 1986 film *Field of Dreams* about the 1919 Black Sox baseball scandal. New York mayor Ed Koch used it as shorthand to imply: "The more shelters you build, the more people will make themselves homeless to fill them."

In the wake of deinstitutionalization and the decimation of cheap housing, unprecedented budget cuts and policy changes at the federal level entrenched and escalated the crisis. These cuts began with Ronald Reagan, signaling the wholesale abnegation of federal responsibility for decent and affordable housing, and they continued through Bill Clinton's administration. Moreover, over the past decade, due to the Budget Control Act of 2011, the HUD budget has dramatically declined. The one-two punch of lasting budgetary cuts and policy changes are why, unlike in other eras in American history, mass homelessness endures.

To fully appreciate the decimation wrought by Reagan's cuts and Clinton's subsequent carpet-bombing of federal income subsidies for our most destitute neighbors, colloquially known as "welfare reform," it's important to take a moment to appreciate the scaffolding of support constructed by Franklin D. Roosevelt in the midst of, and immediately after, the Great Depression.

## FDR'S NEW DEAL USHERS FEDERAL GOVERNMENT COMMITMENT TO HOUSING

In 1944, as his third presidential term drew to a close, Roosevelt delivered one of the most memorable State of the Union addresses in American history. In it, he returned to an enduring theme of his presidency, initially wrought amid the despair of the Great Depression and steeled by more recent victories in World War II: What can government do to ensure genuine, lasting security for its citizens? FDR asserted that true security for our nation was tied inextricably with economic soundness for *all* Americans: "As I see it, the task of government in its relation to business is to assist the development of an economic declaration of rights, an economic constitutional order. This is the common task of statesman and business man. It is the minimum requirement of a more permanently safe order of things."[2]

FDR's progressive vision for enduring national security lay in individual economic stability culminated with his 1944 Economic Bill of Rights: "In our day these economic truths have become accepted as self-evident. We have accepted, so to speak, a second Bill of Rights under which a new basis of security and prosperity can be established for all regardless of station, race, or creed."[3] It included:

- The right to a useful and remunerative job in the industries or shops or farms or mines of the Nation
- The right to earn enough to provide adequate food and clothing and recreation...
- Freedom from unfair competition and domination by monopolies at home or abroad
- The right of every family to a decent home
- The right to adequate medical care and the opportunity to achieve and enjoy good health
- The right to adequate protection from the economic fears of old age, sickness, accident, and unemployment
- The right to a good education

"All of these rights," FDR concluded, "spell security." Then he emphasized, "We have come to a clear realization of the fact that true individual freedom cannot exist without economic security and independence. Necessitous men are not free men.* People who are hungry and out of a job are the stuff of which dictatorships are made." Economic desperation in Europe had indeed made fertile ground for the rise of Hitler, Mussolini, and Franco.

FDR's "right of every family to a decent home" verbally codified the federal government's growing commitment to housing, which aimed to stem the torrent of Depression-era homelessness. His Federal Housing Act of 1937 had created the Section 8 program, which both funded public housing and gave local and state governments subsidies for private entities to build affordable housing.[4]

Subsequent presidential administrations—from Truman through Carter—accepted and expanded the major public sponsorship of afford-

---

* Roosevelt is quoting Old English property law case, *Vernon v. Bethell* (1762) 28 ER 838 here.

able housing that FDR had established. And not just for low-income families. The Servicemen's Readjustment Act of 1944, also known as the G.I. Bill, gave many returning working-class soldiers access to mortgages at reduced or zero interest rates, with no money down.[5] Black vets, however, did not share in this housing bounty; these mortgages were almost exclusively made available to white servicepeople, with widespread redlining reinforcing housing segregation. Even Richard Nixon, albeit with dubious motives, expanded the pathways of federal housing support to include portable Section 8 vouchers that low-income renters could use to secure units in the private market and take with them when they chose to move.

## "GOVERNMENT IS THE PROBLEM"

This multi-decade, bipartisan commitment to decent, affordable housing was abruptly derailed when Ronald Reagan rolled into the Oval Office in January 1981, trumpeting, "Government is not the solution to our problem, government is the problem."[6] He made quick and vicious work on both budgetary and attitudinal fronts. After famously not recognizing his own HUD secretary at a meeting of urban mayors (Samuel Pierce was Black),[7] Reagan slashed HUD expenditures—both for public housing complexes and portable Section 8 vouchers—from $26 billion to $8 billion.[8] It's impossible to overstate the significance of this carnage. If you are looking for the single, most significant factor that transformed US homelessness from a cyclical ebb-and-flow to a permanent fixture on the American landscape, this is it.

A decade and a half after Lyndon Johnson declared a War on Poverty, Reagan's savaging of HUD resources marked a stark pivot to a war against poor people themselves.[9] Reagan's justification was reflected in his offhand remark, delivered as he strolled across the White House lawn to board a presidential helicopter, "In the '60s we waged a war on poverty, and poverty won." Actually, Johnson's poverty initiatives had driven the poverty rate to decrease dramatically, from 19 to 11 percent in just ten years.[10] But the civil unrest and the concentration of urban decay in the late 1960s and early '70s overrode any rational discourse on what worked to improve the economic footing of our poorest neighbors.

Perhaps as damaging as Reagan's budgetary bloodletting was the toxic rationalization he routinely offered for the wholesale abandonment of housing investments. On January 30, 1984, Reagan appeared on *Good Morning America* and, attempting to blunt rising criticism of his brutal cuts in the face of skyrocketing street homelessness, remarked, "The people who are sleeping on grates…the homeless…are homeless, you might say, by choice."[11] His audacious blame-the-victim rhetoric provoked widespread outrage, but also gave cover to anyone looking to assuage their moral unease at the nation's spiraling destitution. In a return to deeply embedded Calvinistic reasoning, Reagan and his supporters claimed that the fate of homelessness was a result of individual choices and actions. By assiduously diverting attention away from obvious policy and fiscal causes, victim-blaming provided essential insulation against a more disturbing explanation for the status quo: that a return to medieval-level suffering is an undeniable manifestation of late-stage capitalism.

The practical fallout from Reagan cutbacks on cities large and small was devastating. Peter Dreier noted in *The Nation* that, when Reagan left office in 1989, "federal assistance to local governments had been slashed by 60 percent."[12] The effects were disastrous. As Dreier explains, "cities with high levels of poverty and limited property tax bases" were hardest hit, as many "depended on federal aid to provide basic services. In 1980 federal dollars accounted for 22 percent of big city budgets. By the end of Reagan's second term, federal aid was only 6 percent." The consequences of this fiscal carnage cut across every public sector from "schools and libraries, municipal hospitals and clinics, and sanitation, [to] police and fire departments—many of which had to shut their doors." Dreier concludes, "Many cities still haven't recovered from the downward spiral started during the Gipper's presidency."[13]

Niels Frenzen's letter to the *New York Times*, several months into the single term of Reagan's former vice president and Oval Office successor, George H. W. Bush, delivered a prescient query, asking if modern homelessness is an enduring legacy of trickle-down economics: "As our own United States homeless population grows, the question arises whether the causes of homelessness can be explained by a transition to a harsher and crueler form of capitalism under the Bush-Reagan Administrations or, if not explicable by such a transition, is homelessness simply a necessary component to our present brand of capitalism?"[14]

## ED KOCH'S NEW YORK

It was against this backdrop of federal abnegation that Ed Koch reigned as mayor of New York. His tenure predated Reagan's inauguration by three years, and when Reagan took office in 1981, Koch was already dealing with the sudden appearance of thousands of New Yorkers sleeping rough in all areas of the city. In addition to narrowly dodging municipal bankruptcy, wide swaths of the Bronx and central Brooklyn had been completely leveled. One of Koch's early attempts to divert attention away from the grim vista was dispatching workers to place huge stickers of curtains and potted plants in the windows of abandoned, decaying buildings, especially those near expressways used by white commuters. The *New York Times* observed that locals responded to Koch's Potemkin village with "a Bronx cheer."[15]

It was Koch (with the blessing of his State counterpart, Governor Hugh Carey) who settled *Callahan v. Carey*, the landmark case brought by the Coalition that established the right to shelter in New York City for single homeless men (Koch was one of the named plaintiffs). Koch was notoriously contentious, forcing the Coalition to sue him again for women and the Legal Aid Society a third time for families with children. The suits were settled with consent decrees: the judges never actually ruled on the underlying legality, which, plaintiffs contended, was rooted in an amendment to the New York State Constitution adopted after the Great Depression, stating that "aid, care and support of the needy are public concerns and shall be provided by the state."[16] The City, with matching funding from the State for single adults and eventually a portion of funds from the federal government for families, agreed to provide emergency lifesaving shelter only when it appeared their prospects of winning the original case outright were greatly diminished.

In practice, Koch set out to make the emergency shelter he'd agreed to provide as bare-bones and off-putting as possible. The results were upward of 1,200 men sleeping on drill floors in vast armories in upper Manhattan and Brooklyn. Another 1,200 were subsequently quartered on Wards Island in the middle of the East River. Koch's approach reprised the "irreconcilable contradictions" that Michael Katz argued defined nineteenth-century poorhouses, which were "at once to be a refuge for the helpless and a deterrent to the able-bodied."[17]

In the mid-1980s, family homelessness followed on the heels of the single adult crisis and Koch responded with dozens of "welfare hotels"—bleak, decrepit, crime-ridden buildings, many in Manhattan's central business district. The engineered demise of SROs and the loss of thousands of apartments in the Bronx, Brooklyn, and Manhattan had made the situation more dire than any time since the Depression: with the dearth of available affordable housing, these facilities, horrible as they were, quickly filled up.

Despite the unspeakable conditions of most facilities, Koch believed that merely offering this emergency shelter somehow encouraged people to falsely claim homelessness. This "woodwork" or "inducement" theory had long been a trope of right-wing welfare critics. Although such claims have been resoundingly disproven, Koch and subsequent mayors continued to cling vigorously to it.[18] It was incontrovertibly disproven by extreme shelter eligibility denials and ultimately by the complete removal of housing options for homeless families by Michael Bloomberg. His outright denial of housing options for homeless families triggered a vast increase of families with vulnerable children crowded into costly emergency shelters.

As it was with Nixon, Koch's fiercest critics rendered him in a more charitable light when his (2013) obituaries and tributes placed him in more contemporary context. Along lines similar to "Nixon was bad, but remember when he floated the notion of a universal minimum income?" Koch is remembered less for refusing to reform hideous, violent emergency shelters (which he belatedly entertained, and only after he received a full political beatdown) and more for his legacy of permanent housing. In the end, Koch was deemed a pragmatist. Having inherited an urban landscape decidedly more *French Connection* than *Breakfast at Tiffany's*—and with Reagan hacking away at federal funding across the board—Koch chose to lean in to perhaps the only resource he had in abundance: the thousands of abandoned buildings and empty land parcels that the City had seized when owners had forfeited on tax liens or cashed out on post-arson insurance claims. These buildings, shells, and vacant lots were sold off, many for one dollar a piece, to be recycled and rebuilt into affordable housing. Koch's ten-year $5 billion capital plan was the biggest, boldest gamble ever taken by a municipality on its housing future. What's more, fully 10 percent was earmarked to provide housing to homeless New Yorkers.

By the time the *Field of Dreams'* "If you build it, they will come" became a ubiquitous tagline in 1989, Koch had adopted it as his sullen rejoinder whenever he was asked why the homeless crisis seemed to be growing worse, not better. Rather than explaining the timeline inherent in any long-term capital investment scheme, Koch would complain that it didn't matter how much money was thrown at the homeless— the more shelter, as a pipeline to permanent housing, was offered, the more people would "come out of the woodwork" to claim it. Nineteen Eighty-Nine also framed the political fight of his life, running for a rare fourth term as mayor against Manhattan borough president David Dinkins. Dinkins bashed Koch—complaining that the rollout of the housing plan was too slow, as was the downsizing of the most notorious shelters (by either constructing smaller, better run shelters or, preferably, moving shelter residents into permanent housing)—and beat him in the Democratic primary. Dinkins went on to defeat Republican candidate Rudy Giuliani in the closest general mayoral election in New York City history, becoming New York's first African American mayor.

Alas, even Dinkins, the great liberal lion, reversed course just six weeks into his term. He reneged on his yearslong criticism of Koch's homeless policy, along with every campaign promise he'd made on homelessness, going all in with his own version of "If you build it, they will come," announcing he would be taking a closer look at possible inducements to shelter usage. But he needed something resembling a legitimate study to justify full-scale reversal of his long-held conviction in increased investment in permanent housing over restrictions to shelter access. A year later in 1991, with homelessness surging and his mayoralty in disarray, Dinkins appointed Andrew Cuomo, son of (and former advisor to) New York governor Mario Cuomo and founder of the nonprofit Housing Enterprise for the Less Privileged (HELP), which provided transitional shelter for homeless families, to head a commission ("The Way Home Commission") to "study the problem of homelessness" and make recommendations. I testified that the time for studies had long past; affordable housing with appropriate services had already been proven many times over to be the most practical and economical solution. Later, even the right-wing *New York Post* editorial page chimed in in agreement ("Give the devil her due, she's right on one point"). When Cuomo's commission finally released its report, it was no shock that chief among the recommendations was privatizing the shelter system. What was surprising was the suggestion to undo New York's right to shelter and institute a work-for-shelter scheme. It's important to note that Cuomo's pronouncement set the stage for undercutting access to emergency shelter and ultimately gave Rudy Giuliani (who would run for mayor again in 1993 and use it in his campaign to beat Dinkins) cover for Rudy's overt contempt for and draconian treatment of homeless adults and children.

### MYTH 7 "THERE IS NO SHORTAGE OF HELP AVAILABLE FOR THE HOMELESS— THEY JUST NEED TO ACCESS IT"

Of all the myths surrounding homeless and indigent people, this one is perhaps the most galling, as it diverts investments in housing-based solutions in favor of more outreach workers to engage homeless people and direct them to a mythical bounty of existing services. Parallel arguments are often made with respect to welfare or food stamp benefits.

Somehow, the inability of poor people to secure a toehold on the first rung of the housing ladder has been reduced to a communication issue. Help and resources exist, this myth insists, it's just a question of connecting people with an imaginary bounty of siloed public benefits. Conveniently, in claiming that existing benefits are already sufficient, this myth also obscures the structural factors at play in creating homelessness, once again shifting blame to the victim.

Understanding how we got waylaid in such a sick eddy entails surveying the basic context of welfare relief in the US. In the early 1900s, there was a patchwork of various state programs called mothers' pensions, which aimed to support (mostly white) widows so they could stay at home and raise their children. A key feature of these programs was encouraging mothers to *not* work outside the home. The same was true of the federal incarnation, Aid to Dependent Children (ADC), created as part of the Social Security Act of 1935. Women who bore children out of wedlock or were divorced were largely excluded, as were women of color: 96 percent of those receiving mothers' pensions were white.[19]

As federal oversight increased in the 1940s and 1950s, racial discrimination within the program dwindled. By the early 1960s, the program had been rebranded Aid to Families with Dependent Children (AFDC) and 40 percent of recipients were Black. The US Supreme Court handed AFDC applicants a landmark victory in 1968's *King v. Smith*, essentially ruling that AFDC was an entitlement, and must be made available to anyone meeting the needs test upon application.[20]

Remember, the original genesis of mothers' pensions had been to deter women—white widowed women in particular—from seeking paid work in the first place. Expectations for Black mothers have always been far different, as they were regularly employed in the lowest levels of the service sector as maids, housekeepers, farm workers, and nannies. As the ranks of AFDC recipients shifted from white to Black, and as caseloads swelled, a public backlash began to brew in the late 1960s and throughout the '70s. Reagan fanned the flames of resentment with his tropes about "welfare queens"—apocryphal Black mothers who

"gamed" the system—and slashed overall funding to the program significantly in his first term.[21]

Setting aside Reagan's racist hyperbole, one significant flaw to the
AFDC funding framework has long been its "phaseout rate." For every
dollar earned by a recipient, a dollar was deducted from their cash benefit check, a practice virtually everyone agreed discouraged recipients
from working outside the home.[22] Reagan, in addition to cutting funding to AFDC outright, also accelerated the phaseout rate, which para-
doxically only further deterred recipients from finding work.[23]

Democrat Bill Clinton, running for president in 1992 against incumbent George H. W. Bush, exploited this backlash, declaring that he
would "end welfare as we know it." It was a central theme in his campaign, and once elected, Clinton enlisted a number of progressives to
join his administration to develop a working model for an AFDC replacement—one with guaranteed subsidized jobs, along with access to
healthcare, transportation, and childcare.[24] Clinton initially released a
plan that capped cash benefits at two years, at which point those who
could not find a job in the private sector would be given a government
job. But the price tag associated with genuine reform turned out to be
more than twice that of a basic AFDC grant of roughly $5,000 per year
per family—a total increase of over $13 billion per year.[25] When Repub-
licans won House and Senate majorities in the 1995 midterm, the odds
of legitimate welfare reform dimmed significantly.[26]

America's poor lost out big time. In the ensuing backroom horse-
trading of basic sustenance, House Speaker Newt Gingrich proposed
converting welfare into that epic Republican subterfuge we've seen so
often deployed to gut funding to poor Americans: block-granting funds
to individual states.

Instead of an entitlement to cash benefits (which has the intrinsic
flexibility to cover everything from rent to outgrown sneakers), Congress would allocate a set amount of welfare funding to the States, with
which they could then choose for themselves amongst a myriad of ways
to spend the money under a new greatly expanded umbrella of options.
As we saw previously with the debacle of deinstitutionalization, the wide

discretion given to states under the guise of "states' self-determination," "progress," and "creativity" led to huge amounts of spending pulled away from the neediest and diluted into a vast array of questionable programming.

Clinton's top advisor on poverty issues, Peter Edelman, resigned in protest, excoriating the president in a blistering assessment published in *The Atlantic*. In it, Edelman, who had been in public service since the '60s, recalled a 1967 speech he had helped Robert Kennedy craft. Kennedy's speech "called the welfare system bankrupt and said it was hated universally, by payers and recipients alike. Criticism of welfare for not helping people to become self-supporting is nothing new." Edelman concluded that "the bill that President Clinton signed is not welfare reform. It does not promote work effectively, and it will hurt millions of poor children by the time it is fully implemented."[27]

Clinton himself described the final product, the Personal Responsibility and Work Opportunity Reconciliation Act, as "a decent welfare bill, wrapped in a sack of shit."[28]

Since the law transformed the AFDC entitlement into the block-granted Temporary Assistance for Needy Families (TANF), monthly caseloads have plummeted dramatically—even though, according to the Center on Budget and Policy Priorities (CBPP), "poverty and deep poverty remained widespread." Moreover, "for every 100 families in poverty, only 21 received cash assistance from TANF, down from 68 families when TANF was enacted in 1996." CBPP estimates that if AFDC had continued, relief would have reached 3.4 million impoverished American families, in 2020—a staggering "2.3 million more families than TANF actually reached."[29]

There is widespread consensus that Clinton's welfare reform, even mitigated somewhat by the subsequent enactment of the Earned Income Tax Credit, gutted the income of poor Americans, leaving, as researchers from the University of Kentucky summarized, "the most vulnerable single mothers either running in place or falling behind."[30] It has also indisputably increased deep poverty, or the number of families living on less than 50 percent of the poverty level.[31] The most egregious effect of block-granting has been the startling shift away from cash assistance to cover basic needs (food, clothing, and housing). In 1996, roughly 79 percent of TANF spending went to cover basic needs; in 2020, a mere 21 percent of TANF expenditures did.[32] Because states are given such broad authority to spend the $16.5 billion annually, funds are increasingly diverted away from families with the lowest incomes and toward everything from tax breaks to tuition assistance for families with incomes well over the federal poverty guidelines. As University of Wisconsin researcher Timothy Smeeding told *Vox*'s Dylan Matthews: "If the goal of welfare reform was to get rid of welfare, we succeeded. If the goal was to get rid of poverty, we failed."[33]

In contrast to the convoluted history of AFDC and TANF, housing subsidies have never been codified as an entitlement. As a result, only one in five households eligible for housing support actually receives federal housing subsidies.[34] The bottom line: thanks to Democrats and Republicans alike, there is simply not enough help available for our poorest neighbors.

As we'll see in the next section, Clinton's successful undoing of federal subsistence cash benefits—particularly the freedom he gave to states and localities, allowing them to require recipients to work in exchange for welfare—provided the essential legal scaffolding for a similar attempted savaging of New York City's right to shelter by Rudy Giuliani. The glue binding both Clinton's and Giuliani's attack on lifesaving protections for our poorest neighbors is another Calvinistic trope: handouts create dependency.

### MYTH 8  "HANDOUTS CREATE HOMELESSNESS"

In the early 1990s, after his stint as US attorney for New York's Southern District, Rudy Giuliani eventually landed at a middling firm known as Anderson, Kill, Olick & Oshinsky. Although it wasn't a blue-chip firm, Giuliani still managed to pull in $500,000 a year for doing very little work. Popular opinion held that the firm, looking for a rainmaker, hoped to cash in on the star power of the then most famous public law enforcement official in the country. During his time at the

Southern District, Giuliani had made headlines indicting the kingpins of the New York mafia's Five Families, as well as dozens of corrupt Wall Street CEOs. His track record of mafia convictions outshone his relatively meager successes in the financial district. But on both fronts, the tabloid and television press soaked up every twist and turn and gave Giuliani a platform for shameless self-promotion and braggadocio. His background in chasing criminals would greatly color his approach to homelessness as mayor.

In the summer of 1993, my Coalition predecessor, Bob Hayes, and I were invited to brief Rudy Giuliani on homelessness as he headed into his second general election for mayor. This was the first time I actually met the man. We waited nearly an hour for his arrival, making small talk with a handful of campaign staffers at the dreary law firm that had gambled on the celebrity lawyer who'd brought New York organized crime to its knees. What they'd gotten instead (multiple press reports relayed) was a mostly indifferent, often absentee colleague who used the midtown digs almost exclusively to plot his second campaign against incumbent David Dinkins.[35]

The meeting itself seemed to go swimmingly. Hayes had told me beforehand that Rudy's homeless platform in his previous 1989 mayoral run had been cribbed nearly word-for-word from Coalition policy briefs, which argued for speeding up the timeline for closure of the city's squalid welfare hotels and increasing investments in supportive housing, SROs, and housing for homeless families.

We briefed Rudy about Dinkins's about-face on the promise to downsize the massive dangerous armory shelters, as well as his embrace of Koch's central myth: increasing affordable housing incentivized indigent New Yorkers to declare themselves homeless and enter the shelter system. We furnished Rudy with detailed reports and graphs decisively undercutting the "woodwork effect" theory, showing that supposed deterrents such as increasing length of stays in shelters or cutting access to affordable housing had the opposite effect—they *increased* the shelter population. In an appeal to both common sense and Rudy's fiscally conservative Republican grounding, we underscored that the current stopgap measure approach—expanded emergency shelter, more frequent hospitalizations, and increased incarceration—*raised* city taxpayer expenditures while bringing us no closer to solving the underlying issue: the dearth of affordable housing.

Rudy seemed reasonably engaged, but then handed virtually all the data off to his rising aide-de-camp Richard Schwartz. The meeting ended with Rudy and Hayes (who, like Rudy, had also reverted to private practice) sharing a laugh, comparing notes on the warm embrace of corporate litigation. They made no effort to hide their shared delight in raking in big bucks in private practice. (Hayes was then at O'Melveny and Myers, working for Exxon in its successful attempt to reduce the multibillion-dollar punitive damages following the *Exxon Valdez* catastrophe. Giuliani's clients included the Mujahideen-e-Khalq and Purdue Pharma.)[36] Walking out of the building, Hayes was delighted, describing the meeting as a "slam dunk" and assuring me there was "not a chance" Giuliani would deviate from the moderate stances of his previous Coalition-inspired 1989 mayoral platform.

In the two subsequent meetings I had with Schwartz in August, he adopted much more of a devil's advocate line of inquiry: wondering aloud if the social contract was ripe for rewriting and repeatedly invoking the new catchphrase "personal responsibility." Clearly it was an emerging go-to concept in Giuliani's camp, the modern-day incarnation of the unshakable Calvinistic axiom, "God helps those who help themselves." Looking back, these not-so-subtle shifts in tone and language should have braced me for the political cyclone to come the following month.

One early evening in mid-September, Schwartz called me to say, "You may not be happy with what we are releasing tomorrow."

"Oh, why's that?" I asked.

"Well...we're not fully onboard with continuing the whole...you know...right-to-shelter thing."

"Oh, that," I replied, deadpan. "What exactly are you proposing?"

He hemmed and hawed and eventually said, "Well, at the end of the day, Rudy feels strongly that limiting shelter stays to ninety days is the best course—you know...to motivate people to move on and get jobs and pull themselves together." Then, suddenly flustered, he added, "This is embargoed until 11 a.m. tomorrow, right?"

I held back my honest take about the plan's practical stupidity—and almost assured political blowback of dumping tens of thousands of homeless New Yorkers on the city's streets—and simply asked if I could see an advance copy of the policy paper. After all, I explained, we had spent untold hours in what I'd assumed were good-faith conversations on the issue. Since I'd no doubt be fielding a barrage of press calls the following morning, I said, "I'd really appreciate looking it over."

I was genuinely shocked that he gave it to me.

Giuliani's plan was even worse than the ninety-day policy Schwartz had let slip over the phone. Rather than downsizing the most notorious shelters, replacing them with smaller, safer facilities, and expanding the pipeline into permanent housing, Rudy was planning a legal full-court press to make shelter eligibility contingent on participation in make-work "workfare" programs, a deterrent strategy already being rolled out in several Southern states as a requirement for basic monthly welfare grants, now permitted in the wake of Clinton's dreadful "welfare reform."

Rudy was scheduled to appear in front of his old stomping grounds at the Manhattan House of Detention the following morning at 11 a.m. Figuring a sizable contingent of campaign press would attend the Giuliani presser, we scheduled a press conference at the same site an hour earlier, at 10 a.m., along with dozens of shelter residents and homeless families and adults sleeping rough. When Rudy arrived on scene, we presented him with a twenty-page rebuttal. The press was primed with a cogent understanding of why dismantling the right to shelter, ejecting several thousands more of our vulnerable neighbors on to the streets, and drastically cutting back on affordable housing access contradicted his central campaign theme of improving New York City's "Quality of Life."

In his previous race against David Dinkins, Giuliani lost by 50,000 votes out of 1.8 million cast, the narrowest margin in city history. He won his second race, in 1993, by an even smaller margin, just 47,000 votes, due largely to a massive turnout of white conservative voters on Staten Island, where a proposition for the borough to secede from NYC helped drive the city's most Republican districts to the polls. Journalist Wayne Barrett, in his extraordinary *Rudy! An Investigative Biography of Rudy Giuliani*, unearthed original documents revealing his entire campaign strategy had hinged on maximizing white voter turnout.[37] Exit polls showed 85 percent of Giuliani's supporters were white. Barrett also reported that Giuliani had told executives at National Public Radio's local affiliate, WNYC, that it would "be a good thing" for the city if the poor left: "That's not an unspoken part of our strategy—that *is* our strategy."

Ironically, Giuliani's threats to evict homeless New Yorkers from emergency shelter after ninety days and eliminate the City's right to shelter proved to be his *least* popular campaign positions, and he was quickly forced to back down. The *New York Times* described his backpedaling in March 1994, a few months after he was sworn in: "Mr. Giuliani and his campaign strategists did not anticipate the force of the reaction against their ideas. Advocates for the homeless dogged him at campaign stops, heckling him and organizing groups of homeless people to show up, as well." William Grinker, a former Koch deputy and chief author of the original campaign policy paper, explained, "The campaign was caught by surprise by the reaction to proposals that were in line with what many other cities were doing." According to the *Times*, "Mr. Grinker said he himself did not anticipate the harsh reaction. 'I probably should have,' he said."[38]

But once in office, Giuliani did press ahead, albeit cautiously. Rather than booting homeless New Yorkers from shelter outright after ninety days, he went to court, attempting to undo the fundamental promise of emergency shelter to New Yorkers who met the need standard for welfare or who were homeless "by reason of physical, mental, or social dysfunction." The administration crafted an argument that shelter was a form of welfare, therefore shelter residents could be compelled to perform workfare in exchange for their cots.

This unprecedented action was only possible thanks to President Bill Clinton's legislative deal to "end welfare as we know it" in 1996. Clinton, in 1994, had vetoed two attempts by the Republican-controlled Congress to allow states to impose time limits on the receipt of basic living grants and food stamps. Democratic support of the federal government's central role in providing affordable housing had diminished so thoroughly that, early on in negotiations to "reform" welfare, to avoid the possibility of any outright veto being overridden, Clinton offered House Speaker Newt Gingrich the wholesale dismantling of the Department of Housing and Urban Development—the realization of a decades-long Republican dream. Clinton's HUD secretary was the same guy who, under Dinkins, had issued a report recommending the razing of the City's right to shelter—Andrew Cuomo. His top lieutenant in charge of the New York/New Jersey region was Bill DeBlasio.

As with the myth surrounding Ronald Reagan creating modern homelessness, it's a myopic shortcut to blame Republicans solely for the savaging of support to provide basic sustenance.

President Clinton and Mayor Giuliani were in lockstep calling for a vastly expanded carceral system—tougher laws, more police, and more prisons. Clinton, like Reagan before him, returned again and again to the theme "The era of big government is over." A Democratic president brought to fruition the Republican agenda to massively deregulate the banking and finance industries.

The impact of this deregulation in large coastal cities—and in New York in particular—was seismic. Clinton-era deregulation kindled New York's economy to grow its investment houses and banking sectors, along with the law firms needed to attend to Wall Street's rapidly evolving needs. Surges in the Dow meant good news for reelection in DC, and the gains realized in the stock market boosted tax revenue, particularly for the home to Wall Street. The DC/NYC win-win was choreographed by Ayn Rand acolyte Alan Greenspan, chair of the Federal Reserve through the Reagan, Bush I, Clinton, and Bush II administrations, working fist-in-glove with Democratic and Republican presidents alike throughout his nearly two-decade tenure (1987–2006).[39] Although wages for middle- and lower-class Americans stagnated throughout Greenspan's entire time at the helm of the Fed, the Dow tripled in value under Clinton. In New York, much of the spoils for the keepers of our increasingly financialized economy were invested in condos and co-ops, fueling massive gentrification throughout Manhattan and deep into Brooklyn, displacing thousands more low-income renters into the ranks of homelessness. The afternoon ritual of spraying blood off the sidewalks in Manhattan's Meatpacking District vanished as the industrial area was converted to multimillion-dollar lofts.

As *NY1*'s political commentator Errol Louis noted recently, there is far more than a mere echo between the overtly racist tones of the Trump presidential campaign in 2016 and of the Giuliani mayoral campaigns in the 1990s—each politician followed the first elected Black person to hold the office. "Backlash in grievance politics and politicians [following] standard, social movements, including the civil rights movement, give rise to equally potent counter-movements. The Dinkins campaign and the election of the first Black mayor of New York City is followed by a backlash," Louis observes.[40] Along these very lines, I believe Clinton's pledge to "end welfare as we know it" and his subsequent caving to Republicans on block-granting and time limits—the hollowing out of basic welfare entitlements—is accurately framed as a reaction to growing ranks of unemployed Black families in the 1960s and '70s seeking assistance.

## RUDY'S RETRIBUTION

In a *GQ* magazine story on Rudy Giuliani's tumultuous career, I recounted a particularly raw encounter I'd had with him on the campaign trail, in which he gave me a look that I could only describe as "I'm gonna win, and you're totally fucked when I do." That imagined speech bubble over Rudy's head at our confrontation in '93 turned out to be more accurate than even I could imagine. As detailed earlier, three West 77th Street townhouses had been awarded to the Coalition in 1988 as part of a plea agreement with the infamous Podolsky landlords. Since the Podolskys' goal was to drive their tenants out, they invested virtually nothing in the buildings' basic upkeep. David Dinkins's commissioner of Housing Preservation and Development (HPD) urged me to apply for federal funding to pay for renovations, which would also include project-based Section 8 certificates (project-based certificates, unlike Section 8 vouchers, cannot be taken away when a resident moves). Local authorities are tasked with ranking the applications based on need and quality of applicant programs, and our application for those brownstones, known colloquially as Coalition Houses, were ranked in the top ten within the applicant pool. Once the application and HPD ranking process was completed, it was standard for the municipality's executive to sign off on the applicant pool, allowing funds to flow directly from DC to the top projects that fell within the localities' dollar amount designation. Programs that provided permanent housing for formerly homeless people were given extra consideration, as our locality had deemed that its greatest need.

In New York City, the executive is the mayor. Dinkins's administrators had begun the seeding of the applications, but by the time the long process was concluded, the mayor was Rudolph Giuliani. Presented one evening with the list being sent off to DC, Rudy drew a red line through two organizations: Coalition for the Homeless and Housing Works. Housing Works, founded in 1990 to fight homelessness among New Yorkers with HIV/AIDS, had been the only other nonprofit in the city to speak out loudly and demonstrate effectively against Giuliani's destructive housing policies.

When we found out that Giuliani had struck our housing from the list, we turned to Clinton's newly minted HUD secretary, New York native Andrew Cuomo. Cuomo dispatched his regional secretary, Bill DeBlasio, on a fact-finding mission. DeBlasio told us that, if our allegations of political retribution were true, HUD would "certainly make the Coalition whole."

The facts were indisputable. The Coalition's application was highly ranked and well within the federal funding allocation for New York City. Our attorney Steve Banks (the Legal Aid Society lawyer who handled our *Callahan* litigation) and I tendered all the relevant evidence and reviewed the process over several hours-long meetings and phone calls with DeBlasio. Weeks later, DeBlasio called to say, although everything we'd provided indeed confirmed that the mayor had vindictively blocked our project from over a million dollars in federal funding: "There's nothing the Secretary can do about this situation."

Apoplectic doesn't begin to describe my reaction to Cuomo stringing us along, only to essentially endorse Rudy's brazen political payback. Although Giuliani's ire inarguably was directed at the two groups most successful at publicly challenging his anti-homeless policies, at the end of the day, who was he hurting here? I wasn't the one living in those Coalition buildings. It was homeless New Yorkers his retribution would effectively harm, by denying them the dignity of permanent homes.

Both this crisis and its subsequent resolution speaks volumes about the core values and toxic power dynamics of Clinton, Giuliani, DeBlasio, and Cuomo. There was, and remains, no doubt in my mind that Cuomo, a master at the political long game, with conservative leanings on homeless policies that aligned closely with Rudy's, calculated that going to bat to rehouse homeless New Yorkers was not a high enough priority to risk alienating Giuliani. DeBlasio had always been only the messenger, never empowered in that role to make a decision that would upend high-level power exchanges in DC. In the end, no one demonstrated a willingness to stand up, not just for housing resources for homeless people but for basic freedom of speech without threat of undue reprisal.

Fortunately, Steve Banks secured a top-tier law firm poised to bring suit in federal court, asserting that HUD had acted improperly by not conducting proper oversight of the application and award system for distribution of Congressional appropriations, as detailed in the *Federal Register*, and that the Coalition and homeless New Yorkers stood to suffer significant damages in retaliation for protected free speech. The hefty legal papers were FedExed directly to Cuomo with a note saying, as a courtesy, we were providing an advance copy of the suit we intended to file the next day in federal court, in hopes of negating the need to do so.

The following morning, DeBlasio called and said, "After reviewing all the materials, we'll be restoring the Coalition's original ranking and making necessary arrangements to release the capital grant."

## A POLITICAL JENGA TOWER

A bird's-eye view of the policymaking landscape in New York and DC in the mid-1990s lays bare a political Jenga tower of interconnected agendas across the Democrat-Republican spectrum, with officials successfully advancing their careers off the backs of the most vulnerable Americans.

At least Giuliani was up-front in his contempt for the poor. DeBlasio was struggling to find solid footing. But Cuomo, given wide latitude by Clinton, was endlessly calculating the political upside or downside to any given situation. Later in his tenure as governor of New York, he tried to recruit me to be his, as he put it, "homeless czar." But during our discussions one striking moment drove home the arm's-length distance with which virtually all elected leaders hold the needs of our poorest neighbors. We were chatting about the scope of the potential role one late Friday afternoon in his office. Cuomo across the low coffee table was shuffling three or four documents.

"You know what we do here on the weekend?" he asked, picking the papers up a half a foot and letting them drop back down on the table. "We do this. We take our work and this is what we do. We let it go. And then we pick it back up on Monday. I don't have the sense that's something you've ever gotten used to. Am I right?"

He was right about one thing. My working for him would not have been a good fit.

Giuliani, a month before his post-9/11 political resurrection as "America's mayor," held one of his daily press briefings and was asked by a reporter if he'd been informed that, for the first time in New York City's history, the number of people in emergency shelter had eclipsed 25,000. When I watched it that night on TV, it was the only time I can remember seeing Rudy visibly shocked. Rather than a typical bellicose rejoinder, he sputtered, "I'll have someone get back to you later today."

So much ink and airtime has been misspent analyzing the mythic fall of Rudy Giuliani. Ta-Nehisi Coates squarely nailed the underlying error in this popular narrative, writing in *The Atlantic*: "Much chin-stroking has been dedicated to understanding how Giuliani, once the standard-bearer for moderate Republicanism, a man who was literally knighted, was reduced to inciting a riot at the U.S. Capitol. The answer is that Giuliani wasn't reduced at all. The inability to see what was right before us—that Giuliani was always, in [Jimmy] Breslin's words, 'a small man in search of a balcony'—is less about Giuliani and more about what people would rather not see."[41]

The last two years of Giuliani's second term saw record homelessness, his histrionic verbal attacks against any and all perceived adversaries, the public meltdown of his marriage and his subsequent affair with an underling, and the implosion of his Senate campaign against Hillary Clinton—all of which formed a waft of failure around his future political ambitions. On the issue of homelessness, Giuliani lost his case to dismantle the *Callahan* decree at the trial level; one of his last vengeful acts in office was filing an appeal. In late November 1999, while Giuliani was locked in major litigation around the decree and as the number of homeless New Yorkers increased dramatically, a young woman walking in midtown was struck in the head with a piece of brick by an unknown attacker. Giuliani, without any evidence whatsoever, declared that the assailant had been a homeless mentally ill person. He ordered the NYPD to begin arresting any homeless people on the street who refused to immediately enter the shelter system. It was unhinged by even Rudy Giuliani standards.

It takes a lot in a city the size of New York to shake its foundation, but after this draconian order, people became truly enraged at Giuliani. The Coalition's pro bono ad company drew up a memorable full-page ad, which ran in the *New York Times* after the attack. Against a black-and-white stock photograph of a homeless man, pushing a shopping cart with a sad, far-off look in his eyes, the caption read:

Deranged, Deluded and Dangerous.
But Enough About Mayor Giuliani. Let's Talk About the Homeless.

It concluded with a short message encouraging people to not be distracted by Giuliani's sideshow and included a tear-off postcard addressed to City Hall, demanding more investment in permanent, affordable housing, including housing with support services for people with mental illness.

The *New York Daily News* conducted a poll, the results of which reflected how smart and compassionate New Yorkers are: 83 percent supported the right to shelter, and close to 90 percent supported increasing the City housing budget for housing our homeless and extremely low-income neighbors. In early December, the Coalition held a massive rally in Union Square to support the homeless, and thousands showed up. Entrance to the VIP section in front of the stage was roped off, its seating reserved exclusively for homeless people.

### BONUS MYTH BROKEN WINDOWS IS FOUNDED ON A LIE

Following Giuliani's November 1993 win, I went with a handful of union leaders and activists to meet with his newly announced choice for police commissioner, Bill Bratton. Bratton, the former head of New York City Transit Police (back when it was considered a separate entity from the NYPD, responsible for crime enforcement in the subway and bus systems), was a fervent champion of the "Broken Windows" theory of policing. I asked him point-blank what his approach to homelessness would be as commissioner. His response was chilling: "Well, Mary, I intend to flush them off the streets. I flushed them out of the subways and I intend to do the same thing across the entire city." I pointed out that—setting aside the legal and moral issues involved—on a practical level, the subway was a relatively small, enclosed system. Where did he think thousands of homeless people who live on the streets would actually be able to go? Bratton replied, "We flushed them out of the subways and we're going to flush them off our streets." His language equating vulnerable humans with sewage was lost on no one.

Because so much of what passes these days as legit homeless policy is predicated on Bratton-championed Broken Windows theory, it's impossible to overstate what historian Bench Ansfield put so succinctly: "The broken-windows theory was founded on a lie."[42]

Its origins can be traced to a now infamous 1982 *Atlantic* article by George Kelling and James Wilson, which badly twisted a 1969 research paper by Stanford University's Philip Zimbardo, by concluding, "If a window in a building is broken and is left unrepaired, all the rest of the windows will soon be broken."[43] Kelling and Wilson's enduring malignant conclusion: law enforcement should come down hard on small acts of disorder or they will metastasize into something far bigger.

Ansfield's 2019 *Washington Post* analysis skillfully dismantles the theory's girding myth, the central support beam of Bratton and Giuliani's approach to policing, beginning with Kelling and Wilson's willful misinterpretation of Zimbardo's original findings. In fact, Zimbardo "wanted to document the social causes of vandalism to disprove the conservative argument that it stemmed from individual or cultural pathology." He did so by parking a car in two very different locations— one in the South Bronx and one in Palo Alto, California. The car in the South Bronx was soon destroyed; notably, the first vandals were a white "well-dressed" family, who were subsequently joined by others. Ansfield summarizes that Zimbardo's "hypothesis was confirmed. The lack of community cohesion in the Bronx produced a sense of anonymity, which in turn generated vandalism."

What became of the Palo Alto car? It sat untouched for a week before the research team drove it to Stanford's campus and, feeling antsy, decided it needed to be "primed." After they did considerable damage to the vehicle, a passerby (who was, as with the Bronx, the intended subject of the study) "joined in after the car was already wrecked." Kelling and Wilson distilled and corrupted this outcome in *The Atlantic* fifteen years later ("One unrepaired broken window is a signal that no one cares, and so breaking more windows costs nothing"). Yet Zimbardo's study had shown exactly the opposite. As Ansfield summarizes, "Anyone—even Stanford researchers!—could be lured into vandalism, and this is particularly true in places like the Bronx with heightened social inequities."

Why does this matter so much? Why is it important to retrace the intentional butchering of a once obscure sociological study and its unending amplification in a mainstream news outlet? Because there is a clear, undeniable throughline between Bratton's belief that "broken windows" policing reduced crime in New York City in the 1990s and its related massive increase in stop-and-frisk incidents (swelling to nearly 700,000 in 2011 alone). Although causal connection between the use of stop-and-frisk (and its progenitor, broken windows) and crime reduction has been thoroughly disproven, the theory lives on as a largely unquestioned, pervasive policy to justifiably disappear countless tens of thousands of visibly poor people from public spaces.[44] Homeless people are avatars of disorder in the construct of Bratton and his ilk—human broken windows, their existence threatens orderly society.

"I believe in order and conformity and the need for everyone to abide by social norms," Bratton wrote in his 1998 autobiography, *Turnaround: How America's Top Cop Reversed the Crime Epidemic*.[45] This obsession with perceived conformity and order—in every sphere, from the physical to the public to the psychological and political—is the hallmark of authoritarianism. Intrinsic to it is the belief that homeless people are the most visible marker of societal disarray. Lensed through this corrupt ideology, our unhoused neighbors aren't human beings—they are walking "broken windows" that need to be removed from sight at all costs (except, of course, for the cost of housing-based solutions), lest they unsettle the nerves of domiciled people and spark others to commit serious crimes.

But numerous recent studies have starkly refuted any causal connection between conditions associated with broken-windows theory and changes in crime rates.

- In January 2019, Daniel T. O'Brien, Chelsea Farrell, and Brandon Welsh of Northeastern University "discovered that disorder in a neighborhood does not cause its residents to commit more crime."[46] Writing in the *Annual Review of Criminology*, they found "no consistent evidence that disorder induces greater aggression or more negative attitudes toward the neighborhood."[47]

- New York City's own Department of Investigation examined quality-of-life summonses and misdemeanor arrests from 2010 to 2015 and found "no empirical evidence demonstrating a clear and direct link between increase in summons and misdemeanor arrest activity and any drop in felony crime."[48]

- Ken Auletta of the *New Yorker* noted in a 2015 profile on Bratton, according to criminologist and Columbia Law School professor Jeffrey Fagan, "There's no good scientific evidence that broken-windows works or has much to do with crime. . . . None of [the few claims for it] stand up to close examination."[49]

In the same *New Yorker* piece, Bratton doubled down on his flawed reasoning, insisting broken windows "is about quality of life, about freedom from fear, about freedom from disturbance." Auletta continues, "Minor crimes—patronizing a prostitute or a drug dealer—had been ignored because they were seen as victimless." Quoting Bratton: "What was not understood was that the victim was the neighborhood." In the same article, the brilliant police reform activist Joo-Hyun Kang strongly rebuked Bratton's take, telling Auletta, "[Broken windows invites] the N.Y.P.D. to go on a fishing expedition. . . . It's basically racial profiling for people under the assumption that they have outstanding warrants."[50]

**MYTH 9** "HOMELESS PEOPLE JUST NEED TO 'GET A JOB' TO LIFT THEMSELVES OUT OF HOMELESSNESS"

One of the most pervasive myths about homelessness is that the key to escaping it is simply working harder or longer. Although the 2008 collapse of the housing bubble loosened the grip of this myth (with more Americans than ever losing their own homes or knowing others who did), the assumption that employment inevitably leads to housing stability remains endemic.

A rare point of agreement across the political spectrum is that housing costs should ideally not exceed 30 percent of a household's income. The genesis of this standard goes back to the late 1800s, when it was assumed a family would devote "a week's wages to a month's rent," or 25 percent of the family's total income, leaving the remaining wages to cover all other household expenses.[51] That 25 percent standard was used in establishing federal housing assistance programs throughout the 1960s and 1970s. In the 1980s, federal legislation increased it to 30 percent, embraced as the norm ever since.

However, at or near minimum wage, it is virtually impossible to secure decent affordable housing, even when working full-time. Each year, the National Low Income Housing Coalition calculates the actual cost to secure either a one- or two-bedroom rental home. With each passing year, the numbers grow grimmer. In 2022, the NLIHC's estimated national hourly housing wage—"the hourly wage full-time workers (working 40 hours, 52 weeks per year) must earn to afford a rental home, at HUD's fair market rent, without spending more than 30 percent of their incomes"—was $25.82. With the federal minimum wage pegged at $7.25 per hour since 2009, "the average minimum-wage earner must work 96 hours per week (nearly two and a half full-time jobs) to afford a two-bedroom rental, or 79 hours per week (two full-time jobs) to afford a one-bedroom rental" at fair market rents. For working parents, this scenario is impossible, given the competing fiscal and scheduling demands of childcare, transportation, food, and healthcare. One single parent interviewed for the 2022 survey was working three jobs to keep their family housed, "but later had to quit one to have time to sleep."[52]

In high-cost coastal states, the affordability gap is even more dire. The 2022 housing wage was $37.72 in New York State; in Washington, DC, $34.33; in California, $39.01.[53] For the first time ever, median rent in the fifty most populous metro areas exceeded $2,000.[54] Put simply, "In no state, metropolitan area or county in the US can a worker earning the federal or prevailing state or local minimum wage afford a modest two-bedroom rental home by working a standard 40-hour work week."[55] More than 40 percent of US workers cannot afford even a one-bedroom fair-market rental with one full-time job. That swells to 60 percent when calculating the portion of workers unable to afford a modest two-bedroom rental home. Martha Galvez, head of the Housing Solutions Lab at the NYU Furman Center, commented in the *New York Times*, "We've been moving in this direction for decades. Since the '70s, rents have been rising faster than incomes."[56] The '70s-era loss of affordable housing as detailed in previous chapters, along with banking deregulations and subsequent financialization of the US economy, precipitated the supply side of this widening gulf between wages and rental costs. The value of the federal minimum wage has now reached its lowest point since 1956.[57] In January 2023, Moody's Analytics declared the typical American renter is now rent-burdened (paying more than 30 percent of their income toward rent), with New York City renters paying 68.5 percent of median income to cover the average rent.[58]

Given the massive and growing gap between the wages of half the nation's workforce and the cost of even the most modest rental housing, the "Go get a job" and "Just work harder" mantras championed by bootstrappers are misguided at best. At its heart, the "Get a job" myth not only rings hollow; it is superb in diverting attention away from one of the main perils of late-stage capitalism: ever more working Americans slipping off the precipice of "barely housed" into homelessness and complete destitution.

In the first in-depth, accurate study of employment among homeless Americans, Bruce D. Meyer of the University of Chicago in June 2021 found that more than half (53 percent) of homeless people under the age of sixty-five had had formal earnings in the year they had experienced homelessness, and an astonishing 40 percent of unsheltered homeless Americans were employed.[59] After examining myriad factors, including population characteristics, geographic mobility, and earnings, drawn from federal census data and an entire decade of government tax records and financial assistance data, Meyer concluded, "People experiencing homelessness are among the most deprived individuals in the United States, yet they are neglected in official poverty statistics and other surveys." It's not that homeless people aren't working—more than half of them are employed, but don't earn enough to make ends meet. The wonderful LA-based advocacy group, Invisible

People, underscored two takeaways from Meyer's findings: "The majority of these [homeless] low-income earners worked part-time. However, even full-time workers earning between $40,000 and $50,000 per year grappled with the unaffordability of housing. These individuals were living in homeless shelters as well, their income topping the charts but still falling desperately short."[60]

### MYTH 10 "HOMELESS PEOPLE JUST NEED TO LEARN TO SAVE"

A corollary to the "Get a job" trope is the myth that, somehow, people become or remain homeless because they lack the know-how to manage money. Billionaire Michael Bloomberg was elected mayor of New York in 2002 and promptly began the most concerted effort of any mayor to restrict entrance eligibility to emergency shelter for homeless families. Giuliani had ridden the tail end of Ed Koch's unparalleled ten-year capital housing program yet was ultimately stunned when the homeless census skyrocketed after the Koch program ended and stopped producing city-funded housing in 1996.[61] Bloomberg subsequently re-upped his predecessors' commitment to Koch's legendary trope, "If you build it, they will come." He enacted intentionally complicated shelter-intake procedures designed to "slam the front door of the system shut." In March 2002, after the new procedures were enacted, author Jennifer Egan, writing for the *New York Times Magazine*, spent weeks with homeless families attempting to complete the arduous intake protocol. In heartbreaking detail, family after family described the toll Bloomberg's new, intentionally arduous "reapplication process" took on its youngest members. If a family was unable to provide complete documentation of their housing history over the previous two years, they were deemed ineligible, remanded to temporary, often one-night placements and ordered to return to reapply. Since all family members were required to be present for the reapplication process, children would routinely miss days and weeks of school. Despite federal legislation mandating that families with children be placed in shelters close to the children's schools, Egan documented numerous instances in which applicant children were placed more than two hours from their school, quoting a homeless mother: "Disaster kept striking little by little… This has to be the bottom."[62] Literal years of court battles ensued against the City, as the vast majority of families initially deemed ineligible for shelter were ultimately found eligible, even though there was no change in the circumstances or documentation.

I spent many nights at the Bronx intake center with Legal Aid lawyers, who were representing homeless families in the class-action litigation. The meetings often went far into the evening. Parents waiting on long lines inside, as youngsters sat outside on the curb, finishing their homework under the arc of street lamps.

Later that year, my son, Quinn, was born. Nursing him late at night, I couldn't help thinking about another new mother—there was always at least one—sitting on a hard plastic chair in the Bronx intake office, trying to soothe her own infant, with no place to wash her child or store their belongings.

New York voters had resoundingly backed two-term limits in 1993 and 1996 for mayors and local elected leaders. But in 2008, Bloomberg did an end run, goading the city council to vote to allow him to run for a third term, at the end of which he eliminated all access to even federal housing resources for families in shelter, including brick-and-mortar NYCHA housing and Section 8 portable vouchers to rent units on the private market.[63] The numbers hit record-high levels, proving categorically that it doesn't matter "if you build it" or not: people will continue to pour into emergency shelters because they simply have no alternative.[64]

As part of his last attempt to disincentivize people from entering the shelters, in 2009, Bloomberg rolled out a new plan, this one to charge "rent" in exchange for emergency shelter. The move was resoundingly denounced by homeless people and quickly became politically toxic to Bloomberg, as voters understood it was in everyone's best interest to allow working people without homes to save whatever earnings they had so they could get back on their feet as quickly as possible. Scores of shelter residents documented that they were currently working—many more than one job—in order to save for security deposits and first month's rent. Just a few short weeks after announcing his plan and in the face of mounting backlash, Bloomberg withdrew the program and invited Steve Banks and me to a rare joint press conference. A victory! But, as the press conference drew to a close, Bloomberg turned to me and said, "You see, Mary, the problem is, these people—they just need to learn how to save money."

To parse this reflection from a man whose net worth exceeds $76 billion: The problem homeless people have isn't that they don't *have enough money* to save. It's that they *don't know how* to save it.[65] A recent study from the University of Chicago showed more than half of homeless Americans in shelter and 40 percent of those without shelter are employed.[66] Coupled with the galaxy of data documenting the growing chasm between wages and rental costs, the myth of profligate homeless people is DOA.

# CHAPTER 5

# WHO WE THINK OF
# WHEN WE THINK OF THE HOMELESS

## MYTH 11 "RUNAWAYS REALLY AREN'T HOMELESS"

Trauma and poverty have long been the two most consistent precursors to youth homelessness in the US; the extraction of labor from unaccompanied youth was the underlying capitalistic driving force from the earliest reformatories in the nineteenth century.

### A BRIEF HISTORY OF HOMELESS YOUTH AND SUBJUGATION

In 1825, the former Society for the Prevention of Pauperism and Crime, newly rebranded as the Society for the Reformation of Juvenile Delinquents (SRJD), opened the first congregate reformatory, the New York House of Refuge (an old arsenal building at Broadway between 23rd and 34th Streets). Its founders considered worthy the reformatory's mission to "rescue" boys "under a certain age, who become subject to the notice of police, either as vagrants, or houseless, or charged with petty crimes...and put [them] to work at such employments as will tend to encourage industry and ingenuity."[1] Note the heavy emphasis on unpaid work; this both enshrined capitalistic ideology and also financially benefited established business owners. The "rescue" was to take place sooner rather than later as the founders believed a new class of "juvenile delinquents" was emerging as a "direct result of morally inferior parents," making it imperative that the process be interrupted somewhere between innocent child and hardened criminal.[2] Then, as now, it is axiomatic that poverty transforms character.

The backdrop to this milestone in history is twofold. First, in 1789, the penitentiary model of rehabilitation was established in Pennsylvania. It sought to take punishment out of the public realm of spectacle (public beatings, whippings, and stockage) and instead isolate convicts so that they could engage in contemplation (sleeping and working in completely isolated cells, in absolute silence). But providing the private plumbing and accommodations for such isolation proved costly, and the New York correctional model, with congregate workspaces, prevailed nationally. The New York model still enforced absolute silence, even in congregate dining and work halls. This literal walling off of correctional efforts from public view ended the communal spectacle of physical punishments (it was also grounded in an emerging belief that isolation would beget penitence). Although advanced as a humane alternative to public corporal punishment, the closeting off of mass punishment created conditions ripe for abuse and degradation.

The second important historical backdrop of the first reformatory was New York City's nineteenth-century population explosion, with the City's census tripling between 1810 and 1840. Amongst concurrent waves of unemployment and homelessness, middle-class citizens were stunned at the large numbers of homeless children, often committing crimes of survival (theft of food or small sums of money to buy food or warm clothing). The founders of the SRJD, seizing on the isolation theme of the penitentiary model, opened their House of Refuge to both boys and girls, who could be remanded to the overseer's custody. Many were given open-ended sentences, their release date at the complete discretion of the reformatory's supervisors.

In public relations efforts, SRJD board members touted its mimicry of the penitentiary system, with highly regimented work structures that ensured youth would gain industrious habits from "constant employment in branches of industry." In other words, once children were given basic on-site training, they were given piecework for various businesses around the city, working seven- or eight-hour days, six days a week, without pay: "Typically, male inmates produced brushes, cane chairs, brass nails, and shoes. The female inmates made uniforms, worked in the laundry, and performed other domestic work."[3]

As this model of juvenile "reform" was replicated in dozens of places across the country, some rumblings of discontent were made public. In 1848 a former reformatory officer, Elijah Devoe, published *The Reform System, or Prison Discipline Applied to Juvenile Delinquents*, in which he denounced "the Refuge as a modern-day dungeon where children were locked up and brutalized."[4] The upper-crust SRJD board fired back with a massive PR effort, culminating in an 1860 *New York Times* article that effectively whitewashed the abuse, declaring the house "confessedly one of the best, its managers having been, from the first, among our most judicious and philanthropic citizens, and having devoted careful and continuous attention to its management.... Its site is an admirable one...the result of careful and critical research.... Here, then, if anywhere, we have a model school on the congregated plan, and we may expect to find all that that system can accomplish for the reformation of juvenile delinquents."[5]

## AUSTIN REED'S FIRSTHAND ACCOUNT OF THE NEW YORK HOUSE OF REFUGE

A few years ago, an astonishing manuscript, meticulously verified by a team of Yale historians, surfaced in upstate New York: a firsthand account of one of the first children imprisoned at the New York House of Refuge, Austin Reed. Beautifully written in heartbreaking detail, *The Life and the Adventures of a Haunted Convict*, published by Random House in 2016, recounts the author's life, beginning not with his remand to the House of Refuge in 1825 at age ten but months earlier with the tragic death of his father. The trauma of his father's death is what "haunts" Reed throughout his life. Following the father's death, Reed's family declines quickly into abject poverty and his mother pushes Reed out of the house, giving him as an indentured servant to a rich landowner in East Avon, New York. Reed (who was multiracial) arrives at the East Avon estate and falls into a deep depression: "Home keeps hanging on my mind." His new master, Mr. Ladd, decides to jolt the boy from his idleness by tying him up in the barn and inflicting a savage whipping. Reed hated the punishment but despised even more the degradation and stigma of being whipped. Volume editor Caleb Smith emphasizes the link between Reed's initial trauma—his father's death—and the violent punishment: "Reed feels that his father's death has exposed him to this mortification, leaving him unprotected and dependent."[6]

Reed flees the Ladd residence but is horrified when he returns to his Rochester home: his mother is a grief-consumed shell of her former self, reduced to taking in laundry to save the last vestiges of the family homestead. His siblings are equally adrift, but they encourage young Austin to take revenge on the man whose whip ripped open his back. Reed eventually makes his way back to East Avon and attempts (unsuccessfully) to burn down the Ladd estate. For this revenge crime, he is sentenced to ten years at the New York House of Refuge, becoming inmate number 1221.

Reed's own account of the House of Refuge is beyond harrowing. Savage whippings were administered frequently with a cat-o'-nine tails: "Reader, these cats are made of cat gut with a small knot made at the end of them and wound around a small wire, then rubbed with shoe maker's wax and attached to a piece of rattan that has a pretty good spring to it, so as when the officer strikes, it leaves a deep cut in the back, causing the tender skin to burst while the blood flows freely down the back from the cut it leaves, leaving the back entirely striped and red."[7] Yet he manages to find solace and camaraderie with the scores of Irish waifs who comprised more than half of inmates, most locked up for theft. (New York City's recorded crime throughout the nineteenth century consisted largely of nonviolent property crimes rather than injury to people.) When boys attempt to escape, the families of the Irish lads take them in and provide cover. Reed jokingly imitates his friends' brogues and phrasing, writing, "Yes, me brave Irish boys, me loves you till the day that I am laid cold under the sod, and I would let the last drop of this dark blood run and drain from these black veins of mine to rescue you from the hands of a full blooded Yankee."[8]

The common enemy of both the penniless Irish boys and Reed is "the merciless 'Hayse'" (Jacob Hays, New York's first police constable), who eventually snares them and brings them back to the House of Refuge. Smith, in his insightful introduction to the memoir, notes the importance of these friendships and affinities in Reed's otherwise dismal life: "At a time when the Refuge was hardening the lines of segregation, Reed was writing about a cross-racial alliance between Irish immigrants and Black Americans, based on their common circumstances and a shared suspicion of police and prisons."[9]

As with virtually all present-day houseless youth, Reed's enduring wish is to return to or recapture some literal and sacred form of stability—*Home*. In the foreword to the book, historians David Blight and Robert Stepto underscore that, from the deathbed scene of Reed's father onward, "the memoir tells of Reed's search for family. Revealingly, Reed almost always capitalizes the word *Home*."

## YOUTH HOMELESSNESS TODAY

Nearly two hundred years have passed since inmate 1221 was remanded to the House of Refuge. But the combined toll of early trauma and poverty remain near constants among homeless youth today. This completely upends the widespread notion that most homeless youth are typically from stable, middle-class homes and have voluntarily taken to the streets for the rebellious thrill of drugs and untethered freedom. Chapin Hall at the University of Chicago recently published a series of in-depth studies on both the scope of youth homelessness in the US and qualitative analyses of factors contributing to their plight.[10] Among their findings:

- In the course of a year, an astonishing 1 in 10, or roughly 3.5 million, young adults (age 18 to 25) and 1 in 30, approximately 700,000, adolescents and teens (age 13 to 17) experience some form of homelessness.
- The HUD-mandated point-in-time estimates (conducted on a single evening in winter each year) significantly undercount

unaccompanied youth and young adults, as they focus solely on persons visibly homeless on the streets and other public spaces, excluding tens of thousands more staying (very short-term) with friends, with other families, or in shelters.[11]

• Homeless youth have often suffered tragic personal loss: roughly 35 percent of kids surveyed (and 40 percent of kids in Cook County's metro Chicago and surrounding neighborhoods) experienced the death of a parent or caregiver.

These findings are drawn from the most comprehensive national qualitative study ever undertaken on homeless youth, comprised of regionally diverse samples, using a narrative mixed-method design. The study found that unaccompanied young homeless people typically experienced early family instability; 23.7 percent had experienced homelessness as children. The study also provided crucial depth on the complexity of interplay between the factors of poverty, instability, and early trauma.

As part of the researchers' qualitative analysis, interviews with homeless youth began with this significant prompt: "If you were to think of your experience with housing instability as a story, *where did your story begin?*" (Emphasis mine.) Study author Gina Samuels explains, "That's a very different question than asking them, 'when did you first become homeless?' The answers we often got were 'My homelessness story begins at birth' or 'When I entered foster care.' So young people see their vulnerability to homelessness starting way before they ever wound up on the street or in a shelter, which has huge implications for when we offer services and how we design interventions."[12] Like Austin Reed, who began his story nearly two centuries before with the death of his father, broadening the narrative lens to include significant events contributing directly to homelessness gives invaluable context and points us toward viable solutions.

The study also highlights the structural problems of generational poverty and family homelessness, along with our nation's highly flawed foster care system, which has contributed significantly to increases in runaway and homeless youth. Foster care as a feeder system for run-away and homeless youth has a particularly sinister history, not surprisingly related to another movement of well-heeled "reformers" seeking to "save" wayward kids.

## THE ORPHAN TRAINS

Not even the House of Refuge could corral the sharply rising numbers of homeless children in New York. Its population swelled to over 1,600 in its first decade alone, and eventually, the facility was reestablished and hugely expanded on Randall's Island in the East River. By the mid-1870s, estimates of the number of homeless children in the city ranged between twenty thousand and thirty thousand. Enter Yale-educated Charles Loring Brace, a wealthy well-connected minister who, after traveling extensively in Europe, returned to New York and was taken aback by the masses of nineteenth-century capitalism's youngest victims. His epiphany: "The best of all Asylums for the outcast child, is the farmer's home."[13] And so, Brace set out to ship homeless, neglected, and impoverished children out west, specifically to Midwestern farms, where they were given over to farm owners as indentured servants.[14] Through his new agency, the Children's Aid Society, an astounding 200,000 children were transported, mostly via trains, between 1854 and 1929 to forced labor arrangements across the country.

Many times, children arrived on trains and were taken to what were essentially public auctions, advertised in advance with posters, where families could select a child or children. To work. Full time. Without pay. All in exchange for a roof over their heads and food.

This systematic extraction of child labor flowed directly from Brace's insistence that poor people themselves—not the larger economic levers of unemployment or rising profiteering of slumlords—were to blame for mass homelessness. If there was any doubt, here's a short excerpt from just one of scores of Brace's articles, "The Life of Street Rats" (1872):

> The "dangerous classes" of New York are mainly the children of Irish
> and German immigrants... There are thousands on thousands in

New York who have no assignable home, and "flit" from attic to attic, and cellar to cellar; there are other thousands more or less connected with criminal enterprises; and still other tens of thousands, poor, hard-pressed, and depending for daily bread on the day's earnings, swarming in tenement-houses, who behold the gilded rewards of toil all about them, but are never permitted to touch them.

All these great masses of destitute, miserable, and criminal persons believe that for ages the rich have had all the good things of life, while to them have been left the evil things. Capital to them is the tyrant.

Not all the children packed off on Brace's trains were truly orphans. Many had been taken from their families, who had been deemed neglectful by local police, and sent away over their parents' protests. The legal underpinning of such early juvenile reform schemes—as well as today's foster care system—is the ancient legal doctrine *parens patriae*, by which the State takes custody of neglected, abandoned, or orphaned children. Based on common law from the United Kingdom, *parens patriae*, Latin for "parent of the country," originally gave "power to the Crown to administer estates of orphans."[15] As the practice evolved in the US, by the mid-1800s, judges almost always rejected parental petitions to keep their children at home, believing that reformatories or farm placements were more schools than penal institutions. Then, as now, it was axiomatic that poverty deforms character. In his introduction to Austin Reed's memoir, editor Caleb Smith describes the perverted impact of this doctrine: "Because it was conducting its business under the auspices of moral instruction, not of imprisonment, delinquents in the reformatory had fewer habeas corpus rights, a weaker claim to relief, than adults charged with crimes. This is one of the paradoxes of juvenile reformation: by portraying its system as an effort to save children, rather than to punish them, the society tightened its hold on the bodies and souls entrusted to its care."[16]

Roxanna Asgarian's 2023 exposé of the American foster care and adoption systems, *We Were Once a Family*, details the central role that foster care played in the murder of a group of six adopted children in 2018, including the evolution of that system from its orphan train roots.[17] She also connects it to the more recent enactment of Bill Clinton's 1997 Adoption and Safe Families Act, which made it far easier for the State to terminate parental rights. This law remains a major factor in the traumatic splintering of birth families. Jessica Winter of the *New Yorker* observed, "A grim truth emerges from *We Were Once a Family*... removing a child from his birth or adoptive home, however horrendous that home may be, and placing him into the foster-care system, is itself a form of trauma."[18]

One-third of homeless youth have previously been in foster care, while nearly half have been in jail, juvenile detention, or prison.[19]

### STRINGING TEMPORARY SITUATIONS TOGETHER AND THE TOLL IT TAKES

It's easy to think of homeless vs. housed situations as a binary, on-off sort of switch. But many homeless youth—facing ever-shifting circumstances—employ a series of stopgap housing solutions before they wind up literally homeless. Teens and young adults describe sleeping on friends' floors or doubling up in dorm rooms before being forced out, perhaps into sleeping in their car or on the streets. According to the 2017 University of Chicago study, some 72 percent of youth "who experienced 'literal homelessness' (generally, sleeping on the streets, in a car, or in a shelter) also said they had stayed with others while unstably housed."[20]

The toll of their unending uncertainty is enormous. Sixty-nine percent of youth surveyed reported mental health problems while being homeless. One-third also reported substance use problems, which require additional investments in harm-reduction solutions.[21]

LGBTQ+ youth face a shocking 120 percent greater risk of homelessness than their peers, reflecting the lack of acceptance they face both inside and outside their homes. New York's wonderful Ali Forney Center is at the forefront of advocating for the needs of these youth, fighting for safe shelter, affordable housing, and a host of mental health and other services. Eighty percent of their clients have been kicked out of their homes, and 62 percent have considered or attempted suicide. Over 40 percent of homeless youth in New York City are LGBTQ+.[22] Until recently, their only option for emergency shelter was congregate facilities, which presented an inherent threat to their personal safety. Data showed that they faced extreme violence even within age-segregated facilities. In 2013, activists from New York City's LGBTQ+ community joined with the Homeless Rights Project at the Legal Aid Society to bring a class action suit on behalf of homeless and runaway youth (ages sixteen to twenty). It successfully culminated in a groundbreaking settlement guaranteeing a separate system of emergency shelter specifically designated for this population, along with important mental health services and steps to successfully transition into permanent housing.[23]

### MYTH 12 "HOMELESS PEOPLE ARE SINGLE ADULTS LIVING ON CITY STREETS"

Since 2007, HUD has conducted its Annual Homeless Assessment on a single night in the last week of January. This point-in-time head count of homeless Americans has been dismissed as wildly inaccurate by advocates, academics, and even the federal government's own watchdog, the Government Accountability Office (GAO). Inaccuracies inherent in the hit-or-miss nature of the study's single-night construct are multiplied many times over by the lack of standardization across cities, towns, and rural districts, contributing to massive undercounts. In 2020, the GAO "found HUD does not closely examine the methodologies local entities are using to produce their counts, leading to confusion and inconsistencies between various agencies and general questions about data accuracy."[24]

In 2022, HUD's annual estimate totaled 530,000 people, up slightly from 2020. As flawed as the process may be, the count is important because it is the basis on which Congress appropriates funds for emergency shelter and other homeless programs across the country. Most of the undercount stems from the exercise itself: because the enumeration only tallies those who are visibly homeless, it essentially attempts to substantiate the existence of people whose very survival is predicated on being invisible. To give a sense of the magnitude of this

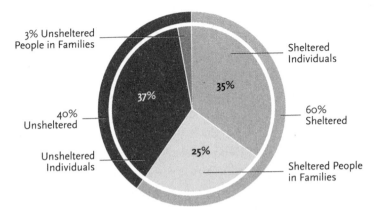

3% Unsheltered People in Families

Sheltered Individuals

37%

35%

40% Unsheltered

60% Sheltered

Unsheltered Individuals

25%

Sheltered People in Families

**Homelessness by household type in the US, 2002.** US Department of Housing and Urban Development, *The 2022 Annual Homelessness Assessment Report (AHAR) to Congress*, December 2022, p. 10.

discrepancy, Seattle's King County point-in-time estimate for 2020 was 11,751. However, comparisons across other databases showed 40,800 people in King County had experienced homelessness in the previous year—not including another 7,300 people who were unhoused and accessed a variety of "homeless healthcare systems but were left out of the other databases."[25] In short, the broadly touted HUD survey had missed three-quarters of Seattle area residents without homes.

So getting to an absolute number of unhoused Americans is complicated. If the proportionality of the HUD analysis is any guide, we can estimate that fully 60 percent of unhoused people are not on the streets but in emergency shelter. Because families are far more likely than individuals to receive emergency shelter, single adults comprise the vast majority of the unhoused people that we see on the streets.

Because single adults are so overrepresented among our neighbors living rough, it's no wonder why our perception negates the reality that families with children make up nearly a third of homeless Americans. And in large cities like New York, the numbers are skewed even more heavily toward families. Roughly 100,000 people will go to sleep tonight in a variety of NYC shelters: congregate (single adult) and family (apartment-style facilities), domestic violence shelters, Safe Havens (places with fewer restrictions for people moving directly off the streets), veteran shelters, small faith-based shelters, and more. An astounding two-thirds are families with children.[26] Since at least 2000, homeless families have comprised the fastest growing segment of the total homeless population, with the number of homeless students increasing over 70 percent in the last decade alone. Over the course of 2022 alone, more than 119,000 students (or one in nine) in New York City experienced homelessness—a 14 percent increase over the previous year. Some 29,000 landed in shelters and 5,500 more slept in abandoned cars and buildings, parks, subway stations, and other public spaces.

Moreover, homelessness is too often imagined (exclusively or primarily) as an urban experience. But a poll commissioned in 2019 by National Public Radio, the Robert Woods Johnson Foundation, and Harvard's T. H. Chan School of Public Health found that fully one-third of rural Americans said, "homelessness is a problem in their communities." The study notes, "The scattered and hidden nature of homelessness in rural places makes it an especially hard problem to measure and address." As Justin Wm. Moyer noted recently in the *Washington Post*, in many ways service providers and advocates in rural communities face even larger obstacles than their urban counterparts when attempting HUD's point-in-time count each late January. For instance, Washington, DC, covers roughly 68 square miles, with thousands of unhoused people. In contrast, "Cumberland County, a 555-square-mile region about 120 miles west of Philadelphia, presents a different challenge. Here, a much smaller number of homeless people—fewer than 100 in 2022—are dotted across a great swath of land in locations unlike urban underpasses and encampments. Small towns. Woodlands. State parks. Farms. Truck stops. Abandoned motels."[27] One service provider volunteering for the HUD count scrambled to cover vast tracks of land in just a few overnight hours. She likened handful of individuals she was able to document as "kind of like an iceberg—you might see a few, and there's more hiding than you know."[28]

## THE PHYSICAL TOLL OF ROUGH SLEEPING AND SHELTER LIVING

The health ramifications for those forced to sleep rough or shelter out-doors are enormous. Unsheltered homeless people have drastically shorter life expectancies, and in rural areas, a greater percentage of the homeless are unsheltered. In this respect, housing is, in fact, health-care—of the most basic and urgent kind.

Harvard-educated (and true hero) physician Jim O'Connell has for nearly forty years been at the front lines of rescuing homeless peo-ple from the worst ravages of disease and illnesses through his work providing lifesaving medical care via the Boston Health Care for the Homeless Program and shelter through the Pine Street Inn.[29] He's also the author of pioneering studies on hypothermia. Contrary to what most assume about cold-related injuries and death, the danger is great-est not on bitterly freezing days or nights, but "in the shoulder season between fall and winter."[30] O'Connell explains that during those days when temperatures hover at or above 40 degrees, homeless people (like the rest of us) become more comfortable, letting their guard down. "But when the temperature plummets into the 20s at night, those who have fallen asleep outside can unwittingly experience extreme hypothermia, especially if they have been drinking alcohol or using drugs, or if their clothing is wet from rain or the ground." The combination of above-freezing temperatures and high humidity—picture the almost stereo-typical image of a homeless person sleeping atop a steam grate—is uniquely dangerous. In extreme cases, individuals as they reach crisis state can fall prey to a phenomenon known as "paradoxical undress-ing." Victims perceive themselves getting warmer and begin shedding clothing. O'Connell explains the underlying assumption: as the body attempts to preserve blood flow to its most vital organ—the heart—"it shuts down blood flow to the limbs and to the brain. And the blood that is reaching the brain is more viscous and not flowing freely."[31] Thus, the deadly hallucinogenic effect sets in.

Hypothermia is just one significant medical issue disproportion-ately affecting unsheltered homeless people. O'Connell and several colleagues documented that over a ten-year period, unsheltered people had three times the mortality rate of their sheltered counterparts and a staggering tenfold higher mortality rate than the housed adult population in Boston.[32] Homelessness accelerates poor health outcomes for chronic diseases. For those remanded to crowded congregate emergency shelters, the conditions increase the transmission of communicable illnesses. In an essay he penned to accompany the study, O'Connell detailed that, beyond the well-documented burdens of mental illness and substance use disorders, homeless people suffer increased rates of "hypertension, diabetes, peripheral vascular disease, respiratory problems, and liver and renal disease. Skin diseases are extraordinarily common and can lead to costly hospital admissions because of cellulitis.... Some conditions, such as diphtheria, pellagra and lice infestations resulting in endocarditis from *Bartonella quintana*, hearken to earlier centuries."[33]

## ONLY THE ECONOMICS SEEM STRAIGHTFORWARD

O'Connell offers one of the most succinct, insightful summations of our modern homelessness crisis: "Only the economics seem straightforward. Housing is a scarce but highly valued commodity. Those least able to compete are doomed to fail; among them are people whose opportunity and choice are limited not only by abject poverty but also by chronic mental illness, substance abuse, physical and sexual violence, illiteracy, complex medical problems and advancing years."[34]

Tracy Kidder delved into O'Connell's life and wisdom in a recent inspirational biography, *Rough Sleepers: Dr. Jim O'Connell's Urgent Mission to Bring Healing to Homeless People*. In it, Kidder teases out a series of logical connections between the healthcare that O'Connell's team provides and the larger, looming health questions implicating housing. If you take nothing else from this book, I hope it's this:

How do you treat H.I.V. in a person who has no place to live? How do you treat diabetes in patients who can't even find their next meals? How do you treat physical illnesses in patients whose activities of daily living are completely determined by the consumption of alcohol or the search for narcotics?[35]

My experience in the Coalition's Crisis Intervention and mobile feeding programs echoed Jim's; convincing those living rough to come in off the streets is virtually always predicated on an offer to move *anywhere other than a shelter* (e.g., a hotel room or SRO apartment). In a single, heartbreaking illuminating exchange between Jim and a schizophrenic person on a bitterly cold night, the man refused help, explaining, "Look, Doc, if I'm at Pine Street, I can't tell which voices are mine and which are somebody else's. When I stay out here, I know the voices are mine and I can control them a little."[36]

O'Connell's Darwinian economic analysis affirms the competitive housing-dependent underpinnings of mass homelessness and this poignant personal exchange perfectly captures the undeniable human need for privacy—the yearning for dignity that a door with a lock provides. Taken together, the macro and the micro urge us to do what is essential: acknowledge the humanity of our homeless neighbors, pivot away from the endemic pathologizing of homeless people (and poor people in general), *and* fully invest in housing-based solutions proven to work.

Princeton sociology professor Matthew Desmond, in his recent book *Poverty, by America*—the follow-up to his Pulitzer Prize–winning treasure *Evicted: Poverty and Profit in the American City*—tackles the larger economic forces sustaining entrenched destitution.[37] Desmond draws upon a passage from Tommy Orange's novel *There There*, in which, amid a rash of suicides on Native American reservations, someone laments, "Kids are jumping out the windows of burning buildings.... And we think the problem is that they're jumping." Stripping away the centuries-old Calvinistic trope that ascribes poverty to moral failure, Desmond concludes, "We've approached the poverty question by pointing to poor people themselves—posing questions about their work ethic, say, or their welfare benefits—when we should have been focusing on the fire."[38]

Kindling the "fire" for our homeless neighbors is a lack of affordable housing. In the next chapter, we'll dissect the modern-day trussing for this essential misdirect and survey investments needed to forge a realistic path toward ending modern mass homelessness.

CHAPTER 6

# BARRIERS AND SOLUTIONS

**MYTH 13** "PEOPLE NEED TO PROVE THAT THEY'RE WORTHY OF AND READY FOR ASSISTANCE"

Much of today's most successful advocacy has been informed by the groundbreaking research of University of Pennsylvania's Dennis Culhane. Malcolm Gladwell amplified Culhane's conclusions in his famous 2006 *New Yorker* article, "Million-Dollar Murray."

## 80-10-10

Shortly after getting his PhD, Culhane spent several weeks in 1991 living in a men's shelter in Philadelphia, observing and later quantifying the stratification of three distinct groups of homeless men. The vast majority (upward of 80 percent) stayed at the shelter for very short periods of time, a few days, at most, and never returned. Culhane noted, "Anyone who ever has to stay in a shelter involuntarily knows that all you think about is how to make sure you never come back."[1]

The second group (roughly 10 percent) stayed about three weeks at a time, most often in winter. Culhane later labeled them as "episodic" users. The third group comprised the remaining 10 percent—the "chronically homeless," who lived in shelters and on the streets for years on end. While only comprising a tenth of the total sheltered homeless population, these chronically homeless individuals consumed over half of the City's total emergency shelter funding.

Although various academics before Culhane had previously attempted to delineate various homeless subpopulations, they had fallen short for two major reasons: First, previous studies hadn't delineated specific causes of homelessness (recently evicted, newly discharged from psychiatric hospitals), characteristics of homeless individuals (from hostile to high functioning), or effects of homelessness (depression, loss of job). Second, none of his predecessors had been given access to the hard data from significant municipalities of actual shelter usage. Culhane was granted access to a huge trove of shelter usage data from New York City and Philadelphia. In analyzing the data over yearslong periods for NYC (1988–1995) and Philadelphia (1991–1995), Culhane and his colleagues were able to not only track specific lengths of stays for individuals but the number of episodes of shelter usage, producing "a more textured explanation of the intensity of homeless experience than based either on duration or recidivism measures alone."[2]

Although their study came with one major caveat—the findings lacked any data on the interlocking relationship between street homelessness and shelter stays (which, particularly among single adults, are often a bracketed respite from sleeping rough, and thus most individuals' episodes and durations of homelessness were longer than what was captured)—Culhane's seminal analysis provided a much-needed wake-up call to policymakers and the public alike: a relatively small segment of the homeless male population was utilizing the vast majority of emergency shelter resources.

This begged the larger question: If most emergency shelter resources were being used by just 10 to 20 percent of homeless New Yorkers and Philadelphians, what about other emergency and stopgap expenditures—emergency room care, long-term hospitalizations, jails, and prisons? Just how much money was being spent to sustain, but not cure, the slow-motion catastrophe of modern homelessness?

## THE PRICE TAG

To answer that question, or to give a sense of proportionality and perspective, Malcolm Gladwell's 2006 *New Yorker* analysis focused on a much smaller city: Reno, Nevada.[3] Gladwell not only tallied Reno's outlays across its various municipal departments, but also detailed expenditures specifically related to one homeless gentleman, Murray Barr. Murray was the personification of Culhane's chronic homeless group. He had been homeless for over fifteen years, spanning the entire career of one Reno police officer whom Gladwell interviewed. A hopeless alcoholic, he was able to frequently detox through a 12-step program but immediately came unglued and was back on the streets once he graduated. Murray was a "happy drunk" who cycled endlessly between hospitals, detox facilities, shelters, and soup kitchens.

It was a very expensive loop, one that never came close to bringing Murray inside for good. Totaling up a decade of costs incurred in shelters, detox, jails, emergency room visits, and hospitalizations, Reno cop Patrick O'Bryan explained succinctly, "It cost us $1 million *not* to do something about Murray."

Traditional "Treatment First" programs, ubiquitous since the mid-1980s, require homeless individuals to be clean, sober, and demonstrate adherence to psychiatric medication *before* being considered for permanent housing. But Murray and countless thousands of other chronically homeless Americans can't quite "prove" themselves "worthy" of receiving permanent housing, so we squander hundreds of millions of dollars each year to provide short-gap shelter, emergency medical support, and soup-kitchen meals that barely allow them to subsist. They are trapped on a Möbius strip of destitution, the twist of which is our collective unwillingness to abandon deeply engrained Calvinistic assumptions about "deserving" versus "undeserving" poor.

The rub in this very public charade is that the cost of truly solving homelessness for the Murrays of our nation would be far less than the reoccurring fortune that we currently sink into essentially ignoring or prolonging it. The paradigm needs to shift from endlessly ameliorating the suffering of homeless people to investing in housing that actually ends their homelessness. But that would require we abandon long-held judgments that dictate a hierarchy of merit among the poor, with the best resources meted out only to the upper tiers of those who are able to "get with the program." Such programs, by the way, are overseen by highly paid bureaucrats and nonprofit executives, running a veritable homeless industrial complex that derives its income from an expanding base of unhoused misery. New York City alone budgeted $2.4 billion on homeless services in 2022, effectively postponing any larger investment to drastically reduce or end homelessness into the distant future.

## HOUSING FIRST

One approach that seeks to shortcut the folly of fixing people in order to be "housing ready" (the "Treatment First" construct) is called Housing First. Its bold approach is up-front in its moniker: First, give housing to unhoused people living rough. Once they've been stabilized, help them work on any underlying issues—health, mental health, employment, substance use, familial estrangement. I became closely involved with this approach as a founding board member of the first group to set it into practice in the late 1990s—Pathways to Housing. I came to know many of Pathways' residents through my late husband, John, who oversaw the clinical staff from outreach to housing.

Through Pathways, John and I became friends with a cadre of homeless and formerly homeless clients. Those friendships could take an odd turn now and again. One resident in particular, Marion, suffered from severe OCD and once threw one of her three cats out her window after it made a mess. John was the only Pathways staffer to argue she be allowed to continue as a client. And so she remained. When John decided eventually to leave Pathways for another job, the staff and clients threw him a going-away party. I arrived, visibly pregnant, and Marion jumped up to introduce herself to me with a huge hug, crying out, "I can't wait to babysit your son!" John watched with amusement—my jaw was hanging open. After an unbearably awkward and silent few seconds, Marion proffered a quick second offer: "Or...I could clean your stove! You know it takes at least two days to do it correctly because you really have to take it all apart. Do you have space in your kitchen for that?"

I nodded numbly as John led me away by my arm. "Yes," I muttered. "We could really use some help with our stove and oven."

Multiple rigorous studies have found that Housing First reduces homelessness and saves money. It's proven particularly effective at helping those who have experienced homelessness for long periods, keeping them stably housed for years. In 2020, the director of the US Centers for Disease Control and Prevention (CDC) appointed an independent panel of public health experts to undertake a systemic review of Housing First programs, which found that it far outperformed standard Treatment First programs.[4] The panel concluded, "Housing First programs decreased homelessness by 88% and improved housing stability by 41%." In the largest of the studies assessed in the CDC meta-analysis, Canada's huge investment in Housing First was found to have yielded significant benefits, with over 62 percent of Housing First clients stably housed after two years, versus just half that number (31 percent) still housed using the Treatment First approach.

The economic savings found across all studies included in the CDC meta-analysis were impressive. Remember Million-Dollar Murray and his cohort of long-term, high-cost homeless neighbors—the 10 percent that comprised Culhane's "chronic homeless" group? The CDC analysis found that for every $10 invested in Housing First for these folks, municipalities saved a staggering $21.72 in emergency shelter, healthcare, and carceral costs.

## HOUSING FIRST SWIMS UPSTREAM, AGAINST MEDIEVAL TIDES

Though Gladwell's piece "Million-Dollar Murray" foregrounds the nascent economic arguments for the Housing First approach, he concludes with a meditation on Calvinistic mores refracted through a modern-day lens, noting that programs like Housing First "have little appeal to the right, because they involve special treatment for people who do not deserve special treatment."[5] His analysis was stunted by the relative newness of the approach when he wrote about it in 2006. The studies available at that time hadn't yet amassed solid evidence that the novel approach led to better overall psychiatric outcomes or reduced dependency on substances. But as the model was replicated across the country, it yielded robust data showing conclusively that Housing First outperforms traditional Treatment First in all areas. A 2015 study found that Housing First residents have far greater engagement with and successful utilization of outpatient alcohol and substance services as well as with both physical and psychiatric healthcare systems than those in Treatment First facilities. They also have markedly reduced alcohol and illicit narcotic usage.[6]

## A CAUTIONARY TALE

There are, however, genuine challenges to the scaling of Housing First to meet the sheer demand. These challenges hobbled its first incarnation, as I witnessed firsthand. Pathways to Housing, and most Housing First programs, don't rely on costly brick-and-mortar construction of new housing units. Instead, they typically rent apartments for their clients on the private market, often in a specific catchment area. (For Pathways, it was initially East Harlem, later expanding into Hell's Kitchen on Manhattan's West Side and eventually into the South Bronx.) This "scattered site" approach hinges on recruiting intensely committed program staff for both the work as well as physical upkeep of the apartments. Small teams are assigned to a set number of clients, usually by location of the apartments, with evening and weekend backup workers filling in as needed. Overseeing those teams and the scores of clients in different buildings and across wide swaths is extremely demanding. It can be daunting to juggle the support to adequately address clients' needs—both acute and chronic—which wax and wane, sometimes without warning.

John kept in touch with dozens of the original Pathways clients long after moving on in his career, and when he died, I was genuinely grateful to spend time with many of them. Marion continued to struggle with her OCD, and I slowly grew alarmed that the Pathways staff seemed less reliably able to support her as they once had. When I hired a new program director at the Coalition (a former Pathways team leader), she clued me in: oversight from top management had disintegrated, leaving the social work teams dangerously adrift. What had once been a labor intense, passionate, mission-driven enterprise had, in many cases, evaporated to drive-by casework. Some teams were literally calling clients from their vans, demanding they come down to the street to receive prescription medications or pantry staples.

The founding ethos of Housing First is to house those who often present as the most troubled and the hardest to reach, those left behind when more established groups choose the more docile, capable, and compliant applicants (a practice known as "creaming"). Given that Pathways' target group has profound, usually long-ignored mental health issues, it is absolutely imperative that staff provide meaningful, proactive support. It's the "make or break" component bolstering long-term housing retention.

Moreover, it's not uncommon for newly housed clients to face an unsettling new challenge: an overpowering sense of isolation. Living through the Covid-19 pandemic gave many of us firsthand experience with the profound loneliness that isolation fuels. As both John and the former Pathways team leader put it, so often what newly housed clients need most is someone to talk to—sometimes for a long time. Finding frontline staff that have the street smarts, the heart, and (most important) the authentic interest to engage with clients is huge. Cornel West, in an interview with Vinson Cunningham, described teaching at Harvard Divinity School as a struggle to bridge the secular and the sacred: "At Harvard you got a site of formation of professional managers. And so they're tied to profession, but not as much the vocation—they're tied to career, not as much to calling.... But we just have to be honest. We got so much cowardliness in the professional-managerial class."[7] That last term, made famous by Barbara Ehrenreich, is almost universally associated with full-on capitalist endeavors, not with the not-for-profit sector. But the professional-managerial class NFP incarnation (the "charitable-managerial class") is alive and well and thriving. At last toll, it accounts for a staggering $1.4 billion in the US economy alone.[8]

Profession versus vocation, career versus a calling. There's a sweet spot that animates the most talented, passionate people I've worked

with. They're strong enough to lean into their vulnerability and comfortable with an acknowledged commonality with any client, meeting them wherever they might be. It's a nearly undefinable flexibility
and strength through commitment. "Radical love and acceptance" was
never a checkbox on a Coalition job application. But as with Dorothy
Day's Catholic Worker movement, it was the X factor that made the
place special. Describing her work, feeding people who showed up each
day, Day remarked, "I've enjoyed getting to know them—they've been
good teachers. You listen to them, hear the troubles they've faced, and
you realize how much courage they have needed to go from one day to
the next. I've met some truly remarkable people, sipping soup or coffee
here."[9] The Catholic Worker, like the Coalition, melded direct service
with advocacy. When Day was a child and witnessed injustice—from
women denied the basic right to vote or desperately poor neighbors
going without food or shelter—she asked her mother why. Her mother
replied, "There's no accounting for justice, it *just* is." She described her
life's work as "trying to account for it, trying to change things a little."[10]
It's through personal service that justice is manifested (personalism).

When genuine caring and radical compassion are shunted in favor
of go along/get along mediocrity disguised as professionalism, bad
things happen. Not just for the people most in need and deserving of
help, but sometimes for entire organizations.

Marion called me one afternoon in 2014, in tears. She had just
received an eviction notice on the door of her tiny studio in Hell's
Kitchen, housing that she'd received through Pathways. I assumed it was
a random mistake and, as a former Pathways board member, mentally
brushed it off as something I could clear up in short order. But as it
turned out, Marion was just the first of hundreds of Pathways residents
to receive eviction notices—scores of whom soon began showing up
at the Coalition's walk-in Crisis Intervention Program. Working with
tireless lawyers at the Legal Aid Society, we uncovered thousands of
motions to evict Pathways clients in NYC Housing Court.

Each tenant, as a stipulation of participating in the Pathways program, had agreed to sign their Social Security Disability Insurance

(SSDI) checks over to Pathways so that the organization could pay their rent on their behalf. In effect, Pathways had become their SSDI "representative payee." Pathways was receiving millions in Social Security benefits, and their top executives were pulling in salaries of over $300,000. But, at some point, the organization—top-heavy with payroll and administrative expenses—just stopped paying their clients' landlords. They stopped doing the exact thing they had agreed to do for each client who signed over their government checks: paying their rent.

Punch-drunk after so many battles with successive mayors and governors, it took a lot to genuinely stun the Legal Aid Society's Judith Goldiner and me. But our outrage surged to new heights when we discovered that the State agency overseeing housing for mentally ill New Yorkers, the Office of Mental Health (OMH), had known about the crisis for over two years and failed to take action, underscoring the too-cozy bond between the professional-managerial class seeded throughout both government *and* nonprofit spheres. The usually unflappable Goldiner told the *New York Daily News*, "It is a scandal. It's appalling."[11]

We successfully pressured OMH to petition the administrative judge to unify all the Pathways cases. She did, assigning them to a single housing court judge in each of the residents' boroughs. In the end, we successfully staved off eviction for the hundreds of Pathways clients.

I don't want to diminish the role that Pathways has played in forging the Housing First model. I'm including the details of its demise in New York for two important reasons. The model itself has been replicated with far tighter fiscal and managerial oversight across the country, building an unparalleled track record of success. Second, and I'm frankly not sure which is more important, it's also an invaluable case study of what happens when a revolutionary idea is nearly destroyed by the slow toxic drip of managerial neglect and the personal collateral damage inflicted on those who can least shoulder it.

Housing First has emerged as the standard for successfully housing our chronically homeless neighbors. HUD, alongside the US Department of Veterans Affairs (VA) and the US Interagency Council on Homelessness (USICH), a lead coordinator between all agencies dealing with homelessness, have all embraced Housing First as the most successful way to house chronically homeless adults with mental health or substance use disorders. The VA was the first agency to significantly invest in Housing First, during the Bush II presidency. Since then, the HUD-Veterans Affairs Supportive Housing (HUD-VASH) program has given permanent homes to over ninety thousand veterans.[12] The VA's unparalleled support of Housing First and priority placements for vets in 137 public housing projects nationwide is the closest our country has come to realizing a right to housing.

Those who dismiss Housing First cynically point to the increasing numbers of homeless Americans, particularly in high-cost coastal cities, despite the significant costs invested in the programs over the years. But those trends are not an indictment of the model or the practical sense it makes. Rather, they directly reflect the sheer scale of need. Each day, in Los Angeles alone, 207 homeless people secure housing, but an additional 227 people fall into homelessness. We've essentially evolved a programmatic system around a crisis; actually *solving* the issue was never the goal.

Getting to a positive tipping point—housing considerably more people than are falling into homelessness on a daily basis—requires a significant increase in funding for permanent housing. Emergency services, including feeding programs, shelters, and mobile healthcare, continue to be invaluable to keep people alive until they can be housed. But it's imperative that we stop deluding ourselves that costly, emergency investments are sufficient to ever right this situation. And investing in both is going to be expensive in the near term.

## FINLAND'S ALL-IN BET ON HOUSING FIRST

Mark Horvath's advocacy organization, Invisible People, has forcefully centered the lived experiences of unhoused and formerly homeless individuals and families in video essays and articles on its popular YouTube channel. His most recent effort is a documentary on Finland's stunning success in eliminating all street homelessness with significant investments in the Housing First model.[13] It provides an unvarnished look at what Housing First, when fully embraced and scaled, looks like.

With unflinching honesty, the documentary shows the struggles of some rehoused adults, who continue to battle substance use and mental health issues. But it also showcases an undeniable success story. In 1985, Helsinki had over two thousand congregate shelter beds, and scores of homeless people died from exposure each year in the region's brutal winters. In the mid-1990s, there were twenty thousand unhoused Finns. Now they have fewer than two hundred total emergency beds, and those are all private accommodations (a shared kitchen or bathroom, but individual sleeping quarters). Those beds are given to people queuing for a Housing First apartment—in US vernacular, these would be considered "Safe Haven" types of shelter. Hemmi, one resident of such short-term accommodation, describes how quickly he was able to move in, as well as how the offer of "my own room with [a] door that locks," was key to convincing him to come in, off the streets. From there, it typically takes months, not years, as is often the case in our country, to move into a private apartment with a lease.

One early champion of the Housing First approach, Jan Vapaavuori, former mayor of Helsinki and minister of housing from 2007 to 2011, observed it "was important from the very beginning that the program was actually led by a center-right politician like me. We needed the ten biggest cities in Finland to be on board, and those ten cities, they had different kind of political majorities. We explained [to] each and every mayor, and a lot of city councilors, and so on, *it is the interest of everyone that we are able to reduce the homelessness.*" This political spade work yielded buy-in from all sectors, because it seeded awareness of "how it makes cities safer, how it makes cities more pleasant, *and that in the long run you even save taxpayers' money.*" (Emphases mine.) He is certain that having solidarity across the political spectrum assured "that these programs and these concepts will be respected, even in the future."

The brilliance of this piece of video journalism is the emphasis it places, alongside the residents' and housing providers' various trials and triumphs, on what the communities of Finland look like as a result of Housing First. *There is virtually no one sleeping rough.* Outreach teams are few—and they have to look far and wide, literally scavenging in hidden urban and suburban crevices, to find a few unhoused people. Once they connect, it is easy to convince them to accept the offer of a private room, which will lead to permanent housing with on-site support services.

Finland determined years ago that a major shift to the Housing First model was expensive, but it was still cheaper than people living on the streets, with all the associated healthcare and carceral expenditures, as well as the hefty price tag associated with people cycling through temporary, congregate shelters. Schools, playgrounds, and entire communities thrive alongside Finland's Housing First apartments. As scholar and activist Juha Kahila puts it, "[Even] if you don't care about people and humanity, those people will care about finance. So, it's always much cheaper to house people and to have the right support for people than that they are sleeping on the streets, in tents, going through the shelters, with this kind of revolving door effect. It's totally doable." Using the Housing First approach, Finland now spends on average 15,000 euros less per year on each homeless person.

Kahila doesn't undersell the fortitude that such a radical change entails or the larger context in which it fully flourishes: "There needs to be a lot of courage to [make] different kinds of decisions regarding affordable housing. [Not just with] Housing First, but also different kind of prevention solutions. So, when people are struggling with their mortgage, or their rent, they need different services to help them before they don't end up being homeless altogether. With the combination of things: prevention, affordable social housing and Housing First, miracles can happen."

The Invisible People crew are uniquely bold in presenting the complex struggles of one young resident, Leevi. Like so many unhoused youth, his homeless story began with a tragedy: his best friend died by suicide. Since then, Leevi has struggled with substance use, and when he allows the cameras inside his Housing First unit, it is an unmitigated chaotic mess. But, as his caseworker observes, a messy apartment is better than having that same mess strewn across the streets. Moreover, the likelihood of Leevi continuing in his recovery is far greater now that he has a home. The case manager explains why the system works: "It's a place where [homeless people in crisis] can feel safe. It's a place where they have a door they can lock. That they can regulate who comes in. They can sleep there in peace." In short, it's far better for Leevi *and* the community. Later in the documentary, the worker gets emotional when responding to the filmmaker's question about those who might ask why addicts or alcoholics are allowed to live there. She replies, "I wouldn't call this a house full of drug addicts—I would call this a house full of *people* who have problems with substances." In turn, she asks the imperative question, "Having people in the streets—who benefits from that? It's not good for them and it's not good for the rest of us. It's just not good for anyone."

This is the simple but complicated essence of Housing First. It recognizes the humanity of each person and responds by honoring their dignity with a private space. It is humane *and* practical. The politician, Vapaavuori, drives this point home: "We used to think that people had to get rid of alcohol in order to be able to live in a flat." After years of cyclical failure—people trying to get clean and sober or compliant with psychiatric medication, only to relapse and have to start from scratch each time—they recognized the waste of time and money. They were brave enough to face reality and invest in what works, not cave in to the out-of-touch moralists, less interested in real solutions than making themselves feel righteous.

Crucially, the apartment helped restore Leevi's hope: "You lose hope when you are on the street, and it means that you die sooner. That's just a fact. It's quite hard to survive on the street. You don't feel part of the society anymore—you are invisible—an outcast. And so if you get a home, you get hope and you start taking care of your life so you can become part of the society again."

Vapaavuori emphasizes this humanistic element is fundamental: "From the beginning, we treated these people as human beings, not as homeless things." When asked what he would say to Housing First skeptics in the US, he replies, "We are a very small country, and you are a big country. You have a lot of money. So, if you want, you can really do this."

Reflecting on Housing First's genesis, he concludes, "Housing First was invented in the US. Make the change!"

## HOUSING FIRST AND THE MURDER OF JORDAN NEELY

Despite the overwhelming evidence in support of Housing First, public discourse continues to cast doubt on it. This argument continues at a high pitch, from local to national stages. I stumbled upon it recently at a joint Manhattan Community Board meeting. Representatives from the not-for-profit Institute for Community Living (ICL) and other Treatment First providers were featured on a panel extolling the virtues of their Intensive Case Management (ICM) approach to homelessness. (ICM is predicated on many outreach workers frequently engaging homeless people living rough, continually guiding them toward medication compliance in advance of providing stable private shelter accommodations or permanent housing.) The organizations were hoping to get a joint resolution supporting increased salaries for their frontline workers and additional funding to increase the number of teams. On the one-page summary of the ICM program, the only mention of its success in housing was couched thusly: "A little over half of the clients who were initially unhoused attained housing and roughly 60 percent of these individuals stayed housed."

In questioning the reps, I tried to clarify and confirm that, indeed, a little over half of a half (60 percent of 50 percent) or between 25 to 30 percent became stably housed (in stark contrast to the 62 percent cited in rigorous studies on Housing First models in North America, detailed above). The ICL medical director declined to give a more exact total number or percentage of stably housed clients, stating bluntly, "Our goal was never housing—it's to keep people out of hospitals and jails."

Okay. Point made and taken. It turns out, a very important distinction.

When the head of another community board's social service committee followed up and asked pointedly what outcomes had been documented as far as preventing people from landing in hospitals or police custody, the medical director demurred and said, "We really don't have those numbers available." The most telling moment came when the ICL leadership made clear that their clients were only referred to housing when they were "clean and sober" and "medication compliant." ICL's "stabilization model" did not prioritize providing their clients with Safe Haven beds (typically semiprivate accommodations) or hotel rooms, either of which has lower bureaucratic barriers to entry and provides more privacy and safety, the top priority for our street-bound neighbors. These options are far and away what homeless people sleeping rough yearn for the most, and having them in the frontline workers' arsenal is *key* to convincing folks to come in off the streets. I pointed out that the research is incontrovertible: access to low-threshold, private accommodations greatly increases the success rates of stability, sobriety, connectivity to mental health services, and compliance with medication. I didn't point out that the CEO of ICL is paid over $600,000, or that medical directors of similar organizations make over $1 million per year.

Disturbingly, this meeting took place hours after Jordan Neely, a thirty-year-old homeless man with a long history of mental illness, was grabbed and choked to death by a former marine, Daniel Penny, age twenty-four, on a downtown F train after shouting that he was hungry and thirsty and didn't care if he died. In the days following the vigilante killing, myriad troubling facts emerged. Shortly before his death, Neely had been placed on the City's special Top 50 list of homeless persons most in need of urgent assistance.[14] "The goal of the list is to connect disparate bureaucracies across a vast city, in which a group of people with intense needs regularly interacts with hospital personnel, street social workers and police officers who do not regularly interact with each other," writes reporter Andy Newman. Rather than bolstering beds for long-term psychiatric care and housing with services, we continue this façade of "connecting services," when what's so obviously missing is the stability a home with services would provide.

Newman, a seasoned journalist, has spent decades covering myriad issues for the *New York Times*, most recently focused almost exclusively on homelessness and poverty. On May 3, 2023, two days after Jordan Neely's murder, the *Times* featured an in-depth piece on intensive mobile treatment teams, reflecting half a year's worth of reporting. The main client featured in the piece, "M," needed a temporary accommodation in which to stabilize and had been offered a semiprivate room, but her Treatment First agency denied her request to allow her partner to stay with her. And so, after months of painstaking work, "M" stayed inside for just a single night, then returned to living in a tent with her boyfriend. Eventually, her sister in Wisconsin sent her a ticket to return to her childhood hometown. To an uneducated eye, the takeaway from the piece is the heroic but seemingly futile lengths to which Treatment First outreach workers go, as well as how difficult it is to work with this segment of the population. But far more important is reevaluating the conditional restrictions (or "hoops," as they're colloquially known) that Treatment First clients *must* get through—sobriety and medication adherence—*before* a private room, even a temporary one, is tendered. These preconditions are inherently deterrent and diminish long-term housing attainment.

What's clear is that this approach is *not* working. It didn't work for "M." It didn't work for Jordan Neely. It's not working for the average domiciled New Yorker who continues to see their homeless neighbors in extreme distress in subways, parks, streets, and other public spaces. It's not even working for taxpayers who are footing the expensive bill: the ICM program, per Newman, "costs about $37 million annually…*about $840 per client per week*."[15] (Emphasis mine.)

Yet, New York mayor Eric Adams, California governor Gavin Newsom, and numerous other elected leaders advance a steady drumbeat of false narratives, insisting that expanding costly outreach efforts will yield different results despite shortchanging investments to increase the number of long-term psychiatric beds, Safe Havens, and Housing

First accommodations. Their stance is premised on the trope that most homeless people are overwhelmingly a public danger and must be rounded up and forced into (nonexistent) psychiatric facilities. Democrat Adams recently directed the NYPD to apprehend those exhibiting the inability to care for themselves and forcibly hospitalize them. Jumaane Williams, NYC's public advocate, cut to the heart of Adams's bullshit rhetoric when he declared: "Hospitalization is not a plan. Jordan had been in the hospital. If you place someone in a hospital, if they are released with no continuum of care [including housing], it doesn't really help."

As supporters of vigilante Daniel Penny raised over $2 million for his legal defense in less than ten days, lawyer and political commentator Olayemi Olurin wrote that "abandoning, vilifying, dehumanizing and criminalizing homeless and Black people not only invited the killing of Jordan, but invites an entire city and its press to justify it." As Adams unleashed the massive NYPD to clear the subways and encampments of homeless people, Olurin concluded, "Those with nowhere to lay their heads at night, who are treated as subhuman," are at the mercy of a government "who would rather give them a prison cell than a home."[16]

Olurin, a former public defender, has represented hundreds of unhoused, impoverished New Yorkers, many for evading the $2.90 fare to enter the subway system. Of all the rhetoric hurled on both sides of this sickening culmination of verbal and physical assaults on our unhoused neighbors, Olurin's clarion call captures the essence of tragedy: "Daniel Petty could kill someone for everyone to see and go home, a place Jordan Neely didn't have. That's why he was on the subway in the first place, screaming out for food and water."[17]

As with Joyce Brown thirty-five years ago, the impact and polarization of the Jordan Neely story is impossible to overstate. Penny's savage, expert choking of a homeless man—a man who may have yelled threats and stated he didn't care if he died—immediately became an allegory for a city in decline. Jordan Neely's life and tragic death became a vector of outrage, from both those appalled by the inhumanity of his death to those championing his killer, raining praise and money in support of his actions. The innumerability and anonymity of homeless people was reduced to a single individual, one with a lengthy rap sheet who had recently spent a year at Rikers for assaulting an elderly woman.

What is lost in these sensationalized cases is the notion of a sane center that could hold both sides of a violently split public. That elusive center is supportive housing. In my thirty-plus years of working with unhoused people, I have never once met a person who refused the offer of a private room unattached to any demands of sobriety or mandated medication. Finland's expansive investment in Housing First emphatically supports far greater funding for this approach.

Democrats should be pressing full-court to increase supportive housing, given that they predominantly govern the coastal states and cities with the least housing availability and the highest levels of homelessness. By treating Housing First solutions as an afterthought, they paint themselves into a familiar corner. By not investing in *what actually* works, they face an electorate unwilling to tolerate escalating public disorder, pivoting instead to police-driven strategies designed to boost their law enforcement bona fides. Choosing to lead with carceral plans also intentionally reinforces a false narrative that they are being proactive and specific. In fact, these options rely on police doing what they frankly don't like to do—spend countless hours forcing unwilling subjects into overwhelmed emergency rooms and into underfunded, overcrowded psychiatric triage wards. All to see the same people released a few days later, owing to the Democrats' self-seeded dearth of long-term hospital beds and housing.

The pandemic has worsened many aspects of life for poor Americans. One way is by draining much-needed psychiatric beds. New York alone saw over 850 psychiatric beds repurposed for Covid-related admissions. Less than 60 percent of the affected hospitals have formulated a plan, let alone a timeline, for restoring them. Across the nation, healthcare providers point to a little-known trip wire undermining the restoration of longer-term psychiatric beds: hospitals and states are not reimbursed by private insurers or the government for non-elderly psychiatric hospitalizations. The Kaiser Family Foundation estimates that only 17 percent of inpatient psychiatric care costs (mostly for emergency room and seventy-two-hour stays) are covered by Medicaid.[18] This means that hospitals, increasingly consolidated under megacorporations to maximize profits, were already shedding beds pre-pandemic. And because reimbursements don't begin to cover the cost of operating psychiatric beds, hospitals are slow-walking a return to even pre-pandemic capacity.[19]

This all leads to a logjam of patients on gurneys in ER hallways, unable to get into acute psychiatric beds. Once patients do get stabilized in those acute care beds, they can languish for weeks waiting for an opening in a long-term facility. For patients without a home, a forced, usually frightening, sometimes violent transport to an ER culminates with a seventy-two-hour hold, after which they are discharged to the streets. In New York City, those discharge instructions include a single-ride MetroCard and printed directions to the chaotic intake shelters.

## THE RIGHT'S INVESTMENT IN CONFIRMATION BIAS

The Housing First model was designed to interrupt this futile decades-old cycle of streets, shelters, jails, and hospitals. Why then are cities as sophisticated as New York and states as vast as California still dumping hundreds of millions of dollars each year into Treatment First approaches? The answers can be traced back to the mid-1980s, when advocates began amassing victories such as the McKinney-Vento Act, which directed significant federal resources to build emergency shelters or right-to-shelter initiatives in New York and Washington, DC. In response, new conservatives who created think tanks like the Manhattan Institute joined forces with older, equally reactionary groups, including the Heritage Foundation and the American Enterprise Institute, to, as cultural geographer Don Mitchell puts it, "re-demonize the homeless, reframing homelessness not as a result of economic restructuring, and certainly not as a concomitant and necessary part of capitalism, but rather as a problem of public order."[20]

Over many years—decades—an agglomeration of interest groups, backed by hugely wealthy businesspeople, funneled hundreds of millions of dollars to these reactionary think tanks. Alongside like-minded columnists and pseudo-journalists, they grew increasingly successful in permeating local, regional, and national news outlets to present an unrelenting stream of false narratives designed to degrade public opinion surrounding visibly poor Americans. The steady drumbeat of intentionally seeded narratives diverted attention and resources away from reinvestments in cost-effective housing solutions proven to permanently ameliorate mass homelessness. No expense would be spared to keep the underlying rot of commodified housing in place. If the genesis of homelessness is revealed to emanate not from personal failure but from unchecked capitalism itself, Reagan's strip-mining of the New Deal social safety net would be exposed for its crucial role in subsequent wealth polarization and record homelessness.

The late Nobel laureate Daniel Kahneman detailed the underlying principle of confirmation bias and how repetition is weaponized to occlude in *Thinking, Fast and Slow*: "A reliable way to make people believe in falsehoods is frequent repetition, because familiarity is not easily distinguished from truth."[21]

The Manhattan Institute and its ilk laid the bedrock for more recent billionaire-backed reactionary gambits. Meet Joe Lonsdale, Peter Thiel bro and tech investor who founded the Cicero Institute, which is almost exclusively dedicated to advancing ordinances nationwide to criminalize homelessness and delegitimize the Housing First model. Lonsdale and Thiel founded Palantir, a kind of dystopian data-mining company that holds government contracts for the NSA, predictive policing, battlefield management, and ICE surveillance. As activist Rosemary Fister points out, this MO fits neatly with "that Silicon Valley mystique of 'disrupting' industries"—but in this case the disruption is trained on proven solutions to homelessness, access to higher education, and healthcare for all."[22]

In 2022, the Cicero Institute created a model bill—a template that could be easily modified for adoption across states and localities—to make camping on public land illegal. It's called the Reducing Street Homelessness Bill of 2022, and as of July 2023, it has been introduced in nine states: Arizona, California, Georgia, Mississippi, Oklahoma, Tennessee, Texas, Washington, and Wisconsin.[23] Cicero's biggest "win" to date has been in Tennessee, where it is now "a felony for homeless people to camp on public land, punishable by up to six years in prison and the loss of voting rights," according to the National Coalition for the Homeless, which has closely tracked this initiative. The template legislation also stipulates that local jurisdictions not enforcing anti-camping laws would be stripped of federal and state funding.[24] It also, ominously, would require outreach teams to include police officers—because nothing inspires trust quite like a sidearm.

While a considerable amount of the Cicero Institute's efforts go toward constructing legal frameworks to criminalize people without homes in order to disappear them, the group also disseminates an extraordinary amount of misinformation to undercut proven, cost-effective housing-based solutions. When the City of Denver created a Social Impact Bond in 2016 to provide housing for unhoused individuals with multiple arrests and jail sentences, the Cicero Institute worked tirelessly to discredit it, despite rigorous studies by the Urban Institute documenting that 86 percent of participants remained housed through year one and 77 percent through year three. On a national level, Lonsdale and his institute have also worked assiduously to discredit the highly successful HUD-VASH program, which gives Section 8 housing vouchers to homeless military veterans, by falsely claiming it "encouraged drug use."

Taking a page from the Manhattan Institute playbook, Lonsdale leverages his wealth and connections to mainstream his most retrograde social theories, planting a mixture of misleading information and outright lies in major news outlets and their opinion pages. His 2022 *Wall Street Journal* op-ed, "Housing First Foments Homelessness in California," correctly points out that California is the state with the highest number of homeless people, but quickly pivots to assign causality to the State's "failed approach to homelessness...built around the 'Housing First' model."[25] That's some top-shelf audacity—akin to blaming CPR for the death of drowning victims. Rather than reckoning with the most recent, exhaustive analyses proving that the primary cause of homelessness is the low-vacancy/high-cost conditions in highly desirable coastal locations, Lonsdale strategically diverts readers to an older discredited fringe theory—"cities must build about ten new permanent subsidized homes to get even one person off the street." The study that Lonsdale cites took the total amount of federal funding for *all* homeless assistance (not limited to housing) and divided it by the number of homeless people enumerated by the annual HUD point-in-time count. You can see why the conclusion, amplified by Lonsdale, is laughable. Because the casual reader can hardly be expected to track down the original study, *Journal* subscribers get exactly what they signed up for: another dollop of reassurance that modern mass homelessness is a result of poor personal choices and itinerant pathology.

The temptation to look away is powerful, especially reassured that those humans you see suffering in plain sight just didn't try as hard as you did on the ever-equal ladder of meritocracy. George Orwell wrote, while reflecting on his days fighting Franco's fascists in Spain: "I saw newspapers in London retailing these lies and eager intellectuals building emotional superstructures over events that never happened."[26]

You'd think that such bold-faced lies would never see the light of day—or that, if they did, they'd die a quick death from exposure to the sunlight of truth. But here's the rub: the size of the lie and the commitment to it successfully distorts, confuses, and ultimately distracts from actual, credible evidence to the contrary. My former colleague at the Coalition, Patrick Markee, provided an epic takedown of this phenomenon, evoking a very useful term coined years ago by Paul Krugman: "zombie lies."[27] Markee takes down Manhattan Institute (now American Enterprise Institute) mainstay Howard Husock, cutting the legs out from under one of his most outrageous lies: "Housing subsidies cause homelessness!" Yes, you read that correctly. Husock, cited as an "expert" on WNYC in 2014, cautioned Bloomberg officials against creating incentives (that is, offering housing vouchers to homeless families) that would make them declare themselves homeless to jump the waiting line, thus, in his alternate reality, manufacturing more homelessness.

He made this claim with absolutely *no* evidence to support it, in the face of a mountain of well-grounded, thoroughly vetted evidence refuting it.

I'm no fan of William F. Buckley, but rewatching his 1969 interview with Noam Chomsky recently made me realize that as wrong as he may have been, as irritating and as rude (how many times can a man interrupt another person?) as he was, I'm willing to consider that he wouldn't stray beyond the bold outline of an island he considered the truth. He didn't just throw out a series of astonishing lies to backhoe an embankment protecting the elite. Within a handful of decades, there's been a clear devolution from Buckley to Reagan to Gingrich to Ann Coulter to Donald Trump, similar to the nosedive from Sandra Day O'Connor to John Roberts to Samuel Alito, Brett Kavanaugh, and Amy Coney Barrett. The destructive force of well-funded, highly coordinated right-wing attacks on poor and homeless Americans is a corollary to Naomi Klein's thesis in *The Shock Doctrine*: lie big enough often enough and have enough unlimited unrestricted cash along with corporate and school-chum connections and you can successfully addle the public into believing anything. Even that a shortage of housing is unrelated to homelessness—or, even more appalling, that providing decent, affordable housing will only make things worse.

The stakes could not be higher or more relevant. As of this writing, the US Supreme Court is poised to take up the most consequential homeless-related case in a generation: *Grants Pass v. Johnson*, in which the City of Grants Pass Oregon has enforced five separate anti-homeless laws. Steve Berg, of the National Alliance to End Homelessness, wrote, "The local officials in Grants Pass and elsewhere seek the ability to arrest and jail unsheltered people. In Grants Pass, the specific charge was 'camping,' which police interpreted as sleeping with a blanket, pillow, or even a sheet of cardboard to lie on. Officials have been explicit about their hopes that people will go elsewhere."[28] Grants Pass and other localities are attempting to overturn the 2018 landmark decision *Martin v. Boise* (from the Court of Appeals for the Ninth Circuit), which prohibits states from making "it a crime to sleep outside if no inside space is available. These precedents are based on the prohibition in the

Eighth Amendment of the US Constitution, against 'cruel and unusual punishment.'"

The National Homelessness Law Center has been at the forefront of beating back attempts to criminalize survival activities of homeless Americans. Its senior policy director, Eric Tars, commented recently, "In this case, the Eighth Amendment is a really low bar here. But, unfortunately, the City of Grants Pass wants to go under even that very low bar. All the courts have said here is that you can't punish people experiencing homelessness for something as simple as putting a blanket over themselves when there's literally nowhere else for them to go."[29] Like many smaller localities, Grants Pass has no HUD-recognized shelter. In larger cities, like Los Angeles and San Francisco, the need for emergency shelter far outstrips availability. Tars concludes that "unlike some other cities which kind of try to hide the ball and pretend they don't want to criminalize homelessness…somehow they just need the 'tool' of criminalization to address homelessness. In Grants Pass, the cruelty was the point."

In oral arguments for *Grant Pass v. Johnson*, on April 22, 2024, Justice Sonia Sotomayor made quick work getting to the core of the dispute, grilling the lawyer for the City of Grants Pass, Theane Evangelis. First, Sotomayor substantiated the two-tiered system of justice: "The police officers testified that… if a stargazer wants to take a blanket or a sleeping bag out at night to watch the stars and falls asleep, you don't arrest them…. You don't arrest people who are sleeping on the beach, as I tend to do if I've been there a while…. You only arrest people who don't have… a home."

Later in proceedings, Sotomayor drilled deeper: "Your intent— stated by your mayor—is to remove every homeless person and give them no public space to sit down with a blanket or lay down with a blanket and fall asleep."

Evangelis replied, "That's not the intent of the law. And I would like to—" Sotomayor interrupted her, "Why don't you answer the basic question?"

After a few moments of back and forth, Evangelis made another attempt to justify the City's goal of fining and arresting visibly homeless people who cover themselves with a blanket in a town with no emergency shelter capacity, saying, "This is a difficult policy question, Justice Sotomayor. It is. And—"

Sotomayor struck at the heart of the matter, asking, "Where do we put them if every city, every village, every town lacks compassion—and passes a law identical to this? Where are they supposed to sleep? Are they supposed to kill themselves, not sleeping?"

If you think that's an entirely rhetorical question, think again.

## HOMELESSNESS IS A HOUSING PROBLEM

In 2017, Gregg Colburn had just moved to Seattle to start as an assistant professor of real estate at the University of Washington. Like many, he was soon barraged by the local public debate surrounding homelessness, a debate that slanted significantly toward blaming individuals' problems: drugs, alcohol use, job loss, mental health issues. But scant research existed on how market forces in housing influenced actual rates of homelessness in cities across the nation. Colburn partnered with data journalist Clayton Page Aldern to delve deeper, and their resulting 2022 book, *Homelessness Is a Housing Problem: How Structural Factors Explain US Patterns*, provides a lucid, meticulously researched argument that "the homelessness crisis in coastal cities cannot be explained by disproportionate levels of drug use, mental illness, or poverty."[30] If individual pathologies were to blame, places with high rates of these issues—Wisconsin, Kentucky, West Virginia, and Alabama—would have higher rates of homelessness. Instead, they have far lower rates of homelessness compared to what the authors call the "superstar cities"—New York, San Francisco, Los Angeles, and Seattle. High rates of homelessness are driven by housing scarcity.

The authors draw a powerful analogy to a game of musical chairs in which one player, hobbled by crutches, quickly loses the game: "The fundamental cause of [his] chairlessness was a lack of chairs, not his ankle injury. *The rules of the game meant that someone had to lose."* (Emphasis mine.) The high-rent/low-vacancy dynamics of these super-star cities ensure those least able to compete for the limited resource of housing will lose out and default into homelessness.

High-poverty cities like Detroit and Cleveland have low homeless-ness rates—and as with the high-pathology states mentioned earlier, it's because these locations have higher housing vacancy rates and lower rents. Colburn and Aldern also disprove the myth that generous wel-fare benefits attract homeless people, or somehow condition people to work less.

The Manhattan Institute and other right-wing pseudo think tanks have made a lucrative industry out of blaming homelessness on per-sonal pathologies, with absolutely no evidence to back their outlandish theories. They could all neatly fit under the now infamous Rudy Giu-liani January 6 quote, "We've got lots of theories, we just don't have the evidence."[31] (As we've just examined, these theories all lead in one di-rection: cutbacks in individual relief, defunding well-proven housing-based solutions, and the criminalization of homelessness paired with greater investments in an ever-expanding carceral system.) But their central theses simply do *not* hold up to Colburn and Aldern's unflinch-ing scrutiny.

Colburn and Aldern bring down to earth what could otherwise be dismissed as philosophical squabbles about poverty, with real-time, real-world implications: the inability of Democratic mayors and gov-ernors to muster housing resources to solve homelessness in coastal areas is breeding more reactionary demands. Their constituents will only tolerate the disorder that accompanies mass homelessness for so long. Dithering on the part of the Eric Adamses and Gavin Newsoms of the nation inevitably leads to more (and more vicious) cycles of sup-port for stepped-up criminalization. Indeed, both Adams and Newsom have honed their national reputations on "get tough" stances, with little in the way of investments in housing-based solutions. They would fare better by adopting the approach championed by the center-right former mayor of Helsinki, Jan Vapaavuori, who—as we've seen—has been an ardent investor in Housing First: "In Finland and Helsinki, you see less homelessness. Because of the Housing First, this is a safer and more pleasant city, and a better city for visitors, for tourists. It's also a better city for foreign direct investments. Investors rely on this being a clean, safe, pleasant, well-organized city."

The good news is that a meaningful, lasting solution is known, but scaling it to meet demand is going to take time. Our current housing crisis is nearly a half century in the making. We aren't going to end it in a single election cycle. But we have to aim far higher than the relative pittance of increased spending recently advanced by Biden. We need a bold plan—one that greatly increases investments in supportive housing for our neighbors' mental health or substance issues and subsidized housing for extremely low-income households. These must come alongside major investments in housing for working- and middle-class families. One significantly consistently overlooked model to achieve the latter is the limited equity co-op. Which dovetails into the next myth.

## MYTH 14 "INVESTMENTS IN SOCIAL HOUSING HAVE PROVEN TO BE FAILURES"

Homeownership as a validation of personal success is a particularly enduring American myth. In addition to our Founding Fathers enshrining special standing for landowners in the Constitution, the federal government put major skin into pushing homeownership following World War I, when then secretary of commerce Herbert Hoover inaugurated the "Better Homes in America" campaign. As head cheerleader for increased homeownership, Hoover was piggybacking on the Department of Labor's 1917 crusade called "Own Your Own Home"—pushback against the Bolshevik Revolution in Russia. A national association of realtors at the time spun homeownership as a uniquely American antidote to the Reds, with a PR campaign that declared, "Socialism and communism do not take root in the ranks of those who have their feet firmly embedded in the soil of America through homeownership."[32] "The homeowner has a constructive aim in life," declared Hoover.[33]

American homeownership crept up in the decade that followed—from 45.6 percent in 1920 to nearly 48 percent (a total of 3 million new homes)—before the Great Depression hit in 1929, just after Hoover was sworn in as president. Not surprisingly, the Depression triggered a surge in home foreclosures, causing homeownership to dip below pre-Depression levels (43.6 percent) by 1940. FDR pushed back, enacting a series of measures that essentially provided government-backed guarantees for homeowners at risk of default, which stemmed most, but not all, of the housing-related fiscal bloodletting. But more importantly, he created the Federal Housing Administration (FHA) and Federal National Mortgage Association (FNMA), also known as Fannie Mae, agencies that forever changed the terms under which Americans borrowed to buy housing. Rather than scraping together 50 percent or more of a home's selling price and taking out a five- or ten-year loan (the pre-Depression standard), the new federal housing agencies backed riskier mortgages so that prospective homeowners could put 20 percent down and amortize the remaining amount over twenty or even thirty years. This new rubric would abide for over a half century.

After World War II, the Veterans Administration got into the game, boosting VA-issued mortgages as part of the G.I. Bill. Another huge thumb on the scale tilting the nation toward homeownership is the option to deduct any interest paid on mortgages from one's taxable income. In 2016, the cost of the mortgage interest deduction (MID) totaled a staggering $71 billion, *by far the greatest housing subsidy given by our federal government.*[34] And affluent taxpayers (those making over $100,000 a year) reap an astounding 77 percent of this benefit.[35] In comparison, the Low-Income Housing Tax Credit (LIHTC) program—the main vehicle for financing construction, rehabilitation, and preservation of affordable housing—totaled just $8.1 billion that same year.[36] Matthew Desmond, in his 2017 *New York Times Magazine* article, "How Homeownership Became the Engine of American Inequality," captured the stark mismatch of benefit to need, "with affluent homeowners [receiving] large benefits...and most renters, who are disproportionately poor, nothing. It is difficult to think of another social policy that more successfully multiplies America's inequality in such a sweeping fashion."[37]

In the century since Hoover, each subsequent presidential administration has unleashed ever-more ambitious twists to gin up homeownership as both financial and emotional bedrock for Americans. These include the essential legalization of subprime mortgages in the 1980s, as well as Clinton's mid-1990s National Home Ownership Strategy, which required the government-sponsored mortgage backers Fannie Mae and Freddie Mac* to issue half of all their mortgages to moderate- and low-income borrowers. George W. Bush soothed post-9/11 market jitters with a plan called the American Dream Downpayment Act in 2003 to entice Americans into buying homes with the promise of little- or no-down-payment mortgages. Bush declared outright that "owning a home lies at the heart of the American Dream."[38] The underlying assumption that homeownership was a universal goal went unquestioned, and these policies were touted as unequivocal successes. Nationwide homeownership rates topped out at nearly 70 percent by 2005.

The catastrophic 2008 collapse of this government-seeded housing bubble exposed the toxic instability of what had evolved into a multinational Ponzi scheme: subprime mortgages that had been bundled into securities, resold, overvalued, and highly leveraged. Hernan Diaz, in his 2022 Pulitzer Prize–winning novel *Trust*, views the singular bleakness of contemporary American high finance through its historic precedent: the Hoover-era boom/bust cycle. In the novel, a young writer, Ida Partenza, is hired to rework a memoir of the antiseptic aspirational climb of a successful banker. A ghostwriter of sorts, she is tasked with cobbling together a fictitious redemptive arc. It's her anarchist father who deftly nails what otherwise goes unspoken in the current of money: "Stock, shares and all that garbage are just claims to a future value. So if money is fiction, finance capital is the fiction of a fiction. That's what all those criminals trade in: fictions."[39]

---

* Known officially as the Federal Home Loan Mortgage Corporation.

The radical father is amplifying the message of Marx, who wrote in *Capital*: "All capital seems to double itself, and sometimes treble itself, by the various modes in which the same capital, or perhaps even the same claim on a debt, appears in different forms in different hands. The greater portion of this 'money-capital' is purely fictitious. All the deposits…are merely claims on the banker, which, however, never exist as deposits."

The 2008 economic collapse gutted a huge swath of Americans. Nearly all of the banks perpetrating the fraud—with the exception of a mere few—were made whole. No such accommodation was extended to the millions of homeowners left holding mortgages far in excess of their actual home value.

And yet, homeownership continues to endure as Americans' primary vehicle for wealth accumulation and coveted social standing. Wealth inequality at its current zenith has become physically manifest in the zombie skyscrapers that have sprung up in our major cities. They are called "housing," but no one actually lives in them. The capital amassed by one percenters is so vast, it needs a place to go—and so they deposit unimaginable sums in what are essentially vertical safe-deposit boxes. The latest one rising in Manhattan, at 5th Avenue and 29th Street, will reach fifty-four stories. It will "house" just twenty-six families. The developer, Boris Kuzinez, seasoned in laundering money from Russian oligarchs via real estate, explained to the *New York Times*, "It's hard for oligarchs to live in a regular building."[40] Kuzinez and his partners recently asked our local community board for an exemption from the City zoning code so that he could increase the building's below-ground parking spaces from the five allowed as-of-right to twenty-three. "Don't worry," his representatives reassured us. "The spots will only be available for [prospective] unit owners, so you won't have the concern of outsiders coming and going."

"Telling us the spots are exclusively for owners is not the flex you think it is," I replied, echoing the sentiment of my colleagues on Manhattan Community Board Five's Land Use, Housing, and Zoning

Committee. The request was denied. But once completed, the banal tower will block the Empire State Building from nearly every vista to its south, permanently eclipsing the view of New York's most iconic structure for anyone visiting, working, or living in Lower Manhattan.[41]

## BUILDING FOR HUMAN NEED, NOT PROFIT

While securing decent housing feels akin to a real-life Hunger Games for most, labor leaders and other left-leaning groups once sought out a different path during World War I. In 1916, immigrants from Finland founded the Brooklyn Finnish Socialist Club and formed the Finnish Home Building Association to construct member-owned co-op residential buildings in the Brooklyn neighborhood of Sunset Park. Sparked by $500 initial equity contributions from six families, and "comrade loans" from friends and family members of $12,000, they leveraged $25,000 in bank loans. Within a year, the group had completed its first building, and in the decade that followed, nearly thirty of these Finnish-owned co-op buildings dotted Sunset Park. These buildings housed their residents at roughly half the rent charged in the surrounding privately owned buildings. Historian Erik Forman describes the limited equity requirement as the decisive feature of these undertakings: "Members were forbidden from selling their units at a profit to ensure lasting affordability. In a pattern that would be repeated for decades to come, the housing co-ops became part of a local co-op ecosystem that included restaurants, bakeries, and grocery stores."[42]

Forman details subsequent developments and their radical roots, including a 1927 project in the Bronx, the United Workers' Cooperative Colony, planned and constructed by a Yiddish Communist group called United Workers. These buildings eventually housed two thousand New Yorkers. "The Coops," as the development became known, spurred other left-leaning Jewish groups in the Bronx to create even more limited equity developments.[43] Eventually, this fledgling housing solidarity caught the attention of union leaders, who provided the deep pockets to scale the model across New York City.

## ABRAHAM KAZAN AND THE ROOTS OF TRUMP'S DYNASTY

The history of the limited equity co-op movement is so consequential, entire books have attempted to capture its scope. Central to labor's first foray into constructing such housing is the genius firebrand who lit the match: a Ukrainian Jewish immigrant who came to New York in 1904 named Abraham Kazan. Kazan became a garment worker and was radicalized, according to Forman, "by anarchist ideas and a stint on a proto-Kibbutz in New Jersey." His organizing at smaller companies landed him on the staff at the International Ladies' Garment Workers' Union and eventually with the Amalgamated Clothing Workers of America. Historian and activist Glyn Robbins notes that although working conditions were brutal, the garment industry also had "high levels of trade union membership and militancy."[44] It was here that Kazan "became convinced that the private market was neither willing, nor able, to meet the housing needs of working-class people."

In 1925, Kazan set his sights on providing decent, affordable housing for those toiling alongside him and living in squalid tenements in the Lower East Side. Author and Columbia School of Journalism professor Gwenda Blair superbly conjures the camaraderie and aspirations of Kazan's founding group, "a knee-pants maker, a coat tailor, a cloth cutter, a millinery worker, a shirt cutter, and several midlevel union officials, [who] met in a tiny space next to the freight elevator at union headquarters."[45] Building on recent success they'd had in forming buying clubs to slash "the price of staples by eliminating the retail grocer, the group decided to cut the price of housing by eliminating commercial builders and landlords." The audacity of their dream was laughed at by fellow union members, yet they forged ahead. They incorporated as the ACW Corporation and began development plans for a 303-unit project in the Bronx, selling shares to prospective residents for $500, up to half of which enrollees could borrow from the Amalgamated Workers' own Amalgamated Bank.

Kazan's eventual victory in winning over the leaders at the Amalgamated Union marked labor's significant entry into this sphere of affordable housing development, upping its cred considerably. This spurred New York State lawmakers to enact the Limited Dividend Housing Company Law, which conferred tax breaks (as well as condemnation rights—a sweeping power that, as we'll see, was not always utilized for good in later decades) on these co-ops and placed rent restrictions on any rental developments. With Kazan's first co-op venture now bolstered with Albany's imprimatur of respectability, the big dogs at Metropolitan Life Insurance Company stepped up to offer $1.2 million in mortgage backing.

Just one of the many wonders of Kazan's first enterprise, Amalgamated Houses, is the breakneck speed at which it was realized. A groundbreaking ceremony was held on Thanksgiving 1926, residents began moving into Building Number One a year later, and by early 1928, all 303 units were fully occupied. Although Kazan spent much of the Depression just keeping his initial co-ops afloat, the tightly knit, collaborative founding culture was reinforced and manifested via mutual aid among residents. Blair quotes a primary school student who delivered pantry staples to struggling families. "I would put the bag down in front of the apartment door, ring the bell and run. The committee ferreted out who was desperate, but to protect people's dignity everything was done anonymously."[46]

In 1951, Kazan partnered with other unions to create the nonprofit United Housing Foundation (UHF), which strengthened his ability to replicate the model. UHF would eventually build over forty thousand limited equity co-op units, providing more than 100,000 New Yorkers with still affordable, decent (and much sought after) housing. Kazan found a strange political bedfellow in Robert Moses.* Moses initially reviled the rough-edged immigrant but grew to respect Kazan after he completed his second project, Hillman Houses, below budget and on

---

* In Kazan's March 1961 marketing pamphlet *The Story of the Seward Park Cooperative*, the "In Appreciation" on page 20 includes "To the City of New York and its former Slum Clearance Committee ably headed by its chairman Robert Moses and to the Housing and Home Finance Agency we are very grateful."

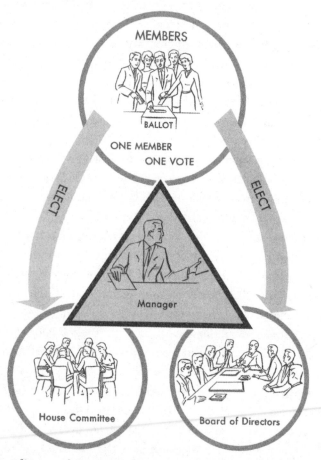

# HOW A CO-OP OPERATES

MEMBERS

BALLOT

ONE MEMBER
ONE VOTE

ELECT

ELECT

Manager

House Committee

Board of Directors

A 1957 diagram from Amalgamated Houses illustrates how limited equity cooperatives govern themselves. *30 Years of Amalgamated Cooperative Housing, 1927–1957*, Amalgamated Housing Corp., 1958, http://graphbooks.com/index.php/happ/detail/30-years-of -amalgamated-cooperative-housing.

time. Moses's public support greatly increased Kazan's clout, allowing him to more widely replicate his limited equity, permanently affordable housing schemes. However, the movement's eventual demise came in the late 1960s at the hands of both New York City mayor Robert F. Wagner (who despised Moses's unparalleled power) and a rival—the very much *for*-profit developer Fred C. Trump, father of Donald.

While Kazan had concentrated his efforts in the Bronx and Manhattan, Fred Trump was the largest developer in Brooklyn.[47] In 1954, a Senate committee declared that Trump "had profiteered on postwar housing," and the resulting backlash from numerous press accounts left him reeling.[48] Around the same time, Robert Moses used the sweeping power of Title I—the urban slum clearance program—to raze a sixty-plus acre plot of land on Brooklyn's Coney Island, intending for Kazan to develop it into permanently affordable housing. But Trump was able to make a critical alliance with Wagner, then on the all-powerful New York City Board of Estimate (the US Supreme Court eventually declared the BOE unconstitutional in 1988 for violating the one-man, one-vote "equal representation" clause in the Constitution). In August 1957, on the eve of what Kazan thought would be a guaranteed approval for his project, Fred Trump filed a last-minute objection and appeared with his lawyer, who read a statement declaring that Kazan's proposal was an "outright giveaway" to "a favored few." The "few" actually totaled nearly 5,200 union families, and Trump's stupefying claim was that Kazan's government-backed affordable housing plan would take "money out of the pocket of taxpayers to subsidize more luxurious housing than they themselves enjoy."[49] What Trump actually feared was that the relative affordability of Kazan's projects would siphon customers away from his more costly for-profit housing complexes.

Robert Wagner, then anticipating a run for mayor, already had the support of most Manhattan and Bronx political machines but badly needed the Brooklyn power brokers who Trump had courted for over a quarter century. And Wagner's enduring hatred and fear of Kazan-ally Robert Moses magnified the political target he'd drawn on Kazan. At the end of the day, Blair observes, "Kazan's single-mindedness, heretofore an asset, would now be his undoing," as Kazan simply refused "to stoop to partisan politics and [specious] alliance building."[50]

Kazan's model of limiting resale speculation may seem more far-fetched and revolutionary today than when early doubters scoffed at him a century ago. His enduring belief in decent housing for people allowed him "to buck the very ethos of American capitalism, to scorn the notion of profits, and yet to build more housing units than anyone else in American history, including Fred Trump."[51]

Trump, with Wagner's backing, won the lion's share of the Coney Island development site. Kazan then fixed his sights on the massive Co-op City in the Bronx, but there, he was eventually turned away by more modern-minded apartment buyers who insisted on the flexibility to sell their apartments for whatever profit the market might yield—a battle culminating in the nation's longest rent strike.[52] The defeat at Co-op City proved too much for Kazan: he and his United Housing Fund never built another unit. In Blair's final analysis, "To the politicians who were doing the deciding, housing was a business, not a sacred trust."

## A GREAT TURN IN THE POSSIBLE*

Today's progressive aspiration to shift the Overton window's spectrum of politically palatable policies is assuredly forward-looking, always casting toward a new and better future. But what if, for housing, the Overton window needs to be temporally reversed? Back to a time before the near-ubiquitous commodification of housing and unquestioned acceptance of it as the primary engine of wealth creation? Before its implied fiscal leverage became central to what writer Lucy Sante called "the nation-long American pursuit of the angle"?[53]

Uncoupling what economists consider housing's two essential functions, utility for consumption ("use value," that is, for shelter) and investment vehicle ("exchange value," for personal wealth growth), is *the*

---

* Legendary photographer Carrie Mae Weems foregrounds protagonists too often forgotten. Her latest collection, published in 2022, is brilliant, and an inspiration: *A Great Turn in the Possible.*

essential step needed to stem the fiscal bleed-out that is destabilizing our economy, undercutting hope to realize meaningful solvency among young people and literally killing our homeless and poorly housed neighbors.

By design and intention, limited equity co-ops (LECs) prohibit significant equity appreciation, placing primacy on their utilitarian purpose (use value) as shelter. The term "co-op," in referring to housing, is usually associated with expensive apartment houses, with watchdog co-op boards demanding impeccable credit histories and deep financial resources from applicants. The roughly 6,400 US housing cooperatives in existence contain over a million units, with an estimated 775,000 market-rate units and 425,000 LEC units.[54] Remarkably, outside the US, durably affordable LECs comprise vast proportions of housing stock in many of the most highly desirable cities, including Vienna, Paris, Singapore, and Vancouver.

## RED VIENNA

Vienna has topped the Economist Intelligence Unit's "Global Liveability Index" for three of the past five years; it was rated the most livable city in the world in 2022.[55] Housing availability, quality, and affordability accounts for fully 20 percent of the EIU's matrix, so it's no surprise the city steadfastly touted for its vibrancy has a deep-rooted affordable housing ethos that allows citizens at every income level to attain stable homes. Fully 60 percent of Viennese people live in government subsidized co-ops or rental buildings. As with New York City, Vienna's first wave of limited equity co-ops was birthed in the aftermath of World War I. But today, New York City clocks in at a dismal fifty-first in the EIU's livability index.[56] Where did the two cities' paths diverge, and can American cities hope to regain lost ground?

"Red Vienna" refers to the sixteen-year period from the end of World War I through 1934 and is a common point of reference for aspirational urban planning and affordable housing creation. As with New York City in the same era, it was left-leaning visionaries who made manifest the dream that all residents could live in housing that was not only affordable, but beautiful and lasting. Vienna during this period was unique in that it was one of the last quasi city-states in Europe, allowing it extensive autonomy in setting tax policy. The Austrian Social Democratic Workers' Party (SDAPÖ), amidst the ascent of the Weimar Republic and rising fascist tides in nearby countries (as well as its own), first gained control in Vienna in November 1918.[57] Journalists Veronika Duma and Hanna Lichtenberger, in *Jacobin*, detail the seeds that swelled support for the SDAPÖ, including "strong labor, feminist, and council movements [which] emerged from widespread hunger, unemployment and homelessness that characterized the [first world] war years."[58] The Social Democrats instituted a progressive tax system that levied surcharges on luxuries such as mansions, villas, cars, horses, and services, including domestic help. Housing conditions immediately after the war were on par with pre-reformist New York: overcrowded firetraps lacking private bathrooms, airless rooms, fetid harbingers of tuberculosis. And so, the Social Democrats put a massively ambitious housing program at the top of their priorities list.

The end of the war saw widespread economic collapse in the wake of the crumbling Austro-Hungarian Empire, and the SDAPÖ were cannily opportunistic, seizing on the financial instability and hyperinflation to buy out private property owners and snap up vast tracts of abandoned buildings and lots. As historian Janek Wasserman put it, "They used that hyperinflationary moment to basically expropriate land and property from people going under—the people who owned a lot of the real estate stock in the city."[59] By 1924, Vienna itself became the largest property owner in the city-state.

A decade later, the SDAPÖ had built over 60,000 new apartments. By the end of the 1930s, fully half of Vienna's current 220,000 city-owned apartments were already constructed.

But equally important to quantity is the *quality* and compositional structure of Vienna's *Gemeindebauten*, or council estates. As housing expert Eve Blau, director of the Davis Center for Russian and Eurasian Studies at Harvard University, highlights, they were "designed to be indistinguishable from private buildings housing the city's bourgeoisie."

Critically, the overarching goal was "to integrate them into the fabric of the city. The buildings' open courtyards were revolutionary, because they did away with the division between public streets and private inner gardens."[60] The complexes also incorporated kindergartens, bakeries, grocery shops, and medical clinics, as well as space for economic stimulus programs: childcare, nursing homes, and public libraries.

Post–World War II, much of Europe and the US would construct cheap, vertical public housing projects outside of city centers. Their intentions may have been good, but the designs paid scant attention to aesthetics or to the integration of the projects into surrounding neighborhoods, reinforcing segregation, social ghettos, and a burgeoning reliance on cars. But from the jump, Vienna's guiding principle was to weave government-sponsored housing seamlessly into the city, making it alluring for middle-class families, who would flock to it alongside working-class and poor residents.

As *Jacobin*'s Duma and Lichtenberger remarked, "These housing complexes were usually multistory apartment blocks with green inner courtyards that provided residents with natural light and strengthened community ties and solidarity. The city connected these blocks to local infrastructure—like consumer cooperatives and schools—making residents' daily lives easier by cutting down travel and shopping time." The critical truss undergirding its sustained success was that "neither the complexes nor the various companies and services established to support them were intended to make a profit."[61] The decommodification of shelter endures in Vienna because its social housing is not a series of disconnected, shitty, decaying, walled-off loci of despair, but beautifully designed, spatially integrated homes intended to increase connectivity and joy in their residents. "Public housing in the United States was designed to fail," said Saoirse Gowan of the Democracy Collaborative. "It was designed to be segregated; it was designed to be low-quality. Even where a few public housing authorities tried to do it very well, it was disinvested from later on."[62]

In 2022, a delegation of tenant organizers from America toured Vienna. Among them was Julie Colon from Northwest Bronx Community and Clergy Coalition. Having grown up in public housing herself, Colon remarked that the stark attitudinal difference in Vienna links directly to the fact that over half its residents are living in beautifully designed, cohesive public housing: "We have it ingrained that public things are supposed to be nasty, supposed to be the lowest of the low. But to see what we saw in Vienna, it was like, wow, it is achievable to have housing that is government-owned, for the people, and beautiful. It was really inspiring to see that people had saunas—and directly down the hall, a child care room and a communal kitchen, so you could be chilling and your friends could be making dinner." In the US those things exist, "maybe for the very rich, but it's not for the public, not for the working class."[63]

Austria does not spend more on housing than the US as a percentage of GDP.[64] Because there is no mortgage interest deduction in Austria, it subsidizes multiunit developments rather than individual homeowners. *Vienna chose housing as a human right over profit.* And contrary to what investment bankers and the real estate industry would predict, this choice didn't ruin the City or country's economy. Nor has it drained the residents' inherent motivation to attain employment. *Eighty percent of Viennese residents rent—and their average rents are half the rates in Zurich, Barcelona, and other European cities.*

## JFK AND THE APEX OF FEDERAL INVESTMENT IN AFFORDABLE HOUSING

When Abraham Kazan created the first American LECs in the 1920s, his achievement was made possible in part by New York State's 1927 Limited Dividend Housing Company Law. The second significant boost to finance low and moderate-income housing was also birthed in New York: the Mitchell-Lama Act of 1955. Prime examples of sustained affordable housing created under Mitchell-Lama (and the similar NY Article 5 Redevelopment Corporation) include the Penn South complex in Chelsea and Manhattan Plaza in Times Square. Penn South is a mini city, spanning 8th to 9th Avenues from 23rd to 29th Streets. It has fifteen terraced buildings, along with playgrounds, restaurants, and grocery stores, even its own power plant. The opening ceremony on March 19, 1962, headlined by President John F. Kennedy and Eleanor Roosevelt, would signal the high-water mark of our federal government's commitment to affordable housing for all Americans.

That particular March date is etched in our collective memory, thanks to the indelible footage of Marilyn Monroe breathlessly serenading JFK at Madison Square Garden that evening. But earlier that afternoon, a crowd of more than ten thousand gathered outdoors for Penn South's grand opening. They also welcomed the young president with "Happy Birthday" as he took the stage. His remarks to leaders and union rank and file are as stirring as they are prescient.* According to the *New York Times*, Kennedy squinted "into the blazing sun that broke city heat records" and set aside his prepared speech, imploring Americans to work toward goals most worthy and lasting: those sure to "provide a better life for those who come after us," specifically "the 300 million people who will live in this country in the next forty years."[65]

In a stinging rebuke to the first whiff of the modern-day conservative austerity mindset, Kennedy declared, "There are those who say that the job is done, that the function of the federal government is not to govern, that all the things that had to be done were done in the '30s and the '40s and that now our task is merely to administer. I do not accept that view at all, nor can any American who sees what we still have left to do."[66] Kennedy took the "long view"—that federal investments in affordable housing were central to fulfilling the principal role of government. "It is the task of every generation to build a road for the next generation. And this housing project, the efforts we're making in this city, and state, and in the national government, I believe can provide a better life for the people who come after us, if we meet our responsibility." Like FDR, Kennedy insisted that true national security entails individual economic stability: projects like Penn South provide "the kind of progress on which our ultimate security depends."

He closed with the story of a famous French marshal who told his gardener to plant a tree. The gardener protested that the tree wouldn't

* The original audio of Kennedy's stirring remarks is remarkable and available via WNYC: https://www.wnyc.org/story/jfk-cracks-jokes-and-dedicates-one-manhattans-storied-co-ops.

flower for a hundred years. "In that case," the marshal replied, "plant it this afternoon!" Kennedy finished with riveting urgency: "That's the way I feel about *all* the tasks left undone in this country that will *not* be finished in our time—that we ought to do something about it this afternoon!"

Sadly, the presidents that followed took a decidedly different path, pivoting away from vital funding for new brick-and-mortar projects. Instead, the National Housing Act of 1974 prioritized portable Section 8 rent vouchers. Moreover, slashing investments in affordable housing became a paramount goal of the Reagan and Bush administrations. In 1980, the Reagan administration's "budget authority for HUD assisted housing was cut from \$26.7 billion to \$8.3 billion."[67] What little funding that did still flow from DC took the form of—you guessed it—community block grants to states and local governments. Kennedy's "long view" was eclipsed by a new agenda: taking the federal government out of the business of building or maintaining affordable housing for low- or moderate-income Americans. Unlike the quality construction and financing schemes of union-advanced LECs and Mitchell-Lama units, public housing projects were allowed to deteriorate, and their inherent concentration of poverty fed into a spiral of planned obsolescence.

Republicans and Democrats alike were all too eager to seize on the run-down conditions in projects nationwide, which gave way to the elimination of a long-standing requirement that any demolition of HUD units be replaced on a unit-for-unit basis. Cabrini-Green, the infamous housing project in Chicago's Near North Side, became a shorthand for everything bad associated with HUD housing. In 1997, it was slated for demolition as part of the Chicago Housing Authority's planned diminution of its stock—from 38,000 to 25,000 total units. Using the fig leaf of deconcentrating poverty, Cabrini-Green and other projects across the nation were demolished and replaced with mixed-income communities that had far less capacity to house extremely low-income and homeless families. Janet L. Smith, a professor of urban planning and policy at the University of Illinois at Chicago, argued forcefully in 2002 for a strategy that would empower public housing residents, including conversions to LECs and the creation of land trusts to ensure that new units be protected from speculation: "[We must] reduce the power of private partners in public-private partnerships—the sanctioned means to fund neighborhood revitalization and community development in the US these days. While we work on getting more public funding for affordable housing (e.g., a National Housing Trust Fund), there is an immediate need to re-position the public in these partnerships."[68]

JFK's soaring words reflected the collective American expectation of his time—that the federal government play a major role in providing decent housing. Telling of how far we fell in the forty years that followed: by the millennium, Smith and other progressives were fighting back massive onslaughts of cuts, hoping to merely preserve the existing number of HUD units. Lost in the battle is the invaluable lesson proven over generations: greater tenant control or outright ownership in the form of LECs yields far lower default and higher resident satisfaction than projects directly underwritten by HUD.[69] Fast-forward another two decades to today, and virtually all new government-supported housing is now predicated on public-private partnerships, almost all of which yield a minority percentage of "affordable" units.

## THE ART OF THE DEAL AND THE DECAY OF THE COMMONS

The peerless architect and critic Michael Sorkin was one of the first casualties of the Covid pandemic; his sharp eye and keen, unyielding advocacy for reform in housing and public planning are missed beyond words. In his steely 2016 takedown of a public-private partnership fiasco, Sorkin commented, "Urban morphology maps the flow of cash with concrete precision and the New York skyline is a literal bar graph of investment and return. The manufacture of real estate (what some quaintly refer to as 'architecture') is our leading industry and the art of the deal the epicenter of our creativity."[70] Sorkin references the Trumpian legacy of the "art of the deal"—the expectation that public-private partnerships will reap huge profits for the "private" side of the equation. Because "we now insist that virtually every public enterprise...demonstrably pay for itself," instead of "public construction of housing we have inclusionary zoning, instead of public education we have charter schools and rising college tuition and instead of public healthcare we have the confusions and insufficiencies of a rapacious marketplace."

Like Janet Smith, Sorkin weighs (as should we all) the exchange rate at which these deals are sewn up, as "any trade begs the question of who gets the better of it." These public-private "daisy chains" accelerate the "form follows finance" mentality by which the nominal public planning process is completely abnegated to whatever the market can bear or, more accurately, extract. In New York, enormous luxury towers steadily wall off access to our surrounding rivers, and "Millionaire's Row" on West 57th Street (a series of towers used by Russian, Kazak, and other oligarchs, along with a more casual assortment of millionaires and billionaires looking to park their cash) casts miles of shadow across Central Park. Sorkin concludes, "That we have tipped so far to inducement rather than obligation as a planning strategy is a tragic, indeed Trumpian marker of the decay of the commons."[71]

Here, too, we can learn from Vienna. One of the New Yorkers who traveled there to tour the social housing, Bella DeVaan of the Institute for Policy Studies, interviewed the head of Vienna's public housing authority, Wiener Wohnen, who hails the central role that massive investments in social housing play in the prosperity of a thriving city: "Vienna does not leave rents and land prices solely to the free market. On the contrary: housing is viewed as a public task and part of the services of general interest." Investing close to 500 million euros back into public housing per year, according to Wohnen, "is a great economic play. The high share of subsidized dwellings exerts a price-dampening effect on the private housing market and safeguards good social mix throughout the city. Price control increases local economic activity and quality of life."[72]

# CHAPTER 7

# RESISTANCE VS. REVOLUTION

**MYTH 15** "THERE'S REALLY NOTHING I CAN DO TO MAKE A MEANINGFUL DIFFERENCE"

One of the most important lessons I gleaned from working at the Coalition was the profound difference between waging a ground war and building a movement—in this case, to end homelessness for good. Our ability to see ourselves in our homeless neighbors, to recognize our shared humanity and dignity, is essential to creating the groundswell necessary to solve this crisis. And so, this work is personal.

In eulogizing the incomparable John Berger, Anthony Barnett wrote about the deep connection between the personal and political that animates Berger's work:

> He sought to protect and if necessary salvage and certainly to defend humanity from the inhumanity of consumer capitalism, doing so by revealing the truth of the specific. This gives all his work the quality of resistance. Defiant resistance in the face of likely defeat. The poor, the ill, animals, the prisoner, especially the political prisoner, the migrant, the peasant, the Palestinian: he saw none of them as failures. All in different ways were up against our human fate, so that their experience is the truth of what is being done to us all. He was not sorry for them; it was not a patronizing sympathy that he extended. On the contrary he strove to see life through their eyes—as they see truly.[1]

It's "the truth of the specific" that allows us to understand and appreciate the weight of structural forces at play—because we see the toll they extract on our unhoused neighbors. Recognizing our shared humanity is key to recognizing that housing is essential to be fully human. If it is essential for us personally, how can it not be essential for all? Compassion and empathy allow us to set aside reflexive prejudices and appreciate that both origin and solution to this disaster lie in the wider housing crisis. Homelessness is the most visible evidence that capitalism cannot work without commonsense guardrails, especially those around banking, transportation, and investment created in response to the Great Depression. The massive inequity tearing our nation apart was seeded in reckless deregulation, as well as in the wholesale defunding of housing and mental health care by Democrats and Republicans alike. Slashing New Deal regulations precipitated the seismic shift from a wage-based to an asset-based economy and record income inequality. The resulting rush for hedge funds, oligarchs, billionaires, millionaires, and the merely affluent to park their teeming assets in real estate has increased land values in US coastal cities astronomically, resulting in corresponding record homelessness.

## PEOPLE AREN'T HOMELESS BECAUSE THE SYSTEM IS BROKEN. THEY ARE HOMELESS BECAUSE THIS IS HOW THE SYSTEM NOW WORKS.

Urban planner Peter Marcuse and sociologist David Madden expertly map the unfolding of today's housing instability in their invaluable book, *In Defense of Housing: The Politics of Crisis*. The enclosure of the British Commons was an early precondition for housing commodification: Marcuse and Madden flag it as "a crucial episode in the early development of capitalism." This "violent and complicated process laid the groundwork for the eventual commodification of land on a planetary scale." The contemporary counterpart to the enclosure of the commons "is deregulation, the removal of restrictions placed on real estate as a commodity."[2]

In turn, late-twentieth-century deregulation was the integral precursor to the financialization of housing. From our nation's founding, politicians of every stripe have enshrined homeownership as an essential American aspiration. But as New Deal regulations were abraded during the Reagan era, mortgages—once an instrument to increase homeownership—became profit-making tools themselves, fueling private equity as a major presence in the housing market across the nation.

Deregulation also ushered in a tidal wave of privatization of public housing: "Since the 1990s, more than 260,000 public housing units were either sold off to private owners or demolished in order to sell the land beneath them. . . . The privatization of housing since 1989 has probably constituted the largest transfer of property rights in history."[3]

The devastation wrought by deregulation cannot be overstated, particularly as it relates to soaring housing costs and rising homelessness. An essential condition of globalization, Noam Chomsky observed, is that capital moves freely, not labor. The centrifugal force pulling vast sums of wealth into real estate in a globalized economy is its liquidity. The superrich pour increasing amounts of surplus wealth into real estate, making, as one top broker put it, "luxury real estate the world's new currency."[4] They sleep easy at night. Their investments are secure, as Peter Marcuse notes, "because of the ease with which [they] can be converted into money through loans, debentures, mortgages, and other complex financial transactions. Whether anyone will ever make a home in such buildings is irrelevant."[5]

Financialization and globalization severely distort the value of housing, making it less available to fulfill its essential function: to provide shelter. Because investors are increasingly geographically distanced from their properties, they "reorient the housing system away from local residential needs and disconnect prices from wages in local labor markets."[5] The *Financial Times* reports that "nearly 70 percent of New York City homes purchased in the final quarter of 2023 were bought without a mortgage (in cash-only transactions)."[6]

When speculation rises to a level that it threatens the lives and well-being of over a million people in our country, it's un-American. The last time parasitic inequity was named as such was during the Great Depression, and thirty years before that, amidst the Gilded Age. It's important to call this what it is. Unbridled housing speculation is not only wrong because it is unfair and shafts many who may wind up on the wrong side of any given housing bubble. It's also wrong because its acceleration contributes directly to ever-increasing homelessness. It's not sustainable and it's literally injuring and killing our unhoused neighbors. Even if you don't care about them, realize their treatment is a prologue for what's in store for all of us. As Syracuse University's Don Mitchell observes, "The movements and lives of homeless people are continuously regulated to keep public city space primed for capital accumulation. The kinds of regulatory experiments on the homeless that order the streets and make them safe for capital accumulation implicate all of us and can criminalize us." Mitchell concludes that our homeless neighbors are "an indicator species, as those who are most vulnerable are targeted first.... If it works to order and manage homeless people and we accept it, then it works to manage us and we accept it."[7]

At the clean intersection of the personal and the structural lies the myths bound up in homeownership as proxy for full citizenship, and the corollary, unquestioned evolution of housing as the main investment vehicle for individual wealth creation. And yet mainstream public political debate is virtually silent on the central role housing commodification plays in accelerating wealth inequality and homelessness. To crib Brad Pitt in *Fight Club*, "The first rule of capitalism is, you do not talk about capitalism." Not directly, anyway. Not with the degree of honesty that reveals that American homeownership, where the main goal is equity, places most buyers on the ground floor of a high-stakes Ponzi scheme. Revealing the roots of these myths can help to harness "defiant resistance"—with a revolutionary aspiration of a more hopeful, vibrant America. Decent, affordable housing for all is a keystone to realizing that dream.

## THE ABIDING TAINT OF CALVINISM

In chapter 3, we discussed Calvinism's enduring imprint on our national narrative. There's an essential throughline of Calvinism via the British Puritans, who transplanted their values to colonial America.

They were called Puritans because they wanted to purify the evils of the Catholic Church. Although people often confuse Puritans and the earlier-arriving Pilgrims, they were two distinct populations. Unlike the Pilgrims, who were more radical separatists (seeking to abandon any relationship with their native Church of England), the Puritans hewed to Calvin's call to reform the Protestant Church from within. They were also, owing to the precepts of Calvinism, a self-selecting group with more substantial means and, as historian David Roos puts it, a "divinely ordained arrogance." They traveled to the New World in greater numbers (roughly one thousand in their first voyage in 1630, versus a scant hundred Pilgrims on the *Mayflower* in 1620) with their sights set on investment opportunities and expansion. And expand they did: unlike the Pilgrims, who lost nearly half of their original passengers within a year of arrival, the Puritan ranks grew to over twenty thousand within a decade of making landfall.[8]

Our nation's most durable narrative is the meritocracy canonized in the "American Dream." It manifests today—true to its Calvinistic roots—as excuse to blame poor people for their lot, rather than tackling the structural forces that contribute overwhelmingly to their destitution. The University of Michigan's Matt McManus, in his powerful 2023 examination, "How the Right Rationalizes Inequity: Demanding Reverence and Naturalizing Injustice," delves into the essential reactive nature of the conservative right, who consistently pump "the breaks on progressive ideas."[9] Importantly, McManus digs deeper historically, separating out two distinct theses driving conservative thought—and in the process reveals how the naturally reactive Right succeeds in pushing the progressive Left into a defensive (and debilitating) rhetorical crouch.

The first is *sublimation*, which "entails the association of transcendent qualities with particular persons or whole classes in order to justify their superior status and wealth and their power over others." McManus sums up sublimation's foremost legacy as getting us "to perceive either an individual or an elite group as worthy of deference."

Although McManus does not reference Calvinism directly in analyzing sublimation, its imprint is undeniable. Remember, the base tenet of Calvinism is that God chooses a few people—"the select"—for salvation, while the rest of humanity is condemned to damnation. Faith, rather than good works (action), is the key to redemption. The reflection of God's favor on the chosen is manifested in worldly wealth. Calvinism's two-tiered system privileging a class of spiritual elites provided the historical matrix for the Right's advancement of the sublimation principle.

McManus emphasizes the mystification effect of sublimation, noting the respect and awe it spawns: "When attached to persons and institutions sublime qualities are intended to induce a sense of overpowering reverence and to diminish whatever confidence ordinary people have in their own capacity to critically assess those in power."

The second major (more recent) premise of conservative thought, in McManus's analysis, is *naturalism*. While sublimation's investiture of elite privilege endures, its constructs are easily exposed. But naturalism follows a more straightforward and seemingly undeniable argument: people are by nature endowed with varied intelligence and gifts; therefore, it's only natural that in a capitalistic system, those with superior gifts with have greater means to profit. Naturalism holds that the economic stratification that emerges in capitalism is inevitable and entirely justified, as McManus notes, because it's "not artificially imposed, but instead reflect[s] natural differences of talent."

The effect is intentionally crippling: "The naturalization thesis is intended to generate a feeling of resignation: *This is just how things are, so we'd all better get used to it.*"[10] I would argue that it's best understood as an extension of Calvinism, in which inequities of wealth, status, and power all reflect God's affirmation of those He's selected for redemption.

Naturalism presents a much harder myth for progressives to debunk on two fronts. First, it clothes itself as a neutral presentation of facts. Perhaps most pernicious, as Samuel Moyn asserts in *Liberalism Against Itself* (distilled by McManus), is "how many Cold War liberals internalized conservative arguments about the impossibility of radically improving society because of the natural imperfections of human nature and knowledge." This mutated "American liberalism from a revolutionary creed into a defensive one, *as many liberals gradually turned against the ambitions of the New Deal and the Great Society.*"[11] (Emphasis mine.)

Critically, for many from Obama's generation, the liberalism of our Cold War youth seeded an internalization and tacit acceptance of baseline conservative tenets. "It's taken a long time to start weaning American liberalism off them," concludes McManus.

Sublimation and naturalization together are effective in cloaking conservatism's reactionary, obstructionist core, which, let's face it, has proven unnervingly successful in blocking any attempt by the Left to improve living conditions and odds of success for the lower classes. In fact, their combination is the bedrock of the Right's justification for the unlimited concentration of wealth and power. As author Sean Illing put it, "It's an attempt to neutralize the ambition to improve the world."[12]

## DEREGULATION VIA REZONING AND THE ASCENT OF YIMBYS

Individualism and capitalism form another essential American coupling—success in the US almost universally rests on the assumption of being self-made. Activist Mia Birdsong has written extensively on this nexus and recently commented, "What capitalism has done is, it has inserted the exchange of money. I didn't, you know, get together with a bunch of my friends and build my home. I paid for it."[13] The "go-it-alone" ethos of American capitalism has magnified ramifications for housing and homelessness. There's a tremendous difference between hungry and fed, between naked and clothed, between housed and homeless. But the sheer cost of housing makes bridging the gap between these last two singularly challenging. Marcuse and Madden note that "many people, especially poor and working-class households, need more housing than they can afford. But this form of need does not register with purely profit-oriented developers." Yet even the smartest and most progressive economic theorists (Stiglitz and Chomsky, to name two) in the end settle for arguing for greater access for lower classes to join the homeownership class—essentially building more on-ramps to a flawed and failed system. It is perhaps the most disturbing example of the Left internalizing assumptions from the Right.

The relative cost of housing makes the corresponding incentive to game its development for maximum profit unparalleled. The result is dramatic rises in land values in North American coastal cities—and correspondingly high rates of homelessness in these areas. Patrick Condon of the University of British Columbia puts the extraordinary rise in land values in context: "Since 2010 the value of America's urban land has roughly doubled, or increased in value by $15 trillion. Yearly increases in American GDP were in the range of $1 trillion, meaning that the annual increase in urban land value substantially exceeded total annual GDP growth. Of this $1.5 trillion annual increase in urban land value over 80 percent was attributable to the increase in the value of existing housing."[14]

The Left's embrace of more "on-ramps" for moderate- and lower-class Americans to buy into our highly financialized homeownership scheme is not only a dicey bet for our struggling neighbors; it's also propping up the core cause of modern mass homelessness. Today's hyper-commodification need not be the default setting for housing. Taking active, doable steps to increase nonmarket housing is the only way out of this capitalistic cannibalism. As we saw in the previous chapter, Vienna did it a hundred years ago, and the legacy of that bold gambit is extraordinary. Its success is unassailable. More recently, Vancouver set out in the 1980s to create thousands of nonmarket limited equity co-op projects, which (along with other social housing ventures) now comprise fully 15 percent of its total housing units. If those efforts had continued apace, Condon estimates that over 30 percent of Vancouver housing stock would be nonmarket today.[15]

Remarkably, a vocal contingent of American activists has emerged arguing that commodification has not gone far enough, and that the true solution to the housing crisis (and, by extension, mass homelessness) is complete deregulation of zoning and land use regulations. This group, known as YIMBYs (Yes in My Back Yard), also argues for upzoning, or allowing all land parcels to be developed as densely as possible. In a *New*

*York Times* op-ed, economist Ed Glaeser argued that in order to make cities more affordable, we need to "reduce the barriers to building and unleash the cranes…end the dizzying array of land use regulations… that increase cost." Well-funded by real estate titans and tech bros, YIMBY groups are adamant that giving developers a freer hand would miraculously solve housing affordability death spiral. Marcuse and Madden note YIMBY's echo of the Reagan rallying cry "Government is not the solution to our problem; government is the problem," noting that for YIMBYs, it's "The hyper-commodification of housing is not the problem; it is the solution." What's lost in their simplistic analysis is the fact that significant upzoning without creating nonmarket housing ensures an outright giveaway to speculative landholders. A laissez-faire approach to upzoning is perilous, as Condon's research proves: "Doubling allowable density without the demand for affordability streams public benefit to private hands and effectively excludes nonprofit developers from the land market." Condon highlights Cambridge, Massachusetts, as a model to follow. In October 2020, Cambridge granted nonmarket developers "double the current zone density" provided they "supply 100 percent [permanently] affordable housing."[16] This type of creative alternative path is essential, given historically high land values, which wealthy investors are both creating and actively exploiting.

In early 2024, New York City's unprecedented glut of unused office space—a consequence of the pandemic-era move to remote work—shows signs of a classic real estate bubble in the making. It is teetering on the brink of potential collapse, which could be catastrophic for the national economy.[17] While all-in conversion of office buildings to housing might sound like a no-brainer, not all buildings are suitable for such conversion. Older buildings are far more likely to be readily converted, as they were designed with templates similar to housing: "Both share a rule of thumb that no interior space be more than 25 to 30 feet from a window that opens," explain Emily Badger and Larry Buchanan of the *New York Times*.[18]

Market conditions surrounding any potential implosion of office space values—and the associated ripple effects across the nation's economy—are changing at a rapid and often unpredictable clip. For years, one New York City real estate titan, Vornado Realty Trust, funneled massive campaign donations to former governor Andrew Cuomo and has subsequently lined the pockets of Governor Kathy Hochul and Mayor Eric Adams. Vornado's largess ensured the two politicians would support its proposal to construct eight colossal office towers around Penn Station, under the guise of producing (unspecified) increased tax revenue to finance badly needed renovations of the Western Hemisphere's busiest transit hub. With the expected assistance of the State via eminent domain, Vornado's plan included razing entire blocks of existing affordable housing (many, if not most, home to elderly tenants), small businesses, and churches, to build office towers and help underwrite the estimated $7 to $10 billion project. Hochul and Adams clung to the inane plan, despite major blowback from fiscal watchdogs, good-government groups, and media outlets across the political spectrum that questioned core financial aspects of the scheme. Then, suddenly, in mid-2023, it was pulled from the table, not in response to public outcry or commonsense reasoning but because the market for new office space had by then evaporated.[19] The sad fact is, New York never needed Vornado's money to renovate Penn Station. Their proposed office towers likely would have yielded little in actual funds and would have left taxpayers on the hook for billions of dollars, like the recent public-private folly that is Hudson Yards, which has cost taxpayers an astonishing $309 million since 2018.[20] Because our political system is predicated on candidates raising vast sums of money, the *demands* of the elite, particularly real estate titans (our modern-day robber barons), always eclipse the *needs* of those scraping to keep a roof over their heads, let alone those with no homes.

## WHY IS NO ONE TALKING ABOUT "THE HOUSING QUESTION"?

Abraham Kazan famously remarked, "Housing should not be subject to politics. It is too basic." A significant host of activists and scholars have pushed back against Kazan's principled but simplistic view. Glyn Robbins (like me, a huge fan of Kazan) pulls no punches, writing, "[Kazan] was wrong. Housing is inherently political. The issues [Kazan faced] are a version of those faced by all forms of nonmarket housing in an economy dominated by private landlordism and property speculation."[21] Robbins, along with Marcuse and Madden, invoke the relevance of Friedrich Engels's 1872 pamphlet *The Housing Question*, which asserts housing instability is a deliberate feature of the capitalist system and offers a clear-eyed analysis of the displacement that follows waves of real estate speculation. Robbins notes, "Engels was especially scathing of the proposition that private home ownership could immunize workers from housing precarity and misery...buying a home has become a source of wealth building for many—but as Engels points out, it is inherently unstable and inequitable and directly serves the interests of the ruling class."[22]

Robbins flags a more updated, distilled version of Engels's argument, found in activist Upton Sinclair's novel *Co-op* from 1935, "It is a question of whether any co-operative can exist alongside a capitalist economy."[23] The complete lack of serious dialogue around this point reflects nonmarket housing's increasing eclipse from the Overton window. This silence is the result of liberals "internaliz[ing] conservative arguments about the impossibility of radically improving society," as described by McManus and Moyn, causing them to abandon New Deal and Great Society aspirations.

Marcuse and Madden describe the housing market as "a struggle between two unequal groups," *which is reinforced by the glaring lack of awareness surrounding its commodification in our economy.* (Emphasis mine.) They are particularly forceful on the omission of nonmarket alternatives from our contemporary political dialogue: "That the basic shape of the housing system is not on any mainstream political agenda is a sign of the power of economic and political elites to make it seem as if fundamental housing questions are basically settled....Communities are at the mercy of corporate real estate actors who know that there are currently no alternatives: either they build or no one does. This monopoly of the private sector needs to end."[24]

Rather than tinkering around the edges to maintain the status quo, any meaningful movement for housing justice must "widen the place of housing in society," writes Robbins, even as he acknowledges that, sadly, "the strength of movement necessary to challenge the norms of capitalist housing still feels a long way away."[25]

## THE ANTIDOTE TO CYNICISM: HOW TO TAKE ACTION

As we've seen, a century ago, Austria's SDAPÖ seized on worldwide financial calamity, snapping up a wide swath of businesses and empty lots, harnessing land control, and enacting progressive taxation to develop the miracle that is Vienna's vibrant, nonmarket housing system. The US today very well might be teetering on the brink of similarly cataclysmic (but potentially opportune) times. Start-up guru Reza Chowdhury recently quoted a real estate investment banker: "In New York, buildings are selling for less than the value of the land they sit on. We are seeing prices lower than they have been in 20 years in absolute dollar terms."[26] The markers of a real estate bubble are being flagged in nearly every quarter—the financial sector, the press, among government watchdogs. At this same moment, in many cities, real estate funded YIMBY groups push for unprecedented upzoning. Their simplistic "supply and demand" pablum is entirely self-serving to their real estate industry masters, drowning out the proven solution to this problem: nonmarket housing.

This is another stark example of how we are compelled to fight a ground war—to stave off a wholesale giveaway to for-profit developers via unchecked rezoning—when we could be building momentum to procure empty office buildings and other unused or underused parcels for conversion into 100 percent affordable housing. Building an authentic and flourishing movement requires manifold replication of nonmarket housing models, proven to be both humane and cost-effective.

## DREAM BIGGER

How big were the dreams of those in Vienna over a century ago, on the heels of perhaps the most brutal war in modern history? And more recently the dreams of the Finns when they committed to fund

Housing First projects at a scale that ended homelessness in their nation?

It's not that we don't know what to do. The question is: Do we have the courage to do it? Do we have the courage to admit that the hyper-financialization of housing has created a permanent, growing class of precariously housed and homeless Americans? Can we not only dream big enough about a different way, but take the steps necessary to get us there? Through dint of effective advocacy, healthcare as a human right has been embraced, if not yet fully realized. Housing too is a human right every bit as valid as healthcare. In fact, at its core, housing is the most essential form of healthcare. Activists' success in pushing universal access to healthcare into the foreground of mainstream political debate serves as an inspiration and helps provide a roadmap for our work ahead.

Supporting efforts to increase the supply of your local version of nonmarket housing is the first and foremost thing you can do to effectively combat modern mass homelessness. As the folks at Inequality. org summarize perfectly, "We must protect land and housing from the vagaries of the market by creating community land trusts, cooperative housing and mutual [public] housing on a large scale."[27] They underscore several successful models in wealthy nations, including Sweden, which built hundreds of thousands of limited equity co-ops and public housing units after World War II. Beyond demanding government investments to that end, the calls to action here are manifold, but can be grouped easily into two parts:

*First: Get wise.* Arm yourself with information. Be an advocate for commonsense solutions both nationally and locally. Hannah Arendt, in her masterwork, *The Origins of Totalitarianism*, warns against taking "refuge in cynicism." Megan Garber aptly links Arendt's theory to the current unrelenting barrage of right-wing misinformation: "Propaganda, pumped out as a fog that never lifts, can make people so weary and cynical that they stop trying to distinguish between fact and fiction in the first place: everything as possible, nothing as true."[28] Author and journalist Johann Hari identifies cynicism as both a default reaction to the attention-scattering effects of social media and as an existential threat to democracy around the world.[29] But this very intentional, continual overload of patently false narratives from the Right (as examined earlier) is increasingly *the* central design of their plan—not a bug or a symptom or a by-product—and it has proven sadly successful in distracting from any honest dialogue to sort out best practices or legitimate ways forward.

Jay Rosen, New York University professor of journalism, put it best, coining the phrase "flooding the zone with shit," aka "the firehose of falsehood."[30] This destructive torrent is a daily constant, especially as it relates to homelessness in the US. As I write this, yesterday's example was a *Wall Street Journal* article titled "California Spent $17 Billion on Homelessness. It's Not Working."[31] The article includes several facts that undercut the headline, prominently featuring a woman who works two jobs and still cannot afford housing. That woman, by the end of the article, finally finds a landlord willing to accept her Section 8 voucher and is now safely housed with her adorable dog. The comment section is predictably packed with thousands of subscriber missives, almost all ascribing homelessness to personal failure and demanding that we "lock these people back up" in jails and hospitals and administer forced treatment. A far more accurate headline would have been "California Spent $17 Billion on Homelessness: The Only Thing That Works Is Housing." What are the odds of seeing *that* in a Murdoch prestige broadsheet?

As Nietzsche put it, "They muddy the water, to make it seem deep"— so it's imperative to foreground essential truths.[32] Whether you're in the digital public square or in conversation with friends or new acquaintances, you can push back on myths surrounding homelessness and reframe the crisis with basic facts:

- Homelessness is a housing problem. Places with far higher rates of the pathologies typically associated with homelessness—crime and drug use—have lower rates of homelessness than expensive coastal cities because they have cheaper and more available housing. Authors Gregg Colburn and Clayton

Page Aldern have pulled everything you need to know about this central truth on their website: https://homelessnesshousingproblem.com.

- A person with mental illness or substance-use issues is far more likely to be housed than homeless.
- Overwhelming numbers of studies show that Housing First models lead to better outcomes. They are also cheaper than expensive emergency interventions, and they give chronically homeless people a better chance at sobriety and successful engagement in mental health programs.

The example of misinformation in the *Wall Street Journal* is just one in the seemingly limitless spate of well-funded, targeted right-wing efforts to relegate undesirable people into the carceral system. Efforts to discredit social programs have lately found wider reception, not because people are stupid. People are smart. But even smart people grow weary as elected officials at every level devote endless energy to distracting their constituents from their own incompetence; the result is public cynicism toward any increased social investments, even ones that have been proven to succeed. The Right continues "flooding the zone," writing template laws for cities and states to criminalize survival behavior, proactively pushing the narrative that people are homeless by choice and insisting that treatment must be a precursor to permanent housing. Meanwhile, the Democrats who are in charge of coastal cities and states with high homeless rates have stepped up efforts to sweep homeless Americans from sight—see New York mayor Eric Adams's court motion to undo the forty-year-old right-to-shelter consent decree.

It's imperative not to resign yourself to the paralyzing, cynical view that nothing will really make a difference. The ceaseless bombardment of misinformation, left unchecked, will leave you numb, like Dorothy in the poppy fields of *The Wizard of* Oz—exhausted, yearning for the escape of sleep. Using the instance of Adams's attacks on the right to shelter as one example, ground yourself in the basic, indisputable takeaway:

"Doing away with the right-to-shelter will make New York look a whole lot more like California by relegating thousands more adults and children to the streets—and no one wants that." Period. Full stop. Becoming conversant in the basics of homelessness and housing policy, especially as it impacts your surrounding community, can make a tremendous difference. You can decide where you feel comfortable sharing your base of knowledge: your family, your friends, your kid's school, your place of worship...you name it.

*Second: Seek out opportunities to help your unhoused neighbors directly.* If you live in an urban or mixed-income suburban neighborhood, chances are there are kids at your child's school, or families at your place of worship, who are struggling. Giving money via nonprofit organizations can be a good investment, if you do some basic research to confirm their overhead is low and that most (sometimes all) of your donation will make it into the hands of those most in need.* But I also don't shy away from giving directly to people on the street, in grocery stores, or on public transit. In New York, it might take the form of carrying extra MetroCards preloaded with a week's worth of transit or even just a couple of trips (essentially six dollars for two rides). At fast-food places or grocery stores, you might purchase a couple of gift cards. Having them on hand makes it easier and less awkward to reach out to someone you sense is struggling. It could be a mom with a child or two, standing back from the line at a fast-food place trying to figure out what she can afford to buy to best feed her family. Or a person asking for funds outside a grocery store. Your slipping them a small dollar denomination in the form of a gift card will likely be the highlight of their day. Once you start to make small entreaties into your neighborhood soup kitchen, pantry, or shelter, you'll be amazed how things start to click on both a personal and political level.

---

* Charity Navigator provides access to not-for-profit organizations' tax filings (Form 990s), with breakdowns of overhead versus programmatic/advocacy expenditures. It's a great place to start: https://www.charitynavigator.org.

## RADICAL JUSTICE IS ROOTED IN RADICAL LOVE

George Orwell's *Down and Out in Paris and London* endures as a masterpiece because he effortlessly—and without a whiff of sentimentality—humanizes his fellow travelers and coworker friends he made while living rough in 1928. This is the specificity that connects transcendent writers—Orwell, Berger, Dorothy Day—and lights the way for a revolution in the way we view each other. He ends by acknowledging the complex humanity shared by us all: "I should like to know people like Mario and Paddy and Bill the moocher, not from casual encounters, but intimately; I should like to understand what really goes on in the souls of *plongeurs* and tramps and Embankment sleepers." Orwell concludes, "I can point to one or two things I have definitely learned by being hard up. I shall never again think that all tramps are drunken scoundrels, nor expect a beggar to be grateful when I give him a penny."

Getting to know hundreds (and yet only a relative handful) of homeless Americans over the years has brought me moments of lasting grace. These are each gifts, in and of themselves. Allowing oneself the opportunity to open to that grace is the first step toward radical change. It provides the most essential entryway to understanding—in one's bones—that we're really all in this together.

John Berger reflected on the ubiquity of homeless people with mental illness living in public spaces in 1991, noting that, although we often feel "coerced into 'playing' the role of spectator," it's imperative to reframe that default:

> In 1942, the philosopher Simone Weil wrote: "The love of the neighbor, made of creative attention, is analogous to genius." ... "The love of our neighbor in all its fullness," she said, "simply means being able to ask, 'What are you going through?' It is knowing that the sufferer exists, not only as a unit in a collection, or a specimen in the social category labeled 'unfortunate,' but as a man, exactly like us, who was one day stamped with a special mark by affliction. For this reason it is enough, but it is indispensable, to know how to look at him in a certain way."[33]

He offers the most sublime yet practical advice for effecting revolutionary change alongside our homeless neighbors: "To forget oneself, even for an instant, in order to identify with a stranger and fully recognize him, defies necessity. And this moment of defiance, however small and discreet...liberates a power that cannot be measured by any scale in the natural world. This defiance is not a means, and it has no end."

## "SOMETHING GROTESQUE AND SPECIFIC TO OUR TIME IS BLANKETING US"

These are bleak times as the ranks of unhoused Americans continue to swell, amidst this four-decade, still-unfolding catastrophe. But, as writer Sunny Singh recently put it, "despair is not solidarity. Bearing witness can leave us feeling powerless and hopeless. Find whatever it takes to keep hope burning bright. Despair is not an option. Despair is not solidarity."[34]

It's essential to find inspiration that resonates with you personally. Along with writings by Michael Sorkin, Dorothy Day, Orwell, and Berger, I often find myself returning to the work of filmmaker Charlie Kaufman, including an extraordinary speech he delivered at BAFTA in 2011. "Something grotesque and specific to our time is blanketing us," he noted.[35] It's worth quoting a very short portion of his remarks intact, because he so perfectly captures the corrosive undertow of creeping capitalism:

> It's...ludicrous to believe that—at the very least—mass distraction and manipulation is not convenient for the people who are in charge. People are starving. They may not know it because they're being fed mass-produced garbage. The packaging is colorful and loud, but it's produced in the same factories that make Pop-Tarts and iPads, by people sitting around thinking, "What can we do to get people to buy more of these?" And they're very good at their jobs.... *They're selling you something.* And the world is built on this now. Politics and government are built on this, corporations are built on this. Interpersonal relationships are built on this. And we're starving, all of us, and we're killing each other, and we're hating each other, and we're

calling each other liars and evil because it's all become marketing and we want to win because we're lonely and empty and scared and *we're led to believe winning will change all that. But there is no winning."* (Emphases mine.)

Orwell distilled the inevitable monopolistic drift of capitalism, noting, "The trouble with competitions is that somebody wins them."[36] Left unsaid is someone also loses. And homeless people are perhaps the most visible among capitalism's many losers. Kaufman takes an even deeper cut with, "There is no winning," reflecting the existential dread when measuring one's worth against any internalized capitalist scale of victory: money, land, beauty, fame. No amount of these will ever be enough to fill the hole if that's the one you've chosen to dig for yourself. Connection, empathy, sharing your authentic self—these are the things that abide and offer promise of genuine fulfillment. Giving our poorest neighbors the chance to realize the same is predicated on them having the privacy, security, and sanctity of a modest home of one's own.

Most importantly, Kaufman insists, "Don't allow yourself to be tricked into thinking that the way things are is the way the world must work and that in the end selling is what everyone must do. Try not to."

## KEEPING A TENDER HEART

In the end, I think the biggest challenge is keeping a heart both open and tender.

I've noticed that when I get sick—whether it's the first pang of certain illness, a flush of fever or throb in my throat—my first thought is always, "I've got to get home." I try (I'm not always mindful enough to remember, but I try) in that moment to pause and imagine for an instant what it must be like to have no home to go to. I think it's only in that fleeting moment of vulnerability, one can begin to grasp the subjection our unhoused neighbors face each and every day.

One morning long ago when dropping my son off at kindergarten, everything that could go wrong seemed to. I was running late for an important meeting. There was an almost comical torrent of rain. Our train was delayed. Finally, pushing through a wall of wind up the subway stairs, my umbrella jammed and refused to open. My mind could not have been further from my work, let alone the well-being of anyone other than the two of us in the universe.

Just then, my son squeezed my hand quickly a couple of times and said, "I know why you're upset, Mommy."

"Why's that, lamb?" I responded, absentmindedly.

"Because today is *not* a good day to be homeless."

# ACKNOWLEDGMENTS

First and foremost, I have unending gratitude for the thousands of homeless people, and those living precariously (both young and old), I've met and worked alongside over the past three decades. Your friendship, resolve, and spirit inspire me each day.

Catherine Tung of Beacon Press first approached me to write this book and has been the most extraordinary editor I could have hoped for. Thank you for sticking by this rookie author with countless hours of unfailing guidance and good cheer. You have the keenest intellect and sharpest eyes—and always kept me trained on our shared vision of transformative change. Also instrumental was Emily Dolbear, the Walter Payton of line editing (believe me, there is no higher compliment), along with Beacon Press's managing editor, Susan Lumenello.

Of the many extraordinary people who have helped to advocate for the right to housing for our homeless neighbors, there are a couple I must single out, because they have shaped my work and ethos so deeply. For many years, the great Peter Jennings spent untold hours publicly championing the work of the Coalition for the Homeless but also privately volunteered behind the scenes delivering hot meals on the streets and provided an endless source of sage counsel to me. Peter's unfailing good humor, audacity, street smarts, and optimism continue to inspire me and animate my work, nearly twenty years after his death.

Margaret Morton was a professor of photography at the Cooper Union for the Advancement of Science and Art. She spent two decades engaging homeless New Yorkers living rough and documenting their handmade communities through her exquisite photography. Margaret continually welcomed me to accompany her on countless days and nights—from shantytowns in Lower Manhattan to communities dwelling in abandoned underground railroad tunnels uptown. Margaret's quiet, respectful, effortless involvement with our neighbors taught me that humility and an open heart are the true path to affirming our shared dignity.

The late author Paul Auster and his wife, Siri Hustvedt, welcomed me into their own home when I first started working with homeless people. Paul was unendingly generous with his time and advice—writing heartfelt pieces for our newsletter and, alongside his daughter Sophie, delivering dinner to our neighbors on the streets. Paul's innate sense of humility and sly wit inspired (and continues to inspire) me in so many ways.

Finally, my unending thanks to my family, friends, and colleagues. My late husband, John, taught me firsthand (among *so many* more personal things) the gift of limitless compassion for our neighbors without homes. Tremendous gratitude also to my parents, especially my father, Joseph, for his sharp wit and loving devotion to St. Francis. My siblings, Joseph, Michael, Margaret, SallyAnn, Patrick, Brian, and Paul, have given me enduring love and support. And to my son, Quinn: thank you for being a true delight of a person, as well as for all your advice and feedback for this book!

Enormous thanks to my colleagues working to end homelessness over the years, especially Patrick Markee, Judith Goldiner, Josh Goldfein, Tony Taylor, Beverly McEntarfer, Mark Horvath, Keith Summa, David Greenberg, Steve Banks, Kim Hopper, and Mary Ellen Hombs. And finally, thank you to my friends Joan Alker, John Clegg, David Rooney, Ivan Chittick, Patrick McMullan, Brenda Levin, Richard Klein, and Kayce Freed Jennings and my cousin Linda Higgins McCloy—all of whom gave me essential feedback and the encouragement I needed to bring this project to fruition.

# NOTES

**PREFACE**

1. Robert Ellwood, *The Politics of Myth: A Study of C. G. Jung, Mircea Eliade, and Joseph Campbell* (Albany: State University of New York Press, 1999).

2. John Black, "The Meaning of the Word Myth," *Ancient Origins*, August 30, 2012, https://www.ancient-origins.net/human-origins/meaning-word-myth -0061.

**INTRODUCTION**

1. "The Aims and Means of the Catholic Worker," Catholic Worker Movement, from the *Catholic Worker*, May 2019, https://catholicworker.org/aims-and -means.

2. New York Constitution, Article XVII, § 1.

3. Pierce Brown, *Golden Son* (New York: Del Rey, 2015).

**CHAPTER 1: A BRIEF HISTORY OF HOMELESSNESS**

1. Mara Gay, "Why New York Needs a Right to Shelter," *New York Times*, October 15, 2023, https://www.nytimes.com/2023/10/15/opinion/new-york-homeless -shelters.html.

2. Peter Applebome, "Want to Be in Pictures? It Seems Almost Anyone Can, for Five Seconds," *New York Times*, February 2, 1999, https://www.nytimes.com /1999/02/02/movies/want-to-be-in-pictures-it-seems-almost-anyone-can-for -five-seconds.html.

3. Pete Hamill, "How to Save the Homeless and Ourselves," *New York Magazine*, September 20, 1993.

4. June B. Kress, "Homeless Fatigue Syndrome: The Backlash Against the Crime of Homelessness in the 1990s," *Journal of Social Justice* 21, no. 3 (Fall 1994): 85–108, https://www.jstor.org/stable/i29766818.

5. Chris Spolar and Marcia Slacum Greene, "Mitch Snyder Found Hanged in CCNV Shelter," *Washington Post*, July 6, 1990.

6. Malcolm Gladwell, "N.Y. Hopes to Help Homeless by Reviving Single Room Occupancy Hotels," *Los Angeles Times*, April 25, 1993.

7. Thomas Byrnes, "Nurseries of Crime," *North American Review* 149, no. 394 (September 1889): 355–62, https://www.jstor.org/stable/25101862.

8. Jacob Riis, *How the Other Half Lives: Studies Among the Tenements of New York* (1890) (New York: W. W. Norton, 2012).

9. "Thomas Byrnes, New York's Premier Detective," *17th Street*, February 5, 2016, retrieved December 18, 2023, from http://17thstreet.net/2016/02/05/thomas-byrnes.

10. Riis, *How the Other Half Lives*.

11. Paul Groth, *Living Downtown: The History of Residential Hotels in the United States* (Berkeley: University of California Press, 1999), 203–33, 238–46.

12. Brian J. Sullivan and Jonathan Burke, "Single-Room Occupancy Housing in New York City: The Origins and Dimensions of a Crisis," *CUNY Law Review* 17, no. 1 (Winter 2013): 113, https://academicworks.cuny.edu/clr/vol17/iss1/5.

13. Gladwell, "N.Y. Hopes to Help Homeless by Reviving Single Room Occupancy Hotels."

14. Sullivan and Burke, "Single-Room Occupancy Housing in New York City."

15. Sullivan and Burke, "Single-Room Occupancy Housing in New York City."

16. Anthony J. Blackburn, *Single Room Living in New York City: A Report* (New York: Department of Housing Preservation and Development, 1996).

17. Sullivan and Burke, "Single-Room Occupancy Housing in New York City."

18. Sullivan and Burke, "Single-Room Occupancy Housing in New York City."

19. Interview with Anthony Blackburn, in Dennis Hevesi, "Building Homes for the Single Homeless," *New York Times*, April 25, 1999.

20. Sydney H. Schanberg, "New York; Arson and J-51," *New York Times*, July 20, 1982.

21. Joe Flood, "Why the Bronx Burned," *New York Post*, May 16, 2010.

22. Robert Caro, *The Power Broker: Robert Moses and the Fall of New York* (New York: Vintage, 1975); Allyson Ryan, "The Legacy of Robert Moses," *Fordham Political Review*, December 1, 2018.

23. In her documentary *Decade of Fire*, which told the story of the fires in the South Bronx, Vivian Vásquez Irizarry reports, "They chopped up the apartments, squeezing more people into smaller spaces," describing measures taken by speculators to crowd as many people as possible into the old buildings. The speculators cared little about the housing conditions, only about the profit they could generate. *Decade of Fire*, dir. Vivian Vásquez Irizarry, 2020, https://decadeoffire.com; https://www.youtube.com/watch?v=QpbIW_OBu0A.

24. Flood, "Why the Bronx Burned."

25. Flood, "Why the Bronx Burned."

26. Salman Rushdie, "What Kurt Vonnegut's 'Slaughterhouse-Five' Tells Us Now," *New Yorker*, June 13, 2019.

27. Daniel Patrick Moynihan, Memorandum to President Nixon, January 16, 1970, https://www.nixonlibrary.gov/sites/default/files/virtuallibrary/documents/jul10/53.pdf.

28. Peter Kihss, "'Benign Neglect' on Race Is Proposed by Moynihan," *New York Times*, March 1, 1970, https://www.nytimes.com/1970/03/01/archives/benign-neglect-on-race-is-proposed-by-moynihan-moynihan-urges.html.

29. Deborah Wallace and Rodrick Wallace, *A Plague on Your Houses: How New York Was Burned Down and National Public Health Crumbled* (Brooklyn, NY: Verso, 1998).

30. Deborah Wallace and Rodrick Wallace, *Death and Destruction by Algorithm: A Mask for Human Rights Abuses*, April 24, 2018, Christian Regenhard Center for Emergency Response Studies, https://christianregenhardcenter.org/wp-content/uploads/2019/01/wallace-death-and-destruction-by-algorithm-04282018.pdf.

31. Joe Flood, *The Fires: How a Computer Formula, Big Ideas, and the Best of Intentions Burned Down New York City—and Determined the Future of Cities* (New York: Penguin Random House, 2011).

32. Flood, *The Fires*.

33. Joseph B. Treaster, "20 Percent Rise in Fires Is Adding to Decline of South Bronx," *New York Times*, May 18, 1975, https://www.nytimes.com/1975/05/18/archives/20-rise-in-fires-is-adding-to-decline-of-south-bronx-arson-rates.html.

34. Bench Ansfield, "Edifice Complex," *Jewish Currents* (Winter 2022), https://jewishcurrents.org/edifice-complex.

35. Sullivan and Burke, "Single-Room Occupancy Housing in New York City."

36. Schanberg, "New York; Arson and J-51."

37. Irizarry, *Decade of Fire*.

38. Andrew Rice, "Why Run a Slum If You Can Make More Money Housing the Homeless?" *New York Magazine*, November 30, 2013.

39. Associated Press, "Landlords Forfeit Ownership of Buildings to Homeless," June 18, 1987.

40. Sullivan and Burke, "Single-Room Occupancy Housing in New York City."

41. US Census Bureau and New York City Housing and Vacancy Survey 2002.

42. Blackburn, *Single Room Living in New York City*.

43. Noam Chomsky interview, *Requiem for the American Dream*, 2016, available at https://www.youtube.com/watch?v=hZnuc-Fv_Tc; transcript: https://www.mediaed.org/transcripts/Requiem-for-the-American-Dream-Transcript.pdf.

44. Chomsky, *Requiem for the American Dream*.

45. Chomsky, *Requiem for the American Dream*.

46. Alan Greenspan, *Monetary Policy Report to the Congress Pursuant to the Full Employment and Balanced Growth Act of 1978*, https://www.federalreserve.gov/boarddocs/hh/2000/february/fullreport.pdf.

47. Jeff Nilsson, "Why Did Henry Ford Double His Minimum Wage?" *Saturday Evening Post*, January 3, 2014.

48. Henry Ford, *Today and Tomorrow* (1926) (New York: Routledge, 1988).

49. Chomsky, *Requiem for the American Dream*.

50. "The Savings and Loan Crisis and Its Relationship to Banking," in *History of the Eighties*, Federal Deposit Insurance Corporation, https://www.fdic.gov/bank/historical/history/167_188.pdf.

51. Chomsky, *Requiem for the American Dream*.

52. Franklin D. Roosevelt, "On Moving Forward to Greater Freedom and Greater Security," radio address, September 30, 1934, http://docs.fdrlibrary.marist .edu/093034.html.

53. Leilani Farha, "Statement from UN Special Rapporteur on the Right to Adequate Housing," UN.org, March 26, 2019.

54. Gay, "Why New York Needs a Right to Shelter."

55. John Berger, "Keeping a Rendezvous," *The Brick Reader*, 1991.

56. John Berger, *Bento's Sketchbook* (New York: Pantheon, 2011).

## CHAPTER 2: THE ROOTS OF AMERICAN HOMELESSNESS

1. Michael Klarman, *The Framers' Coup: The Making of the United States Constitution* (New York: Oxford University Press, 2016).

2. Peter Linebaugh, Address to the House of Commons, November 20, 2007, *Counterpunch*, https://www.counterpunch.org/2017/11/20/on-the-800th -anniversary-of-the-charter-of-the-forest.

3. Linebaugh, Address to the House of Commons.

4. Noam Chomsky, "How the Magna Carta Became a Minor Carta, Part 1," *The Guardian*, July 24, 2012, https://www.theguardian.com/commentisfree/2012 /jul/24/magna-carta-minor-carta-noam-chomsky.

5. Edgell Rickword, *A Handbook of Freedom: A Record of English Democracy Through Twelve Centuries* (London: Lawrence & Wishart, 1939).

6. Percy Bysshe Shelley, *Declaration of Rights*, 1812, in *The Devil's Walk*, ed. Donald H. Reiman and Neil Fraistat, online resource (College Park: University of Maryland, 2000).

7. William Morris, "Useful Work Versus Useless Toil," 1884, William Morris Internet Archive, https://www.marxists.org/archive/morris/works/1884/useful .htm.

8. Jeanette M. Neeson, "'Commons' Sense: The Failure and Success of British Commons. Property and Commons," *HAL Journal of Open Science* (April 2013), https://hal.science/hal-03380586/document.

9. Karl Marx, "Debates on Law on Thefts of Wood," *Rheinische Zeitung*, 1842, https://territorialmasquerades.net/marx-law-on-thefts-of-wood.

10. Marx, "Debates on Law on Thefts of Wood."

11. Chomsky, "How the Magna Carta Became a Minor Carta."

12. Eula Biss, "The Theft of the Commons," *New Yorker*, June 8, 2022.

13. Biss, "The Theft of the Commons."

14. Neeson, "Commons' Sense."

15. Biss, "The Theft of the Commons."

16. L. P. Curtis Jr., "Landlord Responses to the Irish Land War, 1879–87," *Éire-Ireland* 38, no. 3 (2003): 134–88, Project MUSE, https://doi.org/10.1353/eir .2003.0007.

17. Kurt Aland, *A History of Christianity, Vol. 2.* (Philadelphia: Fortress Press, 1986).

18. Joseph Pohle, "Justification," *The Catholic Encyclopedia, Vol. 8: Infamy-Lapparent* (New York: Robert Appleton Co., 1910).

19. Max Weber, *The Protestant Ethic and the Spirit of Capitalism* (London: Unwin Hyman, 1930), https://www.marxists.org/reference/archive/weber/protestant-ethic.

20. Max Weber, Peter R. Baehr, and Gordon C. Wells, *The Protestant Ethic and the "Spirit" of Capitalism and Other Writings* (New York: Penguin, 2002).

21. Jacek Tittenbrun, "Spirit of Capitalism: Weber, Grossman and Marx," *World Scientific News* 70, no. 1 (2017), https://worldscientificnews.com/spirit-of-capitalism-weber-grossman-and-marx.

22. Ron Shaffer, "Stealing Our Time," *Washington Post*, March 10, 1994.

23. William P. Quigley, "Five Hundred Years of English Poor Laws, 1349–1834: Regulating the Working and Nonworking Poor," *Akron Law Review*, July 2015, https://ideaexchange.uakron.edu/cgi/viewcontent.cgi?article=1471&context=akronlawreview.

24. Michael Coburn, "English Legal History and Materials—Statues of Laborers," Columbia Law School, September 25, 2014, https://moglen.law.columbia.edu/twiki/bin/view/EngLegalHist/StatuteofLabourers.

25. Marilyn Sunderman, "Compassion in Action: Reflections on Matthew 25," Sisters of Mercy, https://www.sistersofmercy.org/compassion-in-action-reflections-on-matthew-25, January 23, 2017. "In Matthew 25, Jesus focuses on the works of mercy as the criteria of the Last Judgment—the need to feed the hungry, give drink to the thirsty, clothe the naked, visit the sick and those imprisoned, shelter homeless people and bury those who have died."

26. Summary from several sites, including Voices of the Victorian Poor, "Indoor vs Outdoor Relief," https://www.victorianpoor.org/pages/indoor-vs-outdoor-relief.

27. The Most Reverend & Right Honourable Justin Welby, "Authorised Liturgy for the Coronation Rite of His Majesty King Charles III," Royal Family website, May 6, 2023, p. 16, https://www.royal.uk/sites/default/files/documents/2023–05/23–24132%20Coronation%20Liturgy_05%20May_0.pdf.

28. Anthony Vaver, *Bound with an Iron Chain: The Untold Story of How the British Transported 50,000 Convicts to Colonial America* (Westborough, MA: Pickpocket Publishing, 2011), and Anthony Vaver, *Early American Criminals: An American Newgate Calendar, Chronicling the Lives of the Most Notorious Criminal Offenders from Colonial America and the New Republic* (Westborough, MA: Pickpocket Publishing, 2014).

29. Vaver, *Bound with an Iron Chain* and *Early American Criminals*.

30. Kenneth Kusmer, *Down and Out, on the Road: The Homeless in American History* (New York: Oxford University Press, 2002).

31. Kusmer, *Down and Out, on the Road*.

32. Kusmer, *Down and Out, on the Road*.

33. John E. Hansan, "Poor Relief in Early America," VCU Social Welfare Library, 2011, https://socialwelfare.library.vcu.edu/programs/poor-relief-early-amer/#.

34. Hansan, "Poor Relief in Early America."

35. Hansan, "Poor Relief in Early America."

36. Hansan, "Poor Relief in Early America."

37. Kusmer, *Down and Out, on the Road.*

38. Kusmer, *Down and Out, on the Road.*

39. Paul Vitello, "Michael Katz, Who Challenged View of Poverty, Dies at 75," *New York Times*, September 4, 2014.

40. Peter Rossi, *Down and Out in America: The Origins of Homelessness* (Chicago: University of Chicago Press, 1991).

41. Billy G. Smith, *The "Lower Sort": Philadelphia's Laboring People, 1750–1800* (Ithaca, NY: Cornell University Press, 1994).

42. Kusmer, *Down and Out, on the Road.*

43. Theda Skocpol, *Protecting Soldiers and Mothers: The Political Origins of Social Policy in the United States* (Cambridge, MA: Harvard University Press, 1995).

44. Nels Anderson, *On Hobos and Homelessness* (1923), ed. Raffaele Rauty (Chicago: University of Chicago Press, 1998).

45. Kusmer, *Down and Out, on the Road.*

46. Kusmer, *Down and Out, on the Road.*

47. Kusmer, *Down and Out, on the Road.*

48. Michael B. Katz, "Poorhouses and the Origins of the Public Old Age Home," *Milbank Memorial Fund Quarterly. Health and Society* (Winter 1984), https://doi.org/10.2307/3349894.

49. Based on Kusmer, *Down and Out, on the Road.*

50. Anderson, *On Hobos and Homelessness.*

51. Anderson, *On Hobos and Homelessness.*

52. Anderson, *On Hobos and Homelessness.*

53. "Tramps and 'Labor,'" *New York Times*, December 23, 1886.

54. Katz, "Poorhouses and the Origins of the Public Old Age Home."

55. Katz, "Poorhouses and the Origins of the Public Old Age Home."

56. Lily Rothman, "How American Inequality in the Gilded Age Compares to Today," *Time*, February 5, 2018, https://time.com/5122375/american-inequality -gilded-age.

57. Henry George, *Progress and Poverty* (Princeton, NJ: Robert Schalken- bach Foundation, 1879).

58. Joseph Stiglitz, "Inequality and Economic Growth," *Political Quarterly*, July 2016, available at Columbia University, https://business.columbia.edu/sites /default/files-efs/imce-uploads/Joseph_Stiglitz/Inequality%20and%20Economic %20Growth_0.pdf.

59. Adam Smith, "Of the Component Parts of the Price of Commodities," book 1, chapter VI, in *The Wealth of Nations*, 1776, https://www.adamsmithworks .org/documents/chapter-vi-of-the-component-parts-of-the-price-of -commodities.

60. David Ricardo, *On the Principles of Political Economy and Taxation* (London: John Murray, Albemarle-Street, 1817).

61. Patrick Condon, "Density, Affordability & the 'Hungry Dogs' of Land Price Speculation," *The Planning Report*, February 18, 2021, https://www .planningreport.com/2021/02/18/patrick-condon-density-affordability-hungry -dogs-land-price-speculation.

62. "Bonus Expeditionary Forces March on Washington," US National Park Service, https://www.nps.gov/articles/bonus-expeditionary-forces-march-on -washington.htm.

63. James Clark, "Smedley Butler's Fiery Speech to World War I Veterans Is Still Relevant Today," *Task and Purpose*, September 6, 2021, https:// taskandpurpose.com/news/marine-medal-of-honor-smedley-butler-bonus -army.

64. Clark, "Smedley Butler's Fiery Speech to World War I Veterans Is Still Relevant Today."

65. "Troops Drive Veterans from Capital; Fire Camps There and at Anacostia; 1 Killed, Scores Hurt in Day of Strife. Few Knew Whiter to Go," *New York Times*, July 29, 1932.

66. Clark, "Smedley Butler's Fiery Speech to World War I Veterans Is Still Relevant Today."

67. Gordon F. Sander, "The Last Time the U.S. Army Cleared Demonstrators from Pennsylvania Avenue," *Politico*, June 7, 2020, https://www.politico.com /news/magazine/2020/06/07/us-army-demonstrations-washington-305913.

68. Kim Hopper, "Research for What? Lessons from the Study of Homelessness," *Bulletin of the American Academy of Arts and Sciences*, May 1991, https:// doi.org/10.2307/3824677.

## CHAPTER 3: HOMELESSNESS IN THE TWENTIETH CENTURY

1. For a terrific summary of growth in institutionalized care across many sectors in the early to mid-1800s, and their subsequent dismantling in the latter half of the century, see Michael Katz's "Poorhouses and the Origins of the Public Old Age Home," *Milbank Memorial Fund Quarterly. Health and Society* (Winter 1984), https://doi.org/10.2307/3349894.

2. "Senate Debates on the Land-Grant Bill for Indigent Insane Persons," Library of Congress, February 21, 1854, https://www.disabilitymuseum.org/dhm /lib/detail.html?id=1222.

3. Graham Warder, "Franklin Pierce's 1854 Veto," *Disability History Museum*, February 10, 2014, http://www.disabilitymuseum.org/dhm/edu/essay.html?id=36.

4. "Collection: Railroad Maps, 1828 to 1900, Land Grants," Library of Congress, https://www.loc.gov/collections/railroad-maps-1828-to-1900/articles-and -essays/history-of-railroads-and-maps/land-grants.

5. "The Homestead Act of 1862," National Archives, https://www.archives .gov/education/lessons/homestead-act.

6. "The Solution to America's Mental Health Crisis Already Exists," editorial, *New York Times*, October 4, 2022, https://www.nytimes.com/2022/10/04/opinion /us-mental-health-community-centers.html.

7. "The Solution to America's Mental Health Crisis Already Exists," *New York Times*.

8. "Public Law 96–398," *Congressional Record*, October 7, 1980, https://www .congress.gov/96/statute/STATUTE-94/STATUTE-94-Pg1564.pdf; E. Fuller Torrey, "Ronald Reagan's Shameful Legacy: Violence, the Homeless, Mental Illness," *Salon*, September 29, 2013, https://www.salon.com/2013/09/29/ronald_reagans _shameful_legacy_violence_the_homeless_mental_illness.

9. *New York Times*, "The Solution to America's Mental Health Crisis Already Exists."

10. From the Appellate Division of the Supreme Court of New York, First Department Ruling, December 17, 1987: "She chooses to use the name Ms. Billie Boggs since she admires a television personality of that name," referring to a local television host, Bill Boggs. Boggs v. Health Hosps. Corp., 132 A.D.2d 340 (N.Y. App. Div. 1987).

11. Jeanie Kasindorf, "The Real Story of Billie Boggs," *New York Magazine*, May 2, 1988.

12. Laura Hirshbein, "O'Connor v. Donaldson (1975): Legal Challenges, Psychiatric Authority, and the Dangerousness Problem in Deinstitutionalization," *American Journal of Legal History* (January 23, 2023), https://academic.oup.com /ajlh/article-abstract/62/4/349/7050971.

13. Josh Barbanel, "Bellevue Unit to Aid Koch Homeless Plan," *New York Times*, September 14, 1987, https://www.nytimes.com/1987/09/14/nyregion /bellevue-unit-to-aid-koch-homeless-plan.html.

14. Judith Lynn Failer, *Who Qualifies for Rights? Homelessness, Mental Illness and Civil Commitment* (Ithaca, NY: Cornell University Press, 2022).

15. Thomas J. Main, *Homelessness in New York City: Policymaking from Koch to de Blasio* (New York: NYU Press, 2016).

16. "Though Homeless, She Copes, She Is Fit, She Survives," excerpts from the decision by Acting Justice Robert D. Lippmann of State Supreme Court in Manhattan ordering the release from the Bellevue Hospital Center of Joyce Brown, *New York Times*, November 13, 1987, https://www.nytimes.com/1987/11/13 /nyregion/though-homeless-she-copes-she-is-fit-she-survives.html.

17. Josh Barbanel, "Homeless Woman to Be Released After Being Forcibly Hospitalized," *New York Times*, January 19, 1988, https://www.nytimes.com /1988/01/19/nyregion/homeless-woman-to-be-released-after-being-forcibly -hospitalized.html.

18. Marianne Yen, "Homeless N.Y. Woman Wins Release from Hospital," *Washington Post*, January 20, 1988, https://www.washingtonpost.com/archive /politics/1988/01/20/homeless-ny-woman-wins-release-from-hospital.

19. Rick Hampson, "What Ever Happened to Billie Boggs?" Associated Press, June 2, 1991, https://apnews.com/article/515e79d71cbab2ab9e404fa58dc88 63a.

20. Kasindorf, "The Real Story of Billie Boggs."

21. "General Recommendation for the Care of Homeless Patients," National Health Care for the Homeless, 2010, https://nhchc.org/wp-content/uploads/2019 /-08/GenRecsHomeless2010-1.pdf.

22. Peter Tarr, "Homelessness and Mental Illness: A Challenge to Our Society," *Brain & Behavior* (November 19, 2018), https://bbrfoundation.org/blog /homelessness-and-mental-illness-challenge-our-society.

23. Scott Hechinger, "A Massive Fail on Crime Reporting by the *New York Times*, NPR," *The Nation*, October 6, 2021, https://www.thenation.com/article /society/crime-reporting-failure.

24. Robert Constantine, Ross Andel, John Petrila, Marion Becker, John Robst, Gregory Teague, Timothy Boaz, and Andrew Howe, "Characteristics and

Experiences of Adults with a Serious Mental Illness Who Were Involved in the Criminal Justice System," *Journal of Psychiatric Services*, May 2010, https://ps .psychiatryonline.org/doi/abs/10.1176/ps.2010.61.5.451.

25. Laurence Roy, Anne G. Crocker, Tonia L. Nicholls, Eric A. Latimer, and Andrea Reyes Ayllon, "Criminal Behavior and Victimization Among Homeless Individuals with Severe Mental Illness: A Systematic Review," *Journal of Psychiatric Services* (October 15, 2014), https://ps.psychiatryonline.org/doi/abs/10 .1176/appi.ps.201200515.

26. R. C. Schwartz and D. M. Blankenship, "Racial Disparities in Psychotic Disorder Diagnosis: A Review of Empirical Literature," *World Journal of Psychiatry* (2014), https://doi.org/10.5498/wjp.v4.i4.133.

27. Schwartz and Blankenship, "Racial Disparities in Psychotic Disorder Diagnosis."

28. R. C. Schwartz and K. P. Feisthamel, "Disproportionate Diagnosis of Mental Disorders Among African American Versus European American Clients: Implications for Counseling Theory, Research, and Practice," *Journal of Counseling & Development* (December 23, 2011), https://doi.org/10.1002/j.1556-6678 .2009.tb00110.x.

29. B. L. Perry, M. Neltner, and T. Allen, "A Paradox of Bias: Racial Differences in Forensic Psychiatric Diagnosis and Determinations of Criminal Responsibility," *Race and Social Problems* (June 12, 2013), https://doi.org/10.1007 /s12552-013-9100-3.

30. S. J. Trierweiler, H. W. Neighbors, C. Munday, E. E. Thompson, J. S. Jackson, and V. J. Binion, "Differences in Patterns of Symptom Attribution in Diagnosing Schizophrenia Between African American and Non-African American Clinicians," *American Journal of Orthopsychiatry* (2006), https://doi.org/10.1037 /0002-9432.76.2.154.

31. Jonathan Metzl, *The Protest Psychosis: How Schizophrenia Became a Black Disease* (Boston: Beacon Press, 2010).

32. Michael Winerip, "Bedlam on the Streets," *New York Times Magazine*, May 23, 1999, https://www.nytimes.com/1999/05/23/magazine/bedlam-on-the -streets.html.

33. Winerip, "Bedlam on the Streets."

34. Winerip, "Bedlam on the Streets."

35. Andy Newman, Nate Schweber, and Chelsia Rose Marcius, "Decades Adrift in a Broken System, Then Charged in a Death on the Tracks," *New York Times*, February 5, 2022, https://www.nytimes.com/2022/02/05/nyregion/martial -simon-michelle-go.html.

36. Newman, Schweber, and Marcius, "Decades Adrift in a Broken System, Then Charged in a Death on the Tracks."

37. Dorothea Dix, "Dorothea Dix Speaks on Behalf of Insane Persons," Memorial to the Legislature of Massachusetts, *Old South Leaflets*, Volume 7, 1843, https://college.cengage.com/history/ayers_primary_sources/dorothea_dix _speaks_insane_persons.htm.

38. Winerip, "Bedlam on the Streets."

39. Janie Har and Adam Beam, "California Governor OKs Mental Health Courts for Homeless," Associated Press, September 22, 2022, https://

apnews.com/article/health-california-san-francisco-gavin-newsom-mental
-0e68288d97959f9ceeb5c5683afa092b.

40. Ethan Geringer-Sameth, "What's Behind the Increased Use of Kendra's Law in New York City?" *Gotham Gazette*, September 27, 2022.

41. Geringer-Sameth, "What's Behind the Increased Use of Kendra's Law in New York City?"

42. Amy Julia Harris and Jan Ransom, "Behind 94 Acts of Shocking Violence, Years of Glaring Mistakes," *New York Times,* November 20, 2023.

43. Harris and Ransom, "Behind 94 Acts of Shocking Violence, Years of Glaring Mistakes."

44. Amy Julia Harris and Jan Ransom, "Kendra's Law Was Meant to Prevent Violence. It Failed Hundreds of Times," *New York Times*, December 21, 2023.

#### CHAPTER 4: OFFERING AID CREATES MORE NEED

1. Walter Leginski, *Toward Understanding Homelessness: The 2007 National Symposium on Homelessness Research. Historical and Contextual Influences on the U.S. Response to Contemporary Homelessness*, US Department of Health and Human Services, August 31, 2007, https://aspe.hhs.gov/reports/toward -understanding-homelessness-2007-national-symposium-homelessness-research -historical-0.

2. Franklin D. Roosevelt, "Campaign Address on Progressive Government at the Commonwealth Club in San Francisco, California," September 23, 1932, at American Presidency Project, https://www.presidency.ucsb.edu/documents /campaign-address-progressive-government-the-commonwealth-club-san -francisco-california.

3. Franklin D. Roosevelt, "State of the Union Message to Congress," January 11, 1944, at American Presidency Project, https://www.presidency.ucsb.edu /documents/state-the-union-message-congress.

4. US Housing Act of 1937, as Amended, Department of Housing and Urban Development, https://www.hud.gov/sites/documents/DOC_10010.PDF.

5. Servicemen's Readjustment Act (1944), at National Archives, https://www .archives.gov/milestone-documents/servicemens-readjustment-act.

6. Ronald Reagan, Inaugural Address, January 20, 1981, at Ronald Reagan Presidential Foundation & Institute, https://www.reaganfoundation.org/ronald -reagan/reagan-quotes-speeches/inaugural-address-2.

7. "Cabinet Aide Greeted by Reagan as 'Mayor,'" Associated Press, June 19, 1981, reprinted in the *New York Times*, June 19, 1981, https://www.nytimes.com /1981/06/19/us/cabinet-aide-greeted-by-reagan-as-mayor.html.

8. Diane Yentel, "Testimony Presented to the United States House of Representatives Financial Services Committee," December 21, 2018, https:// financialservices.house.gov/uploadedfiles/12.21.201_diane_yentel_testimony.pdf.

9. Guian A. McKee, "Lyndon B. Johnson and the War on Poverty," Miller Center of Public Affairs, University of Virginia, https://prde.upress.virginia.edu /content/WarOnPoverty2.

10. Al From, "The War on Poverty Was Not About Welfare. That's Why It Worked," *Politico,* January 8, 2014, https://www.politico.com/magazine/story /2014/01/the-war-on-poverty-was-not-about-welfare-101898.

11. Ronald Reagan, *Good Morning America*, January 30, 1984, https://www
.youtube.com/watch?v=8lSuc6_i79Q; Juan Williams, "Homeless Choose to Be,
Reagan Says," *Washington Post*, February 1, 1984, https://www.washingtonpost
.com/archive/politics/1984/02/01/homeless-choose-to-be-reagan-says.

12. Peter Dreier, "Reagan's Real Legacy," *The Nation,* February 4, 2011,
https://www.thenation.com/article/archive/reagans-real-legacy.

13. Dreier, "Reagan's Real Legacy."

14. Niels W. Frenzen, "Homeless a Product of Capitalism," letter to the
editor, *New York Times*, November 6, 1990, originally published October 23,
1990, https://www.nytimes.com/1990/11/06/opinion/l-homeless-a-product-of
-capitalism-639890.html.

15. William Geist, "Residents Give a Bronx Cheer to Decal Plan," *New
York Times*, November 12, 1983, https://www.nytimes.com/1983/11/12/nyregion
/residents-give-a-bronx-cheer-to-decal-plan.html.

16. New York Constitution, Article XVII, § 1.

17. Michael B. Katz, "Poorhouses and the Origins of the Public Old Age
Home," *The Milbank Memorial Fund Quarterly. Health and Society* (Winter
1984), https://doi.org/10.2307/3349894.

18. Diane Berish, Ian Nelson, Shahla Mehdizadeh, and Robert Applebaum,
"Is There a Woodwork Effect? Addressing a 200-Year Debate on the Impacts of
Expanding Community-Based Services," *Journal of Aging & Social Policy* (June
24, 2018), https://www.tandfonline.com/doi/full/10.1080/08959420.2018.1528115.

19. Jason DeParle, *American Dream: Three Women, Ten Kids, and a Nation's
Drive to End Welfare* (New York: Viking, 2004).

20. King v. Smith, 392 U.S. 309 (1968), https://supreme.justia.com/cases
/federal/us/392/309.

21. Josh Levin, "The Welfare Queen," *Slate,* December 19, 2013, http://www
.slate.com/articles/news_and_politics/history/2013/12/linda_taylor_welfare
_queen_ronald_reagan_made_her_a_notorious_american_villain.html.

22. Kathryn Edin and Laura Lein, *Making Ends Meet: How Single Mothers
Survive Welfare and Low-Wage Work* (Russell Sage Foundation, April 1977).

23. *An Analysis of President Reagan's Budget Revisions for Fiscal Year
1981–1982*, Congressional Budget Office, https://www.cbo.gov/sites/default/files
/97th-congress-1981-1982/reports/81doc11b.pdf.

24. "The New Covenant: Responsibility and Rebuilding the American
Community," Remarks of Gov. Bill Clinton, Georgetown University, October
23, 1991, at http://www.ibiblio.org/pub/academic/political-science/speeches
/clinton.dir/c24.txtp.

25. DeParle, *American Dream.*

26. Richard L. Berke, "Gingrich Promises to Fight Clinton on Welfare
Law," *New York Times,* August 23, 1997, https://www.nytimes.com/1997/08/23/us
/gingrich-promises-to-fight-clinton-on-welfare-law.html.

27. Peter Edelman, "The Worst Thing Bill Clinton Has Done," *The Atlantic*,
March 1997, https://www.theatlantic.com/magazine/archive/1997/03/the-worst
-thing-bill-clinton-has-done/376797.

28. Jonathan Chait, "Bill Clinton, O. J. Simpson, Clarence Thomas, and
the Politics of 1990s Racial Backlash," *New York Magazine*, July 4, 2016, https://

nymag.com/intelligencer/2016/06/clinton-and-the-politics-of-90s-racial
-backlash.html.

29. "Temporary Assistance for Needy Families (TANF) at 26," Center for Budget and Policy Priorities, August 4, 2022, https://www.cbpp.org/research /family-income-support/temporary-assistance-for-needy-families-tanf-at-26.

30. Christopher Bollinger, Luis Gonzalez, and James P. Ziliak, "Welfare Reform and the Level and Composition of Income," University of Kentucky, August 2007, https://citeseerx.ist.psu.edu/viewdoc/download?doi=10.1.1.558.7527&rep= rep1&type=pdf.

31. "A Roadmap to Reducing Childhood Poverty," National Academies of Engineering, Science and Medicine, 2019, https://nap.nationalacademies.org /child-poverty/highlights.html.

32. Shawn Fremstad, *What Do Fertility and Football Have to Do with Clinton-Gingrich Welfare Reform? Read This to Find Out*, Center for Economic and Policy Research, August 18, 2022, https://cepr.net/what-do-fertility-and -football-have-to-do-with-clinton-gingrich-welfare-reform-read-this-to-find -out.

33. Dylan Matthews, "The Legacy of the 1996 Welfare Reform," *Vox*, June 20, 2016, https://www.vox.com/2016/6/20/11789988/clintons-welfare-reform.

34. Sally Corianne Payton, "The Case for More, Not Less: Shortfalls in Federal Housing Assistance and Gaps in Evidence for Proposed Policy Changes," Urban Institute, January 2018, https://www.urban.org/sites/default/files /publication/95616/case_for_more_not_less.pdf.

35. David Margolick and Jane Fritsch, "A Candidate's Colleagues Render a Mixed Verdict," *New York Times*, October 22, 1993, https://www.nytimes.com /1993/10/22/nyregion/a-candidate-s-colleagues-render-a-mixed-verdict.html.

36. Louis Menard, "Was Rudy Giuliani Always So Awful?" *New Yorker*, November 19, 2022, https://www.newyorker.com/magazine/2022/09/26/was-rudy -giuliani-always-so-awful.

37. Wayne Barrett, *Rudy! An Investigative Biography of Rudy Giuliani* (New York: Basic Books, April 2001).

38. Celia W. Dugger, "Giuliani Eases Stance on Plans for Homeless," *New York Times*, March 20, 1994, https://www.nytimes.com/1994/03/20/nyregion /giuliani-eases-stance-on-plans-for-homeless.html.

39. Christopher Hitchens, "Greenspan Shrugged," *Vanity Fair*, December 2000, https://www.vanityfair.com/culture/2000/12/hitchens-200012.

40. WNYC, "The Year of Clinton and Giuliani—How 1993 Helped Give Us the World of 2023: Part Three, Electing Rudy," January 24, 2023, https://www .wnyc.org/story/1993-part-three-electing-rudy.

41. Ta-Nehisi Coates, "Donald Trump Is Out. Are We Ready to Talk About How He Got In?" *The Atlantic*, January 2021, https://www.theatlantic.com /politics/archive/2021/01/ta-nehisi-coates-revisits-trump-first-white-president /617731.

42. Bench Ansfield, "How a 50-Year-Old Study Was Misconstrued to Create Destructive Broken-Windows Policing," *Washington Post*, December 27, 2019, https://www.washingtonpost.com/outlook/2019/12/27/how-year-old-study-was -misconstrued-create-destructive-broken-windows-policing.

43. George L. Kelling and James Q. Wilson, "Broken Windows: The Police and Safety," *The Atlantic*, March 1982, https://www.theatlantic.com/magazine /archive/1982/03/broken-windows/304465; Philip G. Zimbardo, "The Human Choice: Individuation, Reason, and Order Versus Deindividuation, Impulse, and Chaos," *Nebraska Symposium on Motivation*, 1969, https://stacks.stanford.edu/file /gk002bt7757/gk002bt7757.pdf.

44. Donald Braman, "Stop-and-Frisk Didn't Make New York Safer: No Evidence That Invasive Policing Brought Down Crime," *The Atlantic*, March 16, 2014, https://www.theatlantic.com/national/archive/2014/03/stop-and-frisk -didnt-make-new-york-safer/359666. Also see J. MacDonald, J. Fagan, and A. Geller, "The Effects of Local Police Surges on Crime and Arrests in New York City," *PLoS ONE* (2016), https://doi.org/10.1371/journal.pone.0157223.

45. William Bratton, with Peter Knobler, *Turnaround: How America's Top Cop Reversed the Crime Epidemic* (New York: Random House, 2020).

46. Greg St. Martin, "Northeastern University Researchers Find Little Evidence for 'Broken Windows Theory,' Say Neighborhood Disorder Doesn't Cause Crime," *Northeastern Global News*, May 15, 2019, https://news.northeastern.edu /2019/05/15/northeastern-university-researchers-find-little-evidence-for-broken -windows-theory-say-neighborhood-disorder-doesnt-cause-crime.

47. Daniel T. O'Brien, Chelsea Farrell, and Brandon C. Welsh, "Looking Through Broken Windows: The Impact of Neighborhood Disorder on Aggression and Fear of Crime Is an Artifact of Research Design," *Annual Review of Criminology*, January 2019, https://www.annualreviews.org/doi/full/10.1146 /annurev-criminol-011518-024638.

48. Jillian Jorgensen, "NYPD IG: No Link Between Quality of Life Enforcement and Lower Crime," *New York Observer*, June 22, 2016, https://observer .com/2016/06/nypd-ig-no-link-between-quality-of-life-enforcement-and-lower -crime.

49. Ken Auletta, "Fixing Broken Windows: Bill Bratton Wants to Be America's Top Cop. His Critics Say His Legacy Is Tainted," *New Yorker*, September 7, 2015, https://www.newyorker.com/magazine/2015/09/07/fixing-broken -windows.

50. Auletta, "Fixing Broken Windows."

51. Danilo Pelletiere, "Getting to the Heart of Housing's Fundamental Question: How Much Can a Family Afford? A Primer on Housing Affordability Standards in U.S. Housing Policy," *Social Science Research Network* (May 2008), https://papers.ssrn.com/sol3/papers.cfm?abstract_id=1132551.

52. "Out of Reach 2022," National Low Income Housing Coalition, https:// nlihc.org/oor.

53. "Out of Reach 2022," National Low Income Housing Coalition.

54. Chris Arnold, "Rents Across U.S. Rise Above $2,000 for the First Time Ever," National Public Radio, https://www.npr.org/2022/06/09/1103919413/rents -across-u-s-rise-above-2–000-a-month-for-the-first-time-ever.

55. "Out of Reach 2022," National Low Income Housing Coalition.

56. Anna Kodé, "The Typical American Renter Is Now Rent-Burdened, a Report Says," *New York Times*, January 25, 2023, https://www.nytimes.com/2023 /01/25/realestate/rent-burdened-american-households.html#.

57. David Cooper, Sebastian Martinez Hickey, and Ben Zipperer, "The Value of Federal Minimum Wage at Lowest Point in 66 Years," Economic Policy Institute, July 14, 2022, https://www.epi.org/blog/the-value-of-the-federal-minimum -wage-is-at-its-lowest-point-in-66-years.

58. Kodé, "The Typical American Renter Is Now Rent-Burdened, a Report Says."

59. Bruce D. Meyer, "Employment Alone Isn't Enough to Solve Homelessness, Study Suggests," UChicagoNews, June 29, 2021, https://news.uchicago.edu /story/employment-alone-isnt-enough-solve-homelessness-study-suggests.

60. Cynthia Griffith, "Working Homeless: More Than Half of Unhoused People Have Jobs," Invisible People TV, July 21, 2023, https://invisiblepeople.tv /working-homeless-more-than-half-of-unhoused-people-have-jobs.

61. Jonathan Soffer, Ed Koch and the Rebuilding of New York City (New York: Columbia University Press, 2010), excerpted by Gotham Gazette, https://www .gothamgazette.com/624-creating-affordable-housing-how-koch-did-.

62. Jennifer Egan, "To Be Young and Homeless," New York Times Magazine, March 24, 2002, https://www.nytimes.com/2002/03/24/magazine/to-be-young -and-homeless.html.

63. Sally Goldenberg and Erin Durkin, "Bloomberg Tries to Revise History on City Term-Limits Fight," Politico, February 2020, https://www.politico.com /states/new-york/city-hall/story/2020/02/28/bloomberg-tries-to-revise-history -on-city-term-limits-fight-1264298.

64. Renee Lewis, "NYC Homelessness Soared Under Mayor Bloomberg," Al Jazeera America, March 12, 2014, http://america.aljazeera.com/articles/2014/3/12 /record-breaking-nychomelessnessblamedonforprofitsheltersreport.html.

65. "Michael Bloomberg," Forbes, May 29, 2024, https://www.forbes.com /profile/michael-bloomberg/?sh=a72234b14178.

66. Bruce Meyer, "Learning About Homelessness Using Linked Survey and Administrative Data," Becker Friedman Institute, University of Chicago, June 23, 2021, https://bfi.uchicago.edu/insight/finding/learning-about-homelessness -using-linked-survey-and-administrative-data.

## CHAPTER 5: WHO WE THINK OF WHEN WE THINK OF THE HOMELESS

1. Steven L. Schlossman, Love and the American Delinquent: The Theory and Practice of "Progressive" Juvenile Justice, 1825–1920 (Chicago: University of Chicago Press, 1977), 9.

2. Daniel Macallair, "The San Francisco Industrial School and the Origins of Juvenile Justice in California: A Glance at the Great Reformation," UC Davis Journal of Juvenile Law & Policy 7, no. 1 (2003): 4.

3. Christopher A. Mallett and Miyuki Fukushima Tedor, "The History of Juvenile Justice and Today's Juvenile Courts," in Juvenile Delinquency (Thousand Oaks, CA: Sage Publications, 2018), 29, https://us.sagepub.com/sites/default/files /upm-assets/95059_book_item_95059.pdf.

4. Elijah Devoe, The Reform System, or Prison Discipline Applied to Juvenile Delinquents (New York: J. B. M'Gown, 1848), reproduction of original from Harvard Law School Library.

5. "Our City Charities; The New-York House of Refuge for Juvenile Delinquents," *New York Times*, January 23, 1860, https://www.nytimes.com/1860/01/23/archives/our-city-charities-the-newyork-house-of-refuge-for-juvenile.html.

6. Austin Reed, *The Life and the Adventures of a Haunted Convict*, ed. Caleb Smith (New York: Random House, 2016).

7. Reed, *The Life and the Adventures of a Haunted Convict*.

8. Reed, *The Life and the Adventures of a Haunted Convict*.

9. Reed, *The Life and the Adventures of a Haunted Convict*.

10. M. H. Morton, A. Dworsky, and G. M. Samuels, "Missed Opportunities: Youth Homelessness in America. National Estimates," Chapin Hall at the University of Chicago, 2017, https://voicesofyouthcount.org/brief/national-estimates-of-youth-homelessness.

11. M. H. Morton, A. Dworsky, and G. M. Samuels, "Missed Opportunities: Counting Youth Experiencing Homelessness in America," University of Chicago, 2018, https://voicesofyouthcount.org/brief/missed-opportunities-counting-youth-experiencing-homelessness-in-america.

12. Morton, Dworsky, and Samuels, "Missed Opportunities: Counting Youth Experiencing Homelessness in America."

13. Charles Loring Brace, *The Dangerous Classes of New York and Twenty Years' Work Among Them* (New York: Wynkoop & Hallenbeck, 1872).

14. An account from "Western Homes for City Children. Thirty-Five Poor Boys and Girls Sent to Iowa," which appeared in the *New York Daily Tribune* on January 21, 1880: "No mother's tears were shed over the departing waifs, no father's counsel was given to the boys who were to enter upon a new life." Available at National Orphan Train Complex, https://orphantraindepot.org/history/artifacts-of-the-orphan-trains/new-york-daily-tribune.

15. "Parens Patriae Definition & Legal Meaning," The Law Dictionary, https://thelawdictionary.org/parens-patriae, accessed February 14, 2024; Sriradha Rai Choudhuri, "The Doctrine of Parens Patriae," Juris Centre, May 10, 2021, https://juriscentre.com/2021/05/10/doctrine-of-parens-patriae.

16. Caleb Smith, in Reed, *The Life and the Adventures of a Haunted Convict*, xxxi–xxxii.

17. Roxanna Asgarian, *We Were Once Family: A Story of Love, Death, and Child Removal in America* (New York: Macmillan Audio, 2023).

18. Jessica Winter, "Who Decides What a Family Is?" *New Yorker*, March 10, 2023, https://www.newyorker.com/books/page-turner/who-decides-what-a-family-is.

19. Morton, Dworsky, and Samuels, "Missed Opportunities: Youth Homelessness in America. National Estimates."

20. Morton, Dworsky, and Samuels, "Missed Opportunities: Youth Homelessness in America. National Estimates."

21. Morton, Dworsky, and Samuels, "Missed Opportunities: Youth Homelessness in America. National Estimates."

22. The Ali Forney Center, https://www.aliforneycenter.org.

23. "Federal Judge Approves Class Action Settlement in Legal Aid's Landmark Homeless Youth Lawsuit," Legal Aid Society, November 30, 2020, https://

legalaidnyc.org/wp-content/uploads/2020/11/11-30-20-Federal-Judge-Approves
-Class-Action-Settlement-in-Legal-Aids-Landmark-Homeless-Youth-Lawsuit
.pdf.

24. Kyle Swenson, "America's First Homelessness Problem: Knowing Who Is Actually Homeless," *Washington Post*, August 24, 2022, https://www.washing tonpost.com/dc-md-va/2022/08/24/homeless-seattle-hud-statistics.

25. Swenson, "America's First Homelessness Problem."

26. Andy Newman, "A Record 100,000 People in New York Homeless Shelters," *New York Times*, June 28, 2023, https://www.nytimes.com/2023/06/28 /nyregion/nyc-homeless-shelter-population.html.

27. *Personal Experiences of U.S. Racial/Ethnic Minorities in Today's Difficult Times*, NPR, Robert Wood Johnson Foundation, and Harvard T. H. Chan School of Public Health, Spring 2022, https://legacy.npr.org/assets/pdf/2022/08/ NPR-RWJF-Harvard-Poll.pdf; also see https://www.hsph.harvard.edu/horp/ npr-harvard/; Justin Wm. Moyer, "Rural America Has Homeless People Too. But They're Hard to Find," *Washington Post*, February 6, 2023, https:// www.washingtonpost.com/dc-md-va/2023/02/06/homeless-count-carlisle -cumberland-county-pennsylvania.

28. Moyer, "Rural America Has Homeless People Too."

29. Boston Health Care for the Homeless Program, https://www.bhchp.org.

30. Interview with Dr. James O'Connell, "Risks of Living on Street in Bitter Cold: When Not to Walk on By," WBUR, January 31, 2014, https://www.wbur .org/news/2014/01/31/cold-medical-risks-homeless; David Brand, "NYC Shelter Count," *City Limits Magazine*, February 2023, https://citylimits.org/nyc-shelter -count-2022.

31. Interview with Dr. James O'Connell, "Risks of Living on Street in Bitter Cold."

32. Jill S. Roncarati, Travis P. Baggett, James J. O'Connell, Stephen W. Hwang, Francis Cook, Nancy Krieger, and Glorian Sorensen, "Mortality Among Unsheltered Homeless Adults in Boston, Massachusetts, 2000–2009," *JAMA Internal Medicine* (September 2018), https://www.ncbi.nlm.nih.gov/pmc/articles /PMC6142967.

33. James J. O'Connell, "Dying in the Shadows: The Challenge of Providing Health Care for Homeless People," *Canadian Medical Association Journal* (April 2004), https://www.ncbi.nlm.nih.gov/pmc/articles/PMC385355.

34. O'Connell, "Dying in the Shadows."

35. Tracy Kidder, *Rough Sleepers: Dr. Jim O'Connell's Urgent Mission to Bring Healing to Homeless People* (New York: Random House, 2023).

36. Kidder, *Rough Sleepers*.

37. Matthew Desmond, *Evicted: Poverty and Profit in the American City* (New York: Crown, 2016).

38. Matthew Desmond, "Why Poverty Persists in America," *New York Times Magazine*, March 9, 2023, https://www.nytimes.com/2023/03/09/magazine /poverty-by-america-matthew-desmond.html.

CHAPTER 6: BARRIERS AND SOLUTIONS

1. Malcolm Gladwell, "Million-Dollar Murray," *New Yorker*, February 13, 2006, https://www.newyorker.com/magazine/2006/02/13/million-dollar-murray.

2. R. Kuhn and D. P. Culhane, "Applying Cluster Analysis to Test a Typology of Homelessness by Pattern of Shelter Utilization: Results from the Analysis of Administrative Data," University of Pennsylvania School of Social Policy and Practice, 1998, https://repository.upenn.edu/spp_papers/96.

3. Gladwell, "Million-Dollar Murray."

4. Yinan Peng, "Permanent Supportive Housing with Housing First to Reduce Homelessness and Promote Health Among Homeless Populations with Disability: A Community Guide Systematic Review," *Journal of Public Health Management and Practice* 26, no. 5 (2020), https://www.thecommunityguide.org/media/pdf/he-jphmp-evrev-housing-first.pdf.

5. Gladwell, "Million-Dollar Murray."

6. Peng, "Permanent Supportive Housing with Housing First to Reduce Homelessness and Promote Health Among Homeless Populations with Disability."

7. Vinson Cunningham, "Cornel West Sees a Spiritual Decay in the Culture," *New Yorker*, March 9, 2022, https://www.newyorker.com/culture/the-new-yorker-interview/cornel-west-sees-a-spiritual-decay-in-the-culture.

8. "NPOs Added $1.4 Trillion to U.S. Economy: Health of the U.S. Nonprofit Sector by Independent Sector," *NonProfit Times*, July 5, 2022, https://thenonprofittimes.com/report/npos-added-1-4-trillion-to-u-s-economy.

9. Dorothy Day, *The Long Loneliness* (New York: Harper & Row, 1952).

10. Day, *The Long Loneliness.*

11. Greg B. Smith, "Mentally Disabled New Yorkers Face Eviction as Pathways to Housing Program Fails to Pay Landlords," *New York Daily News*, September 7, 2014, https://www.nydailynews.com/new-york/exclusive-mentally-disabled-new-yorkers-face-eviction-pathways-housing-remains-debt-article-1.1930728.

12. "All In: The Federal Strategic Plan to Prevent and End Homelessness," US Interagency Council, December 2022, https://www.usich.gov/All_In_The_Federal_Strategic_Plan_to_Prevent_and_End_Homelessness.pdf.

13. "Finland Solved Homelessness: Here's How," Invisible People, December 23, 2023, https://www.youtube.com/watch?v=ojt_6PBnCJE.

14. Andy Newman, "Jordan Neely Was on New York's 'Top 50' List of Homeless People at Risk," *New York Times*, May 13, 2023, https://www.nytimes.com/2023/05/13/nyregion/jordan-neely-top-50-mental-illness.html.

15. Andy Newman, "They've Spent Years on the Streets. Can Anyone Coax Them Inside?" *New York Times*, May 3, 2023, https://www.nytimes.com/2023/05/03/nyregion/mental-health-intensive-mobile-treatment.html.

16. Olayemi Olurin, "Jordan Neely Killing: Debates About Mental Health, Crime Are Misguided," *Teen Vogue*, May 12, 2023, https://www.teenvogue.com/story/jordan-neely-killing-debates-mental-health-crime.

17. Olurin, "Jordan Neely Killing."

18. MaryBeth Musumeci, Priya Chidambaram, and Kendal Orgera, "State Options for Medicaid Coverage of Inpatient Behavioral Health Services," Kaiser Family Foundation, November 6, 2019, https://www.kff.org/report-section/state-options-for-medicaid-coverage-of-inpatient-behavioral-health-services-report.

19. Pam Marino, "State of Emergency: A Lack of Psychiatric Treatment Beds in California Puts an Enormous Strain on Patients, Staff and the Community," *Monterey County Weekly*, April 6, 2023, https://www.montereycountyweekly.com/news/cover/a-lack-of-psychiatric-treatment-beds-in-california-puts-an-enormous-strain-on-patients-staff/article_11efdca0-d49f-11ed-98ca-e33650a1468a.html.

20. Don Mitchell, "Homelessness, American Style," *Urban Geography* 32, no. 7 (2011), https://doi.org/10.2747/0272-3638.32.7.933.

21. Daniel Kahneman, *Thinking, Fast and Slow* (New York: Farrar, Straus and Giroux, 2013).

22. Rosemary Fister, via Twitter, August 5, 2022, https://x.com/RosemaryFister/status/1555606030679248896?s=20.

23. National Coalition for the Homeless, https://nationalhomeless.org.

24. Kristian Hernández, "Homeless Camping Bans Are Spreading. This Group Shaped the Bills: The Cicero Institute Is Pushing a Model with Residency Limits, Bans on Permanent Encampments, and Penalties for Cities That Refuse to Remove Them," Penn Capital, August 10, 2022, https://www.penncapital-star.com/civil-rights-social-justice/homeless-camping-bans-are-spreading-this-group-shaped-the-bills.

25. Joe Lonsdale and Judge Glock, "Housing First Foments Homelessness in California," *Wall Street Journal*, November 18, 2022, https://www.wsj.com/articles/housing-first-foments-homelessness-in-california-gavin-newsom-government-spending-camp-unsheltered-drug-treatment-psychiatric-care-11668785369.

26. George Orwell, "Looking Back on the Spanish War," August 1942, Sections I, II, III, and VII printed in *New Road*, June 1943, https://www.orwellfoundation.com/the-orwell-foundation/orwell/essays-and-other-works/looking-back-on-the-spanish-war.

27. Patrick Markee, "Fact vs. Fiction: The 'Zombie Lie' That Housing Subsidies Cause a Surge in Homelessness," March 20, 2014, https://www.coalitionforthehomeless.org/2014/03/?cat=2.

28. Steve Berg, "Supreme Court and Homelessness: What the *Grants Pass v. Johnson* Case Could Do," National Alliance to End Homelessness, January 26, 2024, https://endhomelessness.org/blog/supreme-court-and-homelessness-what-the-grants-pass-v-johnson-case-could-do.

29. Cynthia Griffith, "Housing and Legal Experts Weigh in on *Johnson v. Grants Pass* Case," Invisible People TV, March 4, 2024, https://invisiblepeople.tv/housing-and-legal-experts-weigh-in-on-johnson-vs-grants-pass-case/.

30. Gregg Colburn and Clayton Page Aldern, *Homelessness Is a Housing Problem: How Structural Factors Explain U.S. Patterns* (Berkeley: University of California Press, March 2022).

31. Philip Bump, "Many Theories, No Evidence: Giuliani Encapsulates the Entire Trump Era," *Washington Post*, June 22, 2022, https://www.washingtonpost

.com/politics/2022/06/22/lots-theories-no-evidence-giuliani-encapsulates-entire
-trump-era.

32. Vincent J. Cannato, "A Home of One's Own," *National Affairs* (Spring
2010), https://www.nationalaffairs.com/publications/detail/a-home-of-ones-own.

33. Herbert Hoover, *Addresses Upon the American Road, 1933–1938* (New
York: Charles Scribner's Sons, 1938), https://hoover.archives.gov/sites/default
/files/research/ebooks/b3v1_full.pdf.

34. "Estimates of Federal Tax Expenditures for Fiscal Years 2015–2019," Joint
Committee on Taxation (JCX-141-15), December 7, 2015, p. 32, https://www.jct
.gov/publications/2015/jcx-141-15.

35. Matthew Desmond, "How Homeownership Became the Engine of
American Inequality," *New York Times Magazine*, May 9, 2017, https://www
.nytimes.com/2017/05/09/magazine/how-homeownership-became-the-engine
-of-american-inequality.html.

36. "Estimates of Federal Tax Expenditures for Fiscal Years 2015–2019," Joint
Committee on Taxation (JCX-141-15).

37. Desmond, "How Homeownership Became the Engine of American
Inequality."

38. "President Bush's Radio Address to the Nation: Barriers to Minority
Homeownership," Archives, US Department of Housing and Urban Development, June 15, 2002, https://archives.hud.gov/news/2002/homeownradioaddress
.cfm.

39. Hernan Diaz, *Trust* (New York: Riverhead Books, 2022).

40. Sophia Kishkovsky, "A Class Struggle on Moscow's Golden Mile," *New
York Times*, December 18, 2006, https://www.nytimes.com/2006/12/18/world
/europe/18iht-moscow.3941394.html.

41. Michael Kimmelman, "When the Skyscraper You Hate Blocks the Skyscraper You Love," *New York Times*, October 25, 2023, https://www.nytimes.com
/2023/10/25/arts/design/empire-state-building-views.html; "Fifth Avenue Super-
tower Built by Developer with Oligarch Ties Presses Forward," *CityRealty*, March
2, 2022, https://www.cityrealty.com/nyc/market-insight/features/future-nyc/fifth
-avenue-supertower-built-developer-oligarch-ties-presses-forward/54722.

42. Erik Forman, "How Unions Can Solve the Housing Crisis," *In These
Times*, September 24, 2018, https://inthesetimes.com/article/unions-housing
-crisis-labor-coop-apartments-new-york-homeless-rent-control.

43. Forman, "How Unions Can Solve the Housing Crisis."

44. Glyn Robbins, "Review of 'Working Class Utopias: A History of Cooperative Housing New York City,'" *New Sociological Perspectives* (December 2022),
https://nsp.lse.ac.uk/articles/159.

45. Gwenda Blair, *The Trumps: Three Generations of Builders and a President*
(New York: Simon & Schuster, 2001).

46. Blair, *The Trumps.*

47. Jonathan Mahler and Steve Eder, "'No Vacancies' for Blacks: How
Donald Trump Got His Start, and Was First Accused of Bias," *New York Times*,
August 27, 2016, https://www.nytimes.com/2016/08/28/us/politics/donald-trump
-housing-race.html.

48. Blair, *The Trumps.*

49. Blair, *The Trumps*.

50. Blair, *The Trumps*.

51. Blair, *The Trumps*.

52. Robbins, "Review of 'Working Class Utopias.'"

53. Mark Dery, interviews Lucy Sante, "Shelfie: Luc Sante," Thought Catalog, August 13, 2014, https://thoughtcatalog.com/mark-dery/2014/08/374848.

54. "Housing Coops in the U.S.," National Association of Housing Coops, March 2012, http://www.coophousing.org/uploadedFiles/NAHC_Site/Resources/Coop%20Housing%20USA.pdf.

55. "EIU's Global Liveability Index Rebounds as Pandemic Eases," Economist Intelligence Unit, June 23, 2022, https://www.eiu.com/n/eius-global-liveability-index-rebounds-as-pandemic-eases; "Vienna Reclaims Title of the World's Most Liveable City," *The Guardian*, June 22, 2022, https://www.theguardian.com/world/2022/jun/23/vienna-reclaims-title-of-the-worlds-most-liveable-city.

56. "Vienna Reclaims Title of the World's Most Liveable City."

57. See excellent summary via the Weiner Holocaust Library at https://www.theholocaustexplained.org/the-nazi-rise-to-power/the-weimar-republic.

58. Veronika Duma and Hanna Lichtenberger, trans. Loren Balhorn, "Remembering Red Vienna," *Jacobin*, February 2017, https://jacobin.com/2017/02/red-vienna-austria-housing-urban-planning.

59. Jake Blumgart, "Most Liveable City: How Vienna Earned Its Place in Housing History," *City Monitor*, June 22, 2023, https://citymonitor.ai/environment/housing/red-vienna-how-austrias-capital-earned-its-place-in-housing-history.

60. Aitor Hernández-Morales, "How Vienna Took the Stigma Out of Social Housing," *Politico*, June 30, 2022, https://www.politico.eu/article/vienna-social-housing-architecture-austria-stigma.

61. Duma and Lichtenberger, "Remembering Red Vienna."

62. Ally Schweitzer, "How European-Style Public Housing Could Help Solve the Affordability Crisis," National Public Radio, February 25, 2020, https://www.npr.org/local/305/2020/02/25/809315455/how-european-style-public-housing-could-help-solve-the-affordability-crisis.

63. Oksana Mironova, "Reflections on Vienna's Social Housing Model from Tenant Advocates," *The Nation*, January 5, 2023, https://www.thenation.com/article/society/reflections-vienna-social-housing.

64. Ryan Honeywell, "Haus Beautiful," *Governing Magazine*, February 2013, https://drjdbij2merew.cloudfront.net/GOV/GOV_Mag_Feb13.pdf.

65. Richard Hunt, "President Urges Unions to Widen Their Social Aims: Praises ILGWU Housing at Dedication as Example of Progress," *New York Times*, May 20, 1962, https://timesmachine.nytimes.com/timesmachine/1962/05/20/140702372.pdf.

66. "JFK Cracks Jokes and Dedicates One of Manhattan's Storied Co-Ops," WNYC, May 26, 2016, https://www.wnyc.org/story/jfk-cracks-jokes-and-dedicates-one-manhattans-storied-co-ops.

67. Gerald Sazama, "A Brief History of Affordable Housing Cooperatives in the United States," *Economics Working Papers*, 1996, https://opencommons .uconn.edu/econ_wpapers/199609.

68. Janet L. Smith, "HOPE VI and the New Urbanism: Eliminating Low-Income Housing to Make Mixed-Income Communities," Planners Network, Organization of Progressive Planners, April 2002, http://www.plannersnetwork .org/2002/04/hope-vi-and-the-new-urbanism-eliminating-low-income-housing -to-make-mixed-income-communities.

69. Sazama, "A Brief History of Affordable Housing Cooperatives in the United States."

70. Michael Sorkin, "Hudson River Park/Pier 40 Deal Reveals Tangled Web of Collusion That Shapes NYC," *Archpaper*, October 26, 2016, https://www .archpaper.com/2016/10/1-michael-sorkin-hudson-river-park-pier-40.

71. Sorkin, "Hudson River Park/Pier 40 Deal Reveals Tangled Web of Collusion That Shapes NYC."

72. Bella DeVaan, "New Yorkers Visit Vienna for Social Housing Inspiration," Inequality.org, October 24, 2022, https://inequality.org/great-divide/new -yorkers-visit-vienna-for-social-housing-inspiration.

## CHAPTER 7: RESISTANCE VS. REVOLUTION

1. Anthony Barnett, "John Berger, Witness to the Human Condition (1926–2017)," *Open Democracy*, January 2, 2017, https://www.opendemocracy.net /en/john-berger-witness-to-human-condition-1926-2017.

2. Peter Marcuse and David Madden, *In Defense of Housing: The Politics of Crisis* (Brooklyn, NY: Verso, 2016).

3. Marcuse and Madden, *In Defense of Housing.*

4. Jonathan Miller, "Luxury Real Estate as the World's New Currency," *Douglas Elliman Magazine*, October 18, 2012.

5. Marcuse and Madden, *In Defense of Housing.*

6. Madison Darbyshire, "Record Number of Cash Offers Show New York Property Is Only for the Rich," *Financial Times*, March 6, 2024.

7. Don Mitchell, *Mean Streets: Homelessness, Public Space, and the Limits of Capital* (Athens: University of Georgia Press, 2020).

8. David Roos, "What's the Difference Between Puritans and Pilgrims?" History.com, July 31, 2019, https://www.history.com/news/pilgrims-puritans -differences.

9. Matt McManus, "How the Right Rationalizes Inequality: Demanding Reverence and Naturalizing Injustice," *Commonweal Magazine*, June 27, 2023, https://www.commonwealmagazine.org/conservatism-inequality-mcmanus -reagan-burke-de-maistre.

10. McManus, "How the Right Rationalizes Inequality."

11. McManus, "How the Right Rationalizes Inequality."

12. Sean Illing, via Twitter, June 27, 2023, https://x.com/seanilling/status /1673859912550547456?s=20.

13. Mia Birdsong, interview by Julie Beck, "How to Talk to People," *The Atlantic* podcast, June 26, 2023, https://www.theatlantic.com/podcasts/archive/2023/06/building-community-in-individualistic-culture/674493.

14. Patrick Condon, via Twitter, June 25, 2023, https://twitter.com/pmcondon2/status/1673044319446654977.

15. Patrick Condon, "Behold Vancouver, Where There Are Housing Solutions to Be Found," Theroca.com, May 8, 2023, https://www.theorca.ca/commentary/patrick-condon-behold-vancouver-where-there-are-housing-solutions-to-be-found-6970888.

16. "Cambridge, Mass. Adopts Citywide Affordable Housing Overlay—A National Model," *The Planning Report*, March 24, 2021, https://www.planningreport.com/2021/03/24/cambridge-mass-adopts-citywide-affordable-housing-overlay-national-model.

17. Matthew Haag, "A Bleak Outlook for Manhattan's Office Space May Signal a Bigger Problem," *New York Times*, April 25, 2023, https://www.nytimes.com/2023/04/25/nyregion/office-landlords-nyc.html.

18. Emily Badger and Larry Buchanan, "So You Want to Turn an Office Building into a Home? Cities Are Eager, but It's Harder Than You Think," *New York Times*, March 11, 2023, https://www.nytimes.com/interactive/2023/03/11/upshot/office-conversions.html.

19. Patrick McGeehan, "A New Penn Station Is Coming, With or Without Office Towers, Hochul Says," *New York Times*, June 26, 2023, https://www.nytimes.com/2023/06/26/nyregion/hochul-penn-station-vornados.html.

20. Paul Moses and Tim Healy, "The High Price of Empty Office Space: Billions in Tax Breaks, with More to Come," *The City*, December 19, 2023, https://www.thecity.nyc/2023/12/19/tax-breaks-pilot-office-space-nyc.

21. Glyn Robbins, "New York City's Famed Cooperative Housing Is Under Threat," *Jacobin*, April 2023, https://jacobin.com/2023/04/new-york-bronx-amalgamated-housing-cooperative-history-kazan.

22. Glyn Robbins, "150 Years Ago, Friedrich Engels Correctly Assessed What's Wrong with Housing Under Capitalism," *Jacobin*, July 2020, https://jacobin.com/2022/07/housing-question-capitalism-friedrich-engels.

23. Upton Sinclair, *Co-op: A Novel of Living Together* (New York: Farrar and Rinehart, 1936).

24. Marcuse and Madden, *In Defense of Housing*.

25. Robbins, "150 Years Ago, Friedrich Engels Correctly Assessed What's Wrong with Housing Under Capitalism."

26. Reza Chowdhury, via Twitter, June 26, 2023, quoting Will Silverman, managing director at real estate investment bank Eastdil Secured, https://twitter.com/rezac1/status/1673353840089878536?s=51&t=ihuPtM2-FSqt3mXVTDLh4A.

27. "Trendy YIMBY Affordable Housing Activists Are Sheltered in a House of Straw," Inequality.org, November 25, 2018, https://affordablehousingaction.org/trendy-yimby-affordable-housing-activists-are-sheltered-in-a-house-of-straw.

28. Megan Garber, "The Great Fracturing of American Attention," *The Atlantic*, March 5, 2022, https://www.theatlantic.com/culture/archive/2022/03/americans-focus-attention-span-threat-democracy/626556.

29. Johann Hari, *Stolen Focus: Why You Can't Pay Attention—And How to Think Deeply Again* (New York: Crown, 2022).

30. Brooke Gladstone, interview with Professor Jay Rosen, *On the Media*, WNYC, June 9, 2023, https://www.wnycstudios.org/podcasts/otm/segments/cnn-impossible-dilemma-on-the-media; Jay Rosen, via Twitter, October 19, 2020, "Reminder: Flooding the zone with shit, also known as the "firehose of falsehood," is a propaganda method for which there is no known solution. When the people running the government are determined to lower trust in everything—including themselves—there is no way to stop them," https://twitter.com/jayrosen_nyu/status/1318353888521707521.

31. Christine Mai-Duc and Jim Carlton, "California Spent $17 Billion on Homelessness. It's Not Working," *Wall Street Journal*, June 2, 2023, https://www.wsj.com/articles/california-homeless-population-oakland-wood-street-encampment-78d42cc3.

32. Friedrich Nietzsche, *Thus Spoke Zarathustra: A Book for All and None*, 1883–1885, via Project Gutenberg, https://www.gutenberg.org/files/1998/1998-h/1998-h.htm.

33. John Berger, "The Man with the Dishevelled Hair: Looking Misfortune in the Face," *Le Monde diplomatique*, 2011, https://mondediplo.com/1991/01/01gericault.

34. Sunny Singh, Twitter, February 12, 2024, https://x.com/profsunnysingh/status/1757052824813174914?s=51&t=zT1CzZ2qx6Hd39FKc-aPaQ.

35. Charlie Kaufman, BAFTA Screenwriter's Lecture, September 30, 2011, https://www.bafta.org/media-centre/transcripts/screenwriters-lecture-charlie-kaufman.

36. George Orwell, "Review of *The Road to Serfdom* by F. A. Hayek/*The Mirror of the Past* by K. Zilliacus," *The Observer*, April 9, 1944, available at https://maudestavern.com/2008/10/09/george-orwell-review.

Other Books in the Myths Made in America Series

"YOU JUST NEED TO LOSE WEIGHT": And 19 Other Myths About Fat People, by Aubrey Gordon

"I HAVE NOTHING TO HIDE": And 20 Other Myths About Surveillance and Privacy, by Heidi Boghosian

"PRISONS MAKE US SAFER": And 20 Other Myths About Mass Incarceration, by Victoria Law

"THEY TAKE OUR JOBS!": And 20 Other Myths About Immigration (EXPANDED EDITION), by Aviva Chomsky

"YOU CAN'T FIRE THE BAD ONES!": And 18 Other Myths About Teachers, Teachers' Unions, and Public Education, by William Ayers, Crystal Laura, and Rick Ayers

"YOU'RE IN THE WRONG BATHROOM!": And 20 Other Myths and Misconceptions About Transgender and Gender-Nonconforming People, by Laura Erickson-Schroth, MD, and Laura A. Jacobs, LCSW-R

"ALL THE REAL INDIANS DIED OFF": And 20 Other Myths About Native Americans, by Roxanne Dunbar-Ortiz and Dina Gilio-Whitaker

"GUNS DON'T KILL PEOPLE, PEOPLE KILL PEOPLE": And Other Myths About Guns and Gun Control, by Dennis A. Henigan

"YOU CAN TELL JUST BY LOOKING": And 20 Other Myths About LGBT Life and People, by Michael Bronski, Ann Pellegrini, and Michael Amico

"THEY'RE BANKRUPTING US!": And 20 Other Myths About Unions, by Bill Fletcher Jr.